D0917053

Yale Classical Monographs, 1

Dramatic Art in
Aeschylus's *Seven Against Thebes*

William G. Thalmann

New Haven and London   Yale University Press

1978

Published with assistance from
the Horatio McLeod Reynolds Fund.

Designed by John O. C. McCrillis and set in Press
Roman type. Printed in the United States of America
by The Murray Printing Co., Westford, Massachusetts.

Published in Great Britain, Europe, Africa, and Asia
(except Japan) by Yale University Press, Ltd., London.
Distributed in Australia and New Zealand by Book &
Film Services, Artarmon, N.S.W., Australia; and in
Japan by Harper & Row, Publishers, Tokyo Office.

Library of Congress Cataloging in Publication Data

Thalmann, William G., 1947–
    Dramatic art in Aeschylus's Seven Against Thebes.

(Yale classical monographs; 1)
    A revision of the author's thesis, Yale University,
1975.
    Bibliography: p.
    "Index of Aeschylean passages": p.
    1. Aeschylus. Septem contra Thebas.
2. Aeschylus–Criticism and interpretation.
I. Title. II. Series
PA3825.S4T5   1978   882'.01   78–6585
ISBN 0–300–02219–0

Contents

Preface

By its nature, this work will appeal primarily to those who know Greek. In treating the text of the *Seven Against Thebes,* there seemed no alternative to quoting phrases and whole passages in the original. A reader unfamiliar with Greek, however, would probably be able to follow the discussion by referring to C. M. Dawson's translation in the *Prentice-Hall Greek Drama Series,* which is fairly literal and retains the original line numbering.

This monograph is a rather substantially revised version of my doctoral dissertation, submitted to Yale University in 1975.

I have tried to acknowledge as completely as possible my debts on specific points to others who have written on this play. I should like to make such acknowledgement in more general terms here, and to express my respect for their work. Even when I arrived at conclusions different from theirs, their writings stimulated my own thinking. I have not hesitated to register disagreements with them on some matters, but my intention was emphatically not polemical. Rather, I felt I owed it to the reader to indicate the existence of other views than mine.*

I am glad to express thanks of a more personal nature to those who have helped me with advice, encouragement, and criticism (with the customary disclaimer that I alone am responsible for the final product). Professors Thomas Gould and David Claus, after reading the original dissertation, suggested to me in conversation ways in which I could strengthen my arguments. At a later stage, Professor Gould read and criticized an important section of the final chapter. As

---

*Unfortunately, Oliver Taplin's *The Stagecraft of Aeschylus* (Oxford, 1977) became available to me only as this book was going to press. In the light of his discussion of the *Seven* (pp. 129-91), I have not found it necessary to alter what I have written. On some matters our opinions converge; on others they differ (hardly a surprising situation in view of the uncertainties which this play involves). I note only the following points: (1) I find very attractive Taplin's suggestion that the brothers' corpses are brought on while lines 848-53 are delivered and that lines 854-60 introduce the final lament; (2) I disagree on the related questions of what occurs in the shield scene and the authenticity of lines 282-86; (3) I am still persuaded that Eteocles arms himself in the second epirrhematic scene. The latter two points would require more argument than space allows; but I hope I have shown what is gained dramatically in those two scenes if the views I have favored are adopted.

members of the *Yale Classical Studies* Monographs Committee, Professors Thomas Cole and Gordon Williams made comments on an earlier version of this work, which were of great help to me. I am also grateful to a reader for the Monographs Committee for his valuable suggestions, and to an anonymous reader for Yale University Press. And my thanks to my wife, who brought her editorial talents to bear on a manuscript which threatened to become chaotic, and who, throughout the process of writing and rewriting, gave me considerable help of a less tangible nature as well.

I am grateful to Miss Nona Jenkins for her rapid and nearly flawless typing, to Miss Jane Whitehead for compiling the index, and to Yale University for a grant from the A. Whitney Griswold Faculty Research Fund, which enabled me to pay for their services. I have received nothing but kindness and courtesy from Yale University Press. In particular I would like to thank Mr. Edward Tripp, Mrs. Joanne Ainsworth, and Mary-Ellen Patrell.

My deepest debt of all is to Professor C. J. Herington. All through my work on the dissertation and on revising it later, he unstintingly gave me the benefit of his time and of his enviable knowledge and appreciation of Aeschylus. Working with him has been a privilege— and a pleasure.

W.G.T.

New Haven
December 16, 1977

Dramatic Art in
Aeschylus's *Seven Against Thebes*

Introduction

In each of his plays, Aeschylus seems to have exploited to the full all the resources ever known to the Greek theater—plot, structure, imagery, and the various effects created in performance. Not only was he a complete master of each element of drama; he also combined them so skillfully that by working together and reinforcing one another, they produced a unified effect. The present study of the *Seven Against Thebes* will treat these elements in the order mentioned, both individually and in relation to one another. Its ultimate aim will be to recapture the play as a living, dramatic whole.

Aristotle enumerates six elements of tragedy in the *Poetics*.[1] My own list, given above, is in part an adaptation of his, but I have assigned rather broader meanings to certain of his terms. In many respects, his discussion is extremely valuable, even when applied to an Aeschylean play (for which it was never intended); in others, it needs extension and alteration.

The most important element of tragedy, in Aristotle's view, is the plot or μῦθος, by which he apparently means not only the story itself but also what we would call "structure" (λέγω γὰρ μῦθον τοῦτον τὴν σύνθεσιν τῶν πραγμάτων).[2] I would prefer to keep plot and structure distinct as far as possible. *Plot*, as I shall use the term, refers to the events of the story as the poet adapts it to portray a dramatic action (Aristotle's πρᾶξις). Thus an essential part of this study of the *Seven* will be an inquiry, within the limits of the available evidence, into Aeschylus's treatment of the myth of the house of Laius. All the incidents of the story as he used it revealed the progress toward fulfillment of an inherited curse. This fundamental, organizing pattern may, in the last analysis, be called the plot of the Theban trilogy. The dramatic *praxis* was the suffering of three successive generations because of the curse.

Structure, on the other hand, is the arrangement of events chosen for representation into plays of the trilogy and into parts of each play, so that the plot may proceed in an orderly and intelligible fashion. It enables the trilogy as a whole, and each of the com-

1

ponent plays, to have the proper scope and an appropriate beginning, middle, and end—in the manner, as Aristotle says, of a living organism.[3] At least as important as the relation of the parts to the whole, however, is the relation of the parts to each other. Together, through similarity or contrast, the trilogy's three members, and the individual sections of at least the surviving play, clarify and stress the significance of events in the larger design which is the plot.

Even though I shall employ the term *plot* in a more restricted sense than Aristotle does, his argument for the primacy of this element still holds; for of all the aspects of drama it remains most intimately related to the action. The connection between plot and structure is also clearly very close, and the plot and structure of both the Theban trilogy and the *Seven* will be treated together in the first chapter. To distinguish between them at all has the advantage of enabling us to think of the structure as one of several elements which give the plot shape and definition.

Next, Aristotle mentions ἦϑος, the nature or character of the men portrayed. In the main body of my study, this element will not receive much direct attention, chiefly because in my opinion the *Seven* offers only as much characterization as is necessary to the plot (and that is rather little), and also because, of all facets of the play, the character of Eteocles and the related problem of his freedom of action have been the most discussed. The question of how important characterization and the concepts of fate and "free will" are to the *Seven* will be considered in appendix 3. While putting less emphasis on character than is customary, I propose to explore other, more neglected aspects of the *Seven* which I believe illustrate Aeschylus's extraordinary dramaturgical skill.

Aristotle then names two elements which concern speech: διάνοια and λέξις. The first seems to be the intellectual quality of a dramatic personage, as revealed in his words, which enables him to understand his subject or situation and to speak appropriately about it. By the second, Aristotle apparently means little more than "diction" (λέγω δὲ . . . λέξιν εἶναι τὴν διὰ τῆς ὀνομασίας ἑρμηνείαν). These terms refer to such fundamental aspects of speech that they appear restrictive. In his discussion of λέξις later on in the *Poetics*, for instance, Aristotle treats only one form of figurative language, and that is metaphor.[4]

Thus neither term is very helpful in considering the wonderful use

Aeschylus made of language. I shall use instead the word *imagery*, which encompasses both the major themes and the images of the play. A *theme* might best be considered repeated reference, throughout the play, to an event or object by means of the same word or group of words. It may be figurative in varying degrees, or not at all; and it usually is closely related to, and even suggested by, the main concerns of the play. By *image* I mean the transfer of language from one sphere of life to another represented by the drama (the use, for example, of language connected with the sea and navigation to depict the plight of a city under attack). In practice, it will not be necessary to distinguish sharply between *theme* and *image*; but here the choice of the latter term should perhaps be explained.

The word *image* has become very familiar to literary criticism—perhaps excessively so. But though it might justly be dismissed as jargon when indiscriminately applied, this term is useful for interpreting Aeschylus because it stresses that in his hands the phenomena it describes appeal strongly to the senses (principally, though not exclusively, sight) and yet are not physical. An image is suggested verbally and at the same time evokes in the imagination of the reader or spectator a mental picture of a specific action or object. It differs from passages of simple description because it implies, but does not explicitly state, the qualities of the thing it describes. On the other hand, it is not as abstract as a general statement of the type, "the situation of a city under assault is perilous."

This manipulation of language cannot adequately be described by *metaphor* and *simile*, at least in the strict sense of these terms (and if they are used more loosely they are *too* vague). In the *Seven*, for instance, Aeschylus never says outright, through metaphor, that "the city is a ship buffeted by a storm." Once, it is true, he puts the parallel in the form of a simile, when the spy urges Eteocles to "bulwark the city like the helmsman of a ship" (lines 63–64; the translation of the verb is Tucker's). This, however, is to draw attention to the difference between the two terms of the comparison. More often, Aeschylus allows language of the sea to accumulate around mention of the city, as in lines 2–3. The distinction is thereby blurred; the city *is* a ship in an all-but-literal sense. We are left with *image* as denoting a device far more vivid and suggestive than (for example) *simile*.

Concrete is the adjective which best describes Aeschylean imagery, and it is applicable in two ways. First, as has been implied, rather than simply describe a thing or express an idea abstractly, Aeschylus's habit is to present it palpably in the form of an image. In this way he conveys, in a highly compressed manner, all the important attributes of the object. Furthermore, in Aeschylus an image always tends to take actual material form before the eyes of the audience. What starts as an image ends up directly represented.

Since Aeschylus seems to have relied heavily on imagery to clarify the significance of the action, attention to this element is crucial to an understanding of his plays. The imagery of the *Seven* will be examined here in the second and third chapters. Because reservations have often been voiced concerning the study of imagery in ancient literature, a defense of this method will be offered in appendix 2.

None of the elements named so far distinguishes a drama very sharply from a written text. The last two items in Aristotle's list, however, are aspects of performance. As the name implies, the spectacle, or ὄψις, is what the audience saw during a production of the play. It includes not just costumes and masks but all the visual effects, such as the figures of the choral dance. But this category, broad as it is, still does not include all the nontextual elements of a drama. Besides what the spectators saw, there was also what they heard—for instance, the song of the chorus (the other element mentioned by Aristotle, μελοποιία). These aural components of the play are analogous to the spectacle in nature, work simultaneously with it, and supplement its effect.[5] A third feature of the *Seven* also cannot be ignored: the many events which occur out of sight of the spectators but which are, in various ways, made present to their imagination. Since they are reported verbally, these events might seem to belong more with the characteristics of the written text. But they could have been made fully vivid only during actual performance. In fact, much of what the audience witnesses in the play is response to occurrences which are described rather than shown.[6] Thus these unseen events are closely allied to the sights and sounds of the play. In the absence of any term which encompasses the visual, aural, and "offstage" effects, I shall refer to them under the heading *dramatic presentation*.

Many of the effects created in actual production are, of course, lost. But inferences concerning them can be made from the text of the *Seven* in sufficient number and with enough certainty to repay investigation in this area. These inferences will be drawn, wherever possible, during detailed examination of each scene of the play in the last two chapters. Aristotle himself, it is true, considered music, and even more, spectacle, extraneous to the tragic art proper. His reasons for holding this opinion, and the importance of spectacle and related matters of production to the drama of Aeschylus generally, will be discussed in chapter 4. But specific arguments aside, it is hard to conceive how the plays of such a master of the theater as Aeschylus can be fully appreciated, or even understood, without regard for the dramatic presentation. The *Seven Against Thebes* must, I believe, be treated not just as a text but as a *performed* text.

The plot of the *Seven*, as Aristotle persuasively argues in regard to all tragedy, is of paramount importance. The structure, imagery, and dramatic presentation, in close conjunction, articulate the plot. So closely interrelated are these elements that it is somewhat misleading, though necessary for the purpose of study, to consider them in isolation from one another. A spectator in the Theater of Dionysus would not have been able to pause and analyze the function of these elements separately; but he had the advantage over the student or the reader in feeling their combined and simultaneous effect. For all its detail, the discussion which follows is intended to suggest what that experience must have been like.

1

Plot and Structure

Near the beginning of their debate in Aristophanes' *Frogs,* Aeschylus is challenged by Euripides to explain how he made the spectators of his plays better soldiers and citizens. He replies, "by creating a drama full of Ares, . . . the *Seven Against Thebes*. Every man watching it would have yearned to be a warrior."[1] The *Seven* is certainly a play about a war. It is filled to overflowing with fine descriptions, in the high epic spirit, of martial sights, noises, and boasts, as the Argives hurl their grand attack against Thebes. On the part of the city's defenders there is a quiet but no less impressive confidence in the justice of their cause and a determination to protect their homeland. As has often been remarked, much of the play's warlike atmosphere, and the situation of a Greek city threatened by an army of barbaric ferocity, may well have been inspired by Athens' experience of the Persian invasion not much more than a decade before the Theban tetralogy's production in 467 B.C. That was a war in which Aeschylus himself took an active part. It is, perhaps, no accident that in the same passage of the *Frogs* Aeschylus follows his example of the *Seven* with that of the *Persians*, in which he claims that he taught his audience "to be eager always to conquer the enemy."[2]

On these grounds alone the *Seven* merits admiration. Aristophanes expresses a major aspect of its appeal. Some modern critics, although appreciating the play's depiction of war, have declined to see more in it than that. Thus they consider it, as Aristophanes does not, limited in scope. Owen, for instance, thinks the *Seven* inferior to the *Suppliants* and the *Persians*, its subject "less profound."[3] Gilbert Murray, too, says that it "does not deal with its story as a great world-problem" as the other Aeschylean plays do.[4]

Yet the setting of this drama is no ordinary war between states. The Ares here is ambiguous, problematical. In the early part of the play, the terror of the maidens of the chorus is opposed to the masterful figure of Eteocles, the city's leader; there is division inside the city which, unless checked, threatens military disaster. As the play progresses, however, it becomes evident that this division is a symptom of a deeper problem. The war itself has arisen from a quarrel between Eteocles and his brother—a different and potentially graver type of disunity. The danger to Thebes comes not only, and not even originally, from the foreign army, but from within her own ruling house. Eteocles and Polynices are heirs not merely to civil power but also to a curse which afflicts their family. Because of their position, the struggle between them, which is a result of the curse, threatens the whole city, for the city is the issue in the conflict. The maidens of the chorus represent the whole life of the city, its relations with its land and with its gods. This life has been entirely disrupted by the war. And the brothers are isolated from it as men marked by a curse.[5] The general movement of the *Seven* is toward a restoration of equilibrium in the context of the city. That is accomplished by the narrowing of the conflict *from* war between Argos and Thebes *through* the fight at the city gates between the Argive chiefs and the Theban champions *to* the climactic fratricidal duel between the two brothers.

The *Seven Against Thebes*, then (and apparently the trilogy of which it was the last play), portrays the effect of a family curse and thereby examines the problem of inherited guilt. Compared with the lofty theological speculations of the *Oresteia*, it may at first seem tame. Yet its subject is essentially the same, and it raises, in the minds of many critics, similar difficult questions. If the *Oresteia* may be considered Aeschylus's supreme achievement, the *Seven* is the survivor of a trilogy that was, perhaps, not very far behind. The *Seven* may not reach a comprehensive and satisfying solution to the problem of inherited guilt, but the conclusion that it reaches is internally coherent in terms of the extant play and indeed of the trilogy as a whole, so far as that can be reconstructed.

The Theban trilogy appears, moreover, to bear an interesting relation to the *Oresteia*. The climax of the *Seven* (lines 653–719) offers to the audience the spectacle of a family curse taking hold of a descendant of the original transgressor. In this respect it may be considered a forerunner of the ending of the *Choephori*, which shows the onset of madness in Orestes as the Erinyes appear to him, though after the violent act itself. In the *Seven*, the effect of the curse, shown before the deed as Eteocles prepares to face his brother in

combat, is more devastating. As Solmsen observes, the play vividly
portrays the various special characteristics of a curse.[6] It is as if
Aeschylus drew for the *Oresteia* on a conception, developed in the
Theban trilogy, of the way a curse works and how it might be
depicted.

The first step in studying the *Seven* must be to investigate the construction of its plot. Since the *Seven* was the last of three connected
plays, we must inquire how Aeschylus conceived the myth of the
house of Laius. Taking each of the three generations in turn, we shall
ask what events Aeschylus made part of the story, whether portrayed
in the plays or assumed as background. We can then consider how he
organized this material into a trilogy, and finally how he formed the
structure of the surviving play.

THE SHAPING OF THE STORY

In examining Aeschylus's use of the myth, it is important to reject
the assumption, which was common until recently, that the tragedians took their plots entirely from their literary predecessors.[7] That
attitude ignores the organic nature of myth: it never stops growing
and changing shape, even after it has been cast in literary form. Thus
Aeschylus was not bound to any single version previously known. He
was free to choose among familiar elements and to invent new ones
according to his needs. It follows that, in his treatment of the story,
his divergences from his predecessors are especially significant, for if
these can be isolated they should reveal something about his concerns in dramatizing the myth. On the other hand, where he followed
earlier versions, we can ask how these suited his purposes.

That would be a very promising method if the other plays of the
trilogy and more of the earlier literature had survived. Even without
these works, however, it can yield suggestive if not completely certain results. There are scattered references to the Theban legend in
Homer, Hesiod, the lyric poets, and Pindar, and several of the cyclic
epics treated it.[8] Though our knowledge of the story as it existed
before Aeschylus is fragmentary, its outlines can be traced, as Baldry
has done.[9] In that form it looks strange indeed to anyone familiar
with Sophocles' later treatment. It seems too diffuse to be dramatic
material. Aeschylus himself, as Baldry suggests, may have tailored
this myth to the needs of tragedy, and so pointed the way for Sophocles and, after him, for Euripides.

As to the shape Aeschylus gave the story, the loss of the trilogy's first two plays, the *Laius* and the *Oedipus*, severely limits our knowledge. The *Seven* provides almost the only evidence.[10] Plausible guesses can be made from that play concerning some details of the story; about others we can only state possible alternatives. Yet despite the uncertainties it can be said with fair confidence that Aeschylus's guiding principle in handling the myth was the portrayal of a family curse; that when traditional elements fit this scheme he used them; but that when they did not he either invented new ones or incorporated less familiar variants, the sources of which are today unknown.

The Oracle Given to Laius

The curse originated with Laius. But the only information we possess about the circumstances of its origin, given in the second stasimon of the *Seven* (lines 742 ff.), is neither complete nor straightforward. As the chorus look back over the history of the royal family, they do not so much recount the past as allude to it. Their words, in the light of the two preceding plays, must have been intelligible to the trilogy's original audience but are now obscure. The chorus mention a misdeed by Laius, an oracle from Apollo whose terms he failed to meet, and his murder by Oedipus. At least one point is clear. The oracle is not the better known response which apparently figured in earlier versions of the story—a warning to Laius that he would die at the hands of his son.[11] In Aeschylus's version, the issue is the well-being of Thebes, and the birth of Oedipus brings that into question. It seems that Aeschylus was concerned with achieving, from the earliest stages of the story, the tightest possible connection between the city's fortunes and those of its ruling house.

The basic questions which the passage poses are: What was Laius's crime, and how did it bring a curse upon him? What exactly did Apollo tell him? How is the oracle related to the curse and the crime? These are the chorus's words (lines 742–57):[12]

παλαιγενῆ γὰρ λέγω
παρβασίαν ὠκύποινον, αἰῶνα δ' ἐς τρίτον
μένειν, Ἀπόλλωνος εὖτε Λάϊος
βίᾳ τρὶς εἰπόντος ἐν
μεσομφάλοις Πυθικοῖς

χρηστηρίοις ϑνᾳσκοντα γέννας ἄτερ σῷζειν πόλιν,

κρατηϑεὶς ἐκ φιλᾶν ἀβουλιᾶν
ἐγεὑατο μὲν μόρον αὐτῷ,
πατροκτόνον Οἰδιπόδαν, ὅστε ματρὸς ἀγνὰν
σπείρας ἄρουραν ἵν' ἐτράφη
ῥίζαν αἱματόεσσαν
ἔτλα· παράνοια συνᾶγε
νυμφίους φρενώλης.

These lines are almost always understood to mean that Apollo commanded Laius to save the city from some unspecified threat by dying without offspring, or (and this is very hard to get from the text) that Apollo forbade Laius to beget children and told him that by doing so he would destroy the city. Laius disobeyed, and Apollo punished him by death at the hands of his own son and by a curse on the family. Hence the Argive attack on Thebes. Cameron, for instance, writes:

> It would seem that the city was in some danger or other and Laius sought from the oracle some means to save it. Apollo answered that if Laius would die childless the city would be saved. . . .
>
> The task of the three generations is to save the city: Laius from whatever threat caused him to consult the oracle, Oedipus from the Sphinx, and Eteocles from the Argive invasion.

A little later, he concludes:

> The reason for the divine displeasure is that Laius found the recipe for the city's salvation too bitter to himself and tried twice more for the god to propose some other solution. When the oracle three times returned the same answer, he decided to abandon the advice of Apollo and seek his own means to rescue Thebes. Here was his transgression, the hybris which provoked the divine anger.[13]

With few variations, this view has found its way unquestioned into nearly all studies of the *Seven*.[14] It involves several difficulties, however. In the first place, no danger to Thebes which would cause Laius to consult the oracle is known from any ancient source. In itself, of course, this is not a fatal objection; there may have been such a story, or Aeschylus may have devised one. Still, one may reasonably wonder if any threat existed, and so if it really is implied by the phrase εἰπόντος . . . σῴζειν. To judge from the language, that seems unlikely. Whether the participle means "command" or "foretell," it can govern either a present or an aorist infinitive which, though timeless, would still denote the *aspect* of the action by its tense.[15] Thus if σῴζειν here meant "to save," one would expect its tense to be aorist (indicating simple occurrence). I suggest that the present infinitive, implying continued action, means "preserve," and that Apollo's response to Laius was "that by dying without issue he would keep the city safe." The infinitive is, in fact, sometimes translated this way, but without comment or evident consciousness of the distinction involved.[16] Yet that distinction is important and deserves to be made. For if Laius was told that he would maintain the city's safety by dying without offspring, it seems that by begetting a child he would bring Thebes into danger. A prior threat to the city is thus ruled out. Laius's "task" was not to save Thebes from an external peril but to refrain from endangering it from within.[17]

Why, then, did Laius consult the oracle? We do not know. Was it, as some have thought,[18] to seek a remedy for childlessness? That is implied by the more common form of the oracle. But the response as Aeschylus gives it, on any interpretation, does not seem suited to an inquiry of this sort. As Winnington-Ingram has suggested,[19] it seems instead to answer the question πῶς σῴζω πόλιν;—but in the sense (I would now add), "how shall I keep the city safe?" Cases are known, in fact, of states asking oracles not how to cope with immediate or even impending dangers, but how to continue their prosperity and avoid misfortune.[20] Laius could conceivably have made such an inquiry as a young man after being called back from exile to rule Thebes.[21]

As for εἰπόντος, there is no way of deciding between the possible meanings "command" and "foretell."[22] And there is no need to do so. Apollo's answer may have been in the form, "if you do A, then B will follow," like the famous oracle which Croesus received.[23] It would thus have been as much a prophecy as a warning. Or it may have involved an imperative: "preserve the city by dying without offspring," or (with emphasis on the participle θνάσκοντα, as often in Greek) "if you wish to keep the city safe, then die without issue."

In any case Apollo, as Aeschylus records his language, did not directly command Laius not to produce a child or explicitly threaten him with punishment if he did. Instead, he made Thebes' continued security dependent on Laius's fulfilling this condition. Laius's failure to comply would have grave consequences for the city (the Sphinx, perhaps, and the Argive invasion) but not necessarily for himself. Thus what the god orders and what he predicts are finally the same.

The common assumption that Laius was punished for disobeying Apollo's order cannot be reconciled with the character of the response. Moreover, there seems to be no other case in which failure to comply with an oracle incurred not simply the predicted or implied consequences but punishment for an act of disobedience in itself.[24] Thus it is reasonable to doubt that oracles ever worked that way, even in this instance.[25] Two examples will illustrate the distinction.

In the *Choephori* (lines 269–97), Orestes recalls an oracle from Apollo which, he makes clear, *commanded* him to avenge his father (κελεύων, line 270). The god also, he continues, told him what he would suffer if he did not perform this task. This was not a threat but a prediction, as the language of the passage indicates.[26] Furthermore, as several commentators have pointed out,[27] lines 278 ff. are phrased in general terms; the oracle reminded Orestes of the fate of all men who fail to avenge a murdered kinsman. Orestes would be punished for disregard of a religious obligation, not for disobeying Apollo.

Herodotus tells the story of Battus who, having consulted the Delphic oracle on quite another matter, was told to go to Libya and found a city.[28] When, in frustration, he ignored the injunction and went home to Thera, things began to go wrong for him and his compatriots. So he acquiesced and settled on an island off the coast of Libya. But that was not the end of the affair. Failing to prosper in his new home, he again inquired of the oracle, and once more was firmly told to make his home in Libya. Finally he was led to the correct site by the Libyans themselves and founded Cyrene, which ultimately flourished as a result of yet another Pythian pronouncement.

Here is a case of disregard of an oracle; but the consequences were far milder than they are presumed to have been for Laius. And there is no hint that Apollo brought sufferings on Battus out of personal anger, or even that he inflicted them at all. They were merely the result of failure to follow advice which was (to judge from the outcome of the story) in Battus's best interests. And because of the sufferings the god's command was finally obeyed.[29]

Even if one were to ignore these problems and admit that Apollo punished Laius for disobedience, it is hard to believe that Apollo would be the cause of persecution by an Erinys. That would have no parallel, to my knowledge.[30] It seems best, therefore, to separate the oracle and Laius's original transgression—that is, to consider Apollo's warning a sign of some guilty taint in Laius which existed before he consulted the oracle.[31] In the light of this suggestion, let us examine more closely the phrasing of lines 742 ff.

Essential to the traditional association of Laius's crime with the oracle is the assumption that the long clause introduced by εὖτε in line 744 explains the παρβασία of line 743. That is a possible reading. Yet although it does not do violence to the run of the sentence or to the train of thought which leads the chorus to mention Laius, it does not fit particularly well with these either. The chorus have just bewailed "the house's new toils mingled with the old troubles" (lines 740–41). It has often been observed that παλαιοῖσι there is taken up by παλαιγενῆ in line 742. What needs to be stressed, however, is that the context requires not a narrative of Laius's crime but an account of how and why new evils are to be mixed with old. That is what the chorus proceed to give: "for I say that the ancient-born transgression was soon punished, but that it remains till the third generation."[32] The emphasis here is on ὠκύποινον and the accompanying antithesis (crucial to the *Seven*) αἰῶνα δ' ἐς τρίτον μένειν. Thus it is more natural to take the clause beginning with εὖτε as explaining ὠκύποινον than as expansion on παρβασίαν.[33] The precise nature of Laius's misdeed (which the audience presumably knew from the preceding plays) matters here far less than its effects on him in the distant past and on his sons in the imminent future.

"I say that the transgression was soon punished . . . when Laius, in spite of Apollo's having told him"—the oracle is recalled as an attendant circumstance, and then the thread is picked up—"[when Laius] overcome by his own [?] lack of counsel, begot death for himself, the father-slayer Oedipus." Laius's punishment was to die at the hands of his son or (at an intermediate stage) to engender the child who was to destroy him.[34] The immediate agency was his ἀβουλίαι,

a confusion which caused him to ignore the oracle to his own ruin
and so the equivalent of *atê*.[35] This in turn is the effect of the curse
aroused by his crime; Erinyes were often thought to work by derang-
ing their victims' minds and so leading them to commit acts with dis-
astrous consequences.[36]

Compared with the usual interpretation, this way of sorting out the
elements of Laius's history is more consistent with the manner in
which that history is recalled. Certain phrases, therefore, which
can, but need not, imply that Laius's guilt was his flouting of the
oracle should be assigned a milder meaning. Many critics have read
Ἀπόλλωνος . . . βίᾳ (lines 745–46) as a sign of Laius's defiance, and
with reason.[37] But βίᾳ can indicate mere failure to act in accordance
with a warning,[38] and nothing prevents us from taking it this way
here. Line 842 contains a similar ambiguity: βουλαὶ δ᾽ ἄπιστοι Λαΐου
διήρκεσαν. There is apparently a reference here to ἀβουλιᾶν in line
750, except that the negative is now prefixed to the epithet ἄπιστοι.
This can mean "unpersuaded" rather than "disobedient," as it does
in line 876. In that case, line 842 means simply that the birth of
Oedipus ultimately led to his sons' mutual fratricide—an obvious
impossibility if Laius had died childless.[39]

The argument advanced here might seem to make the oracle superfluous to the story. It is fruitless to speculate what might have happened had Laius not inquired at Delphi. But I suggest that Apollo's
admonition performs three functions essential to the story. First,
its implications for Laius are so grave that it provides a measure of
his guilt.[40] Secondly, it throws into relief the atê which is the effect
of the curse, for Laius's begetting of a son could hardly be character-
ized as an act of ἀβουλία if he had not been warned against doing so.
Finally, as I noted earlier, it stresses the involvement of the city in
the troubles of Laius and any descendants he had.

Aeschylus, then, might have envisioned Laius's history as follows.
In his youth, Laius committed a crime and was cursed. Later, he
became ruler of Thebes. Either just before or just after he was
installed, he asked the Delphic oracle how he might continue the
city's prosperity and received the surprising answer that he would
keep Thebes safe if he died without offspring. Later, through some
error, he had a son. Winnington-Ingram has argued persuasively in
favor of the manuscript φίλων in line 750 (as against Wilamowitz's
φιλᾶν), taking the word as referring to Laius's wife. The impetus for

the mistake, he thinks, came from her, for she may have had "dynastic thoughts."[41] In that case she would be the instrument of the Erinys in punishing Laius for his original misdeed.

When Oedipus was born, Laius, realizing his mistake, exposed the child.[42] This was a belated attempt to observe the conditions of the oracle. Presumably, if he were to survive his son, he would die without issue, the oracle's terms would be satisfied, and the city would not be endangered.[43] But this plan failed and Oedipus survived to kill his father.

Though some details are uncertain, this reconstruction seems plausible and consistent. One vital element, however, is missing: What was the act that brought a curse upon Laius and started this series of events?

Laius's Crime

The word παρβασία implies a violation of divinely sanctioned limits on human conduct. In the one known story which tells of a crime by Laius, his deed is of that nature. According to it, Laius as a young man in exile from Thebes found refuge with Pelops, fell in love with the latter's son Chrysippus, and carried him off. Pelops cursed Laius, and in one version Chrysippus killed himself out of shame.[44]

With one possible exception, however, there is no evidence for this story earlier than or contemporary with Aeschylus. It cannot definitely be placed earlier than Euripides who, in his play entitled *Chrysippus,* apparently portrayed the rape as the cause of the misfortunes of the Labdacidae.[45] Can Aeschylus earlier have done the same?[46]

Certainty is clearly impossible. Yet the lack of extant pre-Euripidean sources for the myth is not decisive, and there is one scrap of evidence which might give it greater antiquity. That is the scholion on line 1760 of Euripides' *Phoenissae,* which gives a version of the story and attributes it to one Peisander. The important question is who this Peisander was. Of several men known under that name, only one, mentioned in the *Souda,* can interest us. He was a Rhodian epic poet of the sixth century B.C. who composed a *Heracleia* and to whom, significantly perhaps, other poems were also attributed.[47] If he is the one meant by the scholiast, then there is evidence for epic treatment of the myth before Aeschylus. Perhaps, as several scholars have argued, the scholion contains some later additions to the myth.[48] Even so, the gist of the story is given in the first sentence, and the rest of the note elaborates on it. That sentence refers the tale definitely to Peisander.

If Aeschylus knew the story, in what form would he have used it? By fifth-century Greek standards, Laius's pederasty would not have merited the sort of punishment he received. Chrysippus's subsequent suicide, however, which is mentioned among other places in the "Peisander scholion," would have made Laius culpable. The dying victim might have cursed his abductor and so evoked an Erinys to oppress him. Erinyes, however, need not be associated only with cases of violent death; originally, they probably embodied the curses not only of the dead but of the living as well.[49] In a slightly different account of the myth, when Laius seized the boy, *Pelops* cursed him, praying "that the evil extend as far as his children" ($\mu\acute{\epsilon}\chi\rho\iota\ \pi\alpha\iota\delta\omega\nu$ $\epsilon\ddot{\iota}\nu\alpha\iota\ \tau\grave{o}\ \kappa\alpha\kappa\acute{o}\nu$).[50] In providing for a curse not only on the individual but also on his descendants, this version would fit the requirements of the Theban trilogy very well.[51] Laius would have transgressed the laws of hospitality. There is a good parallel in lines 55–62 of the *Agamemnon,* which imply that Zeus Xenios sent an Erinys against Alexander for the identical offense in the rape of Helen.[52] Thus a curse by Pelops seems preferable to one by Chrysippus.

If this was Laius's crime, the nature of his punishment would have been appropriate. His violation of the guest-host relationship took the particular form of depriving Pelops of a son; what more fitting retribution than to be murdered by his own son? In fact, the distortion of relationships within *all* the generations of Laius's family is intelligible if its source was his own breach of the sanctity of the home. And finally, one of the strange aspects of the oracle he received from Apollo is that he was warned *against* having children, for any Greek would have been concerned with providing himself a son and heir on both religious and social grounds. But the response would accurately reflect his guilt against Pelops.[53]

According to the "Peisander scholion," Hera sent the Sphinx against Thebes because the city did not punish Laius for the rape. In the *Seven* (line 539), the Sphinx is called "the reproach to the city"—a curious phrase if Thebes was merely the passive victim of her ravages. We may reasonably infer from a fragment of the tetralogy's satyr-play *Sphinx* that some god sent the monster,[54] and since Laius's crime struck at Pelops's family, Hera, as patroness of marriage, might have been concerned.[55] But the identity of the god matters less than the connection of the Sphinx with Laius's guilt.[56] If Aeschylus incorporated this into his story (and it is possible, though of course not certain, that he did), it would be one way in which the city was implicated in the misfortunes of the individual family. The Sphinx could only have appeared years after the event, when Oedipus had already reached manhood; but such a lapse of time is not out of the question.

There is no direct reference to the story of Chrysippus in the extant play, although certain lines of the second stasimon can be interpreted as looking vaguely back at it.[57] The silence of the *Seven* on this matter, however, does not rule out Aeschylus's use of the episode. Explicit reference there to the rape would have been unnecessary. Aeschylus need only have alluded to it a few times in one of the preceding plays for the audience to be conscious of it as lying in the background. If, of the three plays of the *Oresteia,* only the *Eumenides* had survived, to what extent would we be aware of the role played by Thyestes' banquet in the disasters which befell the Atreidae? So also, in the Theban trilogy, the last play may have reached a stage in the myth sufficiently distant from Laius's time that the first cause of the troubles seemed remote and not very pertinent, though it was not entirely forgotten.

On balance, then, it seems likely, though definite proof is lacking, that Aeschylus knew and used the Chrysippus myth. It makes intelligible many aspects of the story whose traces we find in the *Seven* (the oracle, the Erinys, and the particular form of her persecution) which are otherwise difficult to explain. Whatever the answer to the question, it does not fundamentally affect my view of the play, though I do think that Aeschylus must have accounted for the curse on the house with some offense by Laius other than disobedience of Apollo.

Oedipus's Sufferings and Curse on His Sons

An essential element in Aeschylus's treatment of the story of Oedipus is a major rearrangement of the family relationships. In the epic version, Oedipus, although he married his mother, evidently did not have his children by her.[58] Whether Aeschylus was the first to make Oedipus's mother the mother also of his children or owed this arrangement to some non-epic variant of the myth, his choice or invention of it is remarkable.[59] The curse, working through the generations, cut off Laius and his descendants from the normal rhythm of life; Aeschylus therefore must have wanted to make the family's composition strikingly abnormal. By making Oedipus not only the father but also the brother of Eteocles and Polynices, he made their birth unnatural; more important, he presented a picture of a family in which the generations were confused and the relations between them. ambiguous. This, as will be argued later, is reflected in the imagery of the *Seven*. Moreover, the extant play contains traces of sexual unease, again in contrast to the normal cycle of the family. Eteocles' vehement dununciation of women in lines 187ff., which has troubled many readers of the play because it goes far beyond what the situation demands, may be traceable at least in part to the anomaly of his birth.

Another innovation, which follows from the first, seems to have been (as Baldry observes) that "there was a long interval, apparently of happiness and prosperity, between the marriage and his discovery of the truth."[60] This would have delayed the *anagnorisis* and made the final catastrophe, when it came, more overwhelming because unexpected.

That climax, in Aeschylus, seems to have involved Oedipus's discovery of his guilt, his self-blinding,[61] and his curse on his sons. The apparently new element here is his self-punishment.[62] What happened to him after that is not known. Did he die immediately? Was he exiled? Did his sons shut him away somewhere, perhaps in the palace itself, as in Euripides?[63] One thing is likely at any rate—that he did not continue to rule in Thebes. According to the *Odyssey*, by contrast, he remained ruler although he suffered,[64] while in the *Thebais* he may have been in some sort of retirement, voluntary or not, by the time he cursed his sons.[65] In any case, Aeschylus had him punished both socially (loss of the kingship) and at his own hands (the self-blinding). This emphasis on pollution as an individual concern has been seen as an advance over the more primitive mechanical conception reflected in the *Odyssey* passage, and as a major step in the adaptation of the myth to drama.[66] Specifically, in Aeschylus, perhaps for the first time, personal guilt occupies the center of attention in the story of Oedipus; and that is crucial to the notion of an inherited curse which affects both the individual and the community.

In the *Odyssey* (XI, 279–80), Erinyes are mentioned in connection with Oedipus: "And for him she [Epikaste] left behind very many sufferings, as many as a mother's Erinyes bring to pass." In the *Seven*, on the other hand, it is a *father's* Erinys (Oedipus's own) which works on his sons (for example, line 70), and it is ultimately the result of Oedipus's own guilt and hence of Laius's earlier crime. Thus the curse is passed from father to son through three generations, a form of patrimony, while the mother, never named in the extant play, is passive. In an important sense, she, like the land, is what the males of this family fight over.

Why Oedipus cursed his sons in the Aeschylean version of the myth is unknown. The text and interpretation of the lines in the *Seven* which refer to this act (785 ff.) are problematical:

$$τέκνοις \; δ' \; ἀραίας$$
$$ἐφῆκεν \; ἐπικότους \; τροφᾶς$$
$$αἰαῖ, \; πικρογλώσσους \; ἀράς \ldots$$

The manuscript reading is given here, but line 785 needs correction because it does not fit the meter (cf. line 778).

Two fragments of the *Thebais* give alternative reasons for the curse: one, that Polynices served a meal to Oedipus using a silver table and a gold cup which were family heirlooms;[67] the other, that the brothers sent him a thigh piece from a sacrifice rather than the customary shoulder.[68] The scholiast who quotes the latter passage says that Aeschylus used a similar version in the *Seven*. Wilamowitz accordingly tried to bring line 785 into agreement with that passage, and to achieve responsion, by emending ἀραίας to ἀρχαίας and accepting the correction of ἐπικότους to ἐπίκοτος. Both reasons given by the epic fragments involve the sons' care of their father and would be appropriate to the situation in the *Seven*. In one version the cause of trouble is inherited family property, in the other an unjust division. One of the main concerns of the extant play is how the brothers will share their inheritance equitably.

Apollodorus gives a different account: that the sons did not intervene when the blinded Oedipus was driven from Thebes.[69] Here again, though in a different sense, it is in care for their father that they are at fault. In Sophocles' *Oedipus at Colonus*, Oedipus complains that his sons, unlike his daughters, have neglected him, and in one passage he connects this reproach with his curses, which he thereupon renews.[70] Cameron plausibly relates this version to the theme of *gerotrophia* in the *Seven*.[71]

All the above accounts rest on one assumption: that a significant interval elapsed between the self-blinding and the curse, during which Oedipus was presumably shut up or in retirement. And they all refer τροφᾶς in line 786 to Oedipus's nurture. Manton, among others, follows Schütz in understanding the word as an allusion to the brothers' upbringing. He thus accepts the latter's argument "that the scholiast was merely misinterpreting ἐπίκοτος τροφᾶς in this passage, and that these words rightly mean that Oedipus was enraged at the thought of having reared the sons of an incestuous marriage."[72] This interpretation requires a correction of line 785 different from that of Wilamowitz, such as Hermann's τέκνοισιν δ᾽ ἀράς.[73] It would have the great advantage of making the self-blinding and curse occur in one climactic fit of rage on Oedipus's part.[74] And it supplies the curse with a motive which would emphasize the perversion of family relationships so important to the myth and to the *Seven*. Oedipus's attitude toward his sons, in fact, would be markedly similar to Laius's position with regard to Oedipus himself—a child also begotten under questionable circumstances, whose father actually tried to dispose of him.

All these versions, however, would fit well with the major themes of the play, and there is no way of deciding finally among them. Not even the precise form of the curse is known. Oedipus's words cannot, at any rate, have been as explicit as they are in the fragment of the *Thebais* quoted by the scholiast on Sophocles, because the *Seven* depends in large part upon the gradual emergence of the curse's full import.[75]

The Quarrel between Eteocles and Polynices

In the third generation, the instrument of the curse is the dispute between the sons of Oedipus. As to its origin in Aeschylus, we are again completely in the dark. In the most common version of the story (followed by Euripides)[76] the brothers agreed to rule Thebes in alternate years, but Eteocles refused to relinquish the power when his year expired. Pherecydes, we are told, said that Polynices was forcibly ejected from Thebes;[77] that also would make Eteocles culpable. According to the same source, however, Hellanicus said that Polynices ceded the kingship to Eteocles in return for the chiton and

necklace of Harmonia and withdrew to Argos. Presumably he would
have been responsible for the conflict if he had turned greedy later
on and demanded the kingship as well.[78] I doubt that Aeschylus used
any of these accounts, because each puts the fault on only one of the
brothers, leaving the other, by implication, blameless.

Cameron argues that Aeschylus followed the version of the myth
recorded by Hellanicus, and so thinks (along with most scholars)
that in the *Seven* "justice is without question solely on Eteocles'
side. The chorus, which has ample opportunity to criticize Eteocles,
never once says he has wronged his brother."[79] No, but neither do
the chorus say the opposite. What they do say, near the end of the
play, is that the brothers suffer a *common* fate as the result of a
mutual act.[80] That may well imply that they share the guilt equally.
Elsewhere in the play, it is true, Amphiaraus sharply rebukes Polynices—not, however, for starting the quarrel, but for invading his
homeland.[81]

The *Seven*, in fact, contains only one indication of the origin of
the dispute: ἦ ζῶντ', ἀτιμαστῆρα τῶς ἀνδρηλάτην ... (line 637, part
of Polynices' threat as reported by the spy). That is essentially the
reading of all the manuscripts.[82] The last word has been emended
to ἀνδρηλατῶν, so that it describes Polynices' intentions, but the
only reason for the change is the assumption that Eteocles is innocent and Polynices guilty.[83] Altering the text to fit a preconceived
view of the characters is risky at best. Left in the accusative, the
word implies that Eteocles drove his brother from Thebes—a charge
which Eteocles never explicitly denies. Thus in the Aeschylean version of the story he must have been as responsible for the quarrel
as Polynices.

Apart from the bare hint in that one line, the text of the *Seven*
does not indicate how the dispute arose. It is a fair inference that
Aeschylus was not concerned with placing the blame clearly on one
side or the other. By the point in the story which the *Seven* treats,
the issues must have become so confused that questions of original
right and wrong would no longer have mattered very much. Probably
each brother could lay claim to justice.[84] That would fit with the
emphasis in the play on their common fate, common blood, and
common heritage. Far more important than their individual claims
are the curse, the fact of the quarrel, and above all, the issue in
mutual slaughter.[85]

Aeschylus evidently contrived the fratricide by making two adjust-ments in the traditional story. He probably devised the matching of a Theban champion against each of the seven Argives at the city gates— a process which ends by opposing Eteocles to his own brother. And although the names of the Argive Seven go back to epic, Aeschylus made an important change in excluding Adrastus from the group of assailants at the gates. That leaves Polynices as the most fitting oppo-nent for Eteocles.[86]

Family and City

The response of the Delphic oracle to Laius implied a close inter-weaving of the city's fortunes with his own. That would be plausible only because at the time Laius was, or was about to become, ruler of Thebes. Of Apollo's warning, Manton remarks, "a paradoxical response, since normally a king would regard it as his duty to provide for the carrying on of his own guardianship of the state by begetting a son."[87] But the Labdacidae are no normal family, because of the taint they carry, and through their position they disrupt the civil life of Thebes. An ordered dynasty would mean political stability, and that is precisely what they cannot provide. In an important sense, the city and its ruling family are one. They grow distinct only in the course of the trilogy's concluding play.

Many readers of the *Seven* have found it difficult to explain why Thebes finally survives. The ultimate consequence of the birth of Oedipus was the Argive invasion; why, in the *Seven*, is this threat averted? Most of the answers which have been offered seem rather desperate. They see Aeschylus relenting at the last and breaking the momentum built up through the trilogy towards Thebes' destruc-tion.[88]

Oracles, however, possess this fiendish characteristic: they are always fulfilled in the end, often in unforeseen ways. So it is in this case, if the response is considered as much a prophecy as a command. Apollo's oracle *is* ultimately fulfilled because Laius *does* die without issue, even though he leaves a son. How does this paradoxical result come about?

Apollo told Laius that he would keep the city safe by dying γέννας ἄτερ. There is a faint ambiguity here, for γέννα can mean either "son" or "family." Laius is finally deprived of the latter in the sense of "continuous line." Because Eteocles and Polynices die childless in the *Seven* (line 828), Laius has left no male descendants beyond the third generation. The difficulty with interpreting the oracle, then, lies in the timing of events. The birth and subsequent survival of Oedipus naturally seem to rule out Laius's compliance with the god's warning. Then either the city must be ruined or the condition imposed on Laius must be met in a more roundabout fashion. The latter is what happens. The stipulation of the oracle is thus satisfied in a manner which would not have been immediately apparent from its wording but which is not incompatible with those terms.[89]

When the end comes in the final play, Apollo, appropriately, oversees it (lines 800-802):

$$\tau\grave{a}\varsigma\ \delta'\ \dot{\epsilon}\beta\delta\acute{o}\mu a\varsigma\ \dot{o}\ \sigma\epsilon\mu\nu\grave{o}\varsigma\ \dot{\epsilon}\beta\delta o\mu a\gamma\acute{\epsilon}\tau a\varsigma$$
$$\ddot{a}\nu a\xi\ \mathrm{A}\pi\acute{o}\lambda\lambda\omega\nu\ \epsilon\ddot{\iota}\lambda\epsilon\tau',\ \mathrm{O}\acute{\iota}\delta\acute{\iota}\pi o\upsilon\ \gamma\acute{\epsilon}\nu\epsilon\iota$$
$$\kappa\rho a\acute{\iota}\nu\omega\nu\ \pi a\lambda a\iota\grave{a}\varsigma\ \Lambda a\acute{\iota}o\upsilon\ \delta\upsilon\sigma\beta o\upsilon\lambda\acute{\iota}a\varsigma.$$

The last word recalls $\dot{a}\beta o\upsilon\lambda\iota\hat{a}\nu$ in line 750. Apollo "brings to completion" on the heads of Oedipus's sons the folly which caused Laius to beget a child. And so the curse which led to that folly is fulfilled. The god supervises the accomplishment of his oracle and guards its veracity. There is no sign that he exacts personal revenge. It is the same when Eteocles describes his race as "god-abhorred" and "hated by Apollo" (lines 653, 691). The family's existence is unnatural and disruptive.[90]

If, then, as I have argued, no earlier threat to the city prompted Laius to consult the oracle, but he himself put its safety in jeopardy by having a son, and if his grandsons' deaths ultimately fulfill Apollo's prophecy, there is no need for the city to be ruined. The story upon which the trilogy was based would thus have followed a perfect curve, from the engendering of a race which should not have been born and the concomitant imperiling of Thebes, to the extinction of that race and the release of the city from danger. By shaping the myth in this way, Aeschylus provided his trilogy with an inner coherence.

THE FORM OF THE TRILOGY

The legend as Aeschylus treated it also had a unifying theme, a family curse that was to last through the third generation. This was

well suited to the requirements of a trilogy: each play dealt with the
misfortunes of one generation.[91] This plan, besides being convenient,
must in itself have stressed that the curse was inherited.

The fragments of the *Laius* and *Oedipus* afford only meager evidence as to what events were dramatized in those plays. The *Laius*
contained a reference (fr. 171)[92] to the exposure of the infant
Oedipus, possibly in a narrative of past events. Perhaps in connection with this was given an account of the oracle Laius had received.[93]
A report (in a messenger's speech?) of the fatal meeting between
Laius and his son at a crossroad may have come later in the same
play.[94] Fragment 172, which gives the location of the crossroad,
shows that Laius cannot have been on his way to Delphi when he fell
in with Oedipus, in contrast to the version of the story followed by
Sophocles. His purpose and destination are unknown. Fragment 173
may reflect something recounted in the same speech—that the
murderer tasted the blood of his victim and spat it out. This, if genuine, is interesting. The act is an attempt to ward off vengeance by
the victim's spirit or Erinys. It has the same object as the mutilation
of Agamemnon's corpse referred to in the *Choephori* (line 439), and
it is to have no more success. But the form of the act in the *Laius*
may have further significance. It is a son who has spilled and now
tastes his own father's blood. In the *Seven*, when Eteocles and Polynices kill each other, their blood mingles on the ground (lines 938–
40)—blood tainted by the guilt which is their heritage. What the
chorus say of them there might be applied to Oedipus and Laius as
well: κάρτα δ᾽ εἰσ᾽ ὅμαιμοι. In fact, as will be argued, blood is a
recurrent theme in the *Seven*. Perhaps it was important to the whole
trilogy.

Fragments 1, 2, and 4 of *Papyrus Oxyrhynchus* 2256 furnish what
appear to be parts of hypotheses to each of the two lost plays. Fragment 1, which probably belongs to the *Laius*, seems to indicate that
Laius spoke the prologue. Fragment 2 is part of an argument, perhaps to the *Oedipus*, which gives essentially the same information as
the hypothesis prefixed to the *Seven* in the Medicean manuscript.
Fragment 4 seems also to concern the *Oedipus*, and apparently
records that the chorus of that play consisted of aged Theban citizens.[95] It breaks off just before telling who delivered the prologue.
To judge from the wording of the fragment, the chorus probably
did not do so; perhaps Oedipus himself did. It is likely, then, that

the prologues of both plays, like that of the *Seven*, were in trimeters and not anapaestic. Moreover, if the chorus of the *Laius* was composed of some group of citizens and if Oedipus played a prominent role in the play that bore his name, then the city and the ruling family would have been represented together on stage throughout the trilogy. That is hardly an uncommon practice in tragedy—one thinks, for instance, of the *Persians* and *Agamemnon*. But in the Theban trilogy, it may have been particularly significant in view of the oracle given to Laius and of the complex relationship between the city and his family.

That is all the fragments reveal. We can reasonably guess that the lost dramas contained certain indispensable events, with others assumed to have occurred in the intervals between plays. (The satyr-play, the *Sphinx*, probably dealt with one of the latter.) The *Laius* must have had the king's departure from Thebes (if he was present to speak the prologue) and a report of his murder. Could there have been a *threnos* over his body at the end? The *Oedipus* would have included the hero's discovery of his identity and guilt, his self-blinding, and apparently his curse on his sons; it might also have presented his death, though that may have been left to the time between the *Oedipus* and the *Seven*. But beyond that we cannot go, and not even all those events need have been portrayed.[96]

The Theban trilogy seems to have been constructed quite differently from the *Oresteia*. The latter shows the effect of a curse on two generations of a family, though its origins are much earlier than Agamemnon's time. The story of Orestes occupies the latter two plays. The *Eumenides* represents the great change in the pattern—in fact, an end to it. The plan of the *Oresteia* is thus A-A-B, with the first two plays, where the curse is at work, practically mirroring each other scene for scene, and the *Eumenides* opposed to them.[97] The Theban trilogy, by contrast, treats *three* generations, and the Erinys wreaks her havoc in the course of each play.

All three plays might then have had the same general plan, particularly if, in the *Laius* and the *Oedipus* as in the *Seven*, the meaning of the curse was revealed suddenly at the climax. Many have found it odd that for the first two-thirds of the *Seven* there is only one reference to the curse, and that Eteocles goes about his preparations for the city's defense as if it did not exist. At line 653 an abrupt change takes place as the curse takes control of him. It was remarked above that in Aeschylus's treatment of the Oedipus myth a long interval of prosperity apparently preceded the *anagnorisis*, and that the climax was thus delayed. Could Oedipus have appeared at the beginning of the second play at the height of his fame and happiness, only later to be revealed, with dreadful suddenness, as a guilty man? One can conceive a similar arrangement in the *Laius*: Apollo's oracle at first apparently satisfied, and then, on Laius's death, a latent problem abruptly revealed. At the risk (surely surmountable) of some monotony, the regularity, and thus the relentlessness, of the curse would be emphasized. The similarity in construction of the plays might add to the horror of the curse's working, much as in the first two plays of the *Oresteia*.

This is speculation, but the Theban trilogy does seem to have proceeded directly through three generations of disaster. Méautis has aptly called it "la trilogie de l'anéantissement."[98] This pattern of calamity provides the context within which the surviving play must be viewed.

THE SYMMETRY OF THE *SEVEN*

The *Seven* presents the consummation of the curse through the fulfillment of Apollo's oracle in an unforeseen and chilling way. As I have observed, this outcome releases the city from the peril brought upon it by Laius's family, and so separates their respective fates. The structure of the play stresses this tendency toward isolation of the family.

Wilamowitz speaks of "eine schöne Symmetrie" in the play, with the shield scene as "das Mittelstück und das Hauptstück."[99] In fact, the *Seven* seems organized in ring composition around the central scene. Framing that on either side is a block of two units, an epirrhematic scene followed by a stasimon (lines 181–286, 677–719; 287–368, 720–91). The two epirrhematic scenes between Eteocles and the chorus are similar in form. The first and second stasima both represent a turning inward by the chorus to assess the situation, and so correspond. In the first, the maidens imagine what the sack of a city is like; in the second, they begin to work out the meaning of the curse. The terror of the parodos (lines 78–180) is answered by the mourning in the third stasimon (lines 822–60). The *kommos* (lines 875–1004) answers the prologue (lines 1–77);[100] Eteocles' reference to the curse in line 70 as μεγασθενής finds bitter confirmation in the chorus's exclamation (lines 977, 988), μέλαιν᾽ Ἐρινύς, ἦ μεγασθενής τις εἶ, and the ring is thus closed.

The one part of the play which does not quite fit this scheme is the short messenger scene (lines 792–820). There the outcome of the war is reported—the city's victory and the death of the brothers. The messenger announces the fulfillment, in an unexpected way, of Eteocles' prayer in lines 264–86: the gods have indeed protected the city, while he and his brother have been destroyed by the family's own divinity, the Erinys. In this sense, the two passages may be said to correspond, although this relation disturbs the symmetry some-what.[101] More generally, however, the messenger scene sums up all that has preceded it; in it are recapitulated many of the important themes and images of the play. At the same time, it leads into the choral lament (lines 822 ff.). The scene thus stands by itself as a summing up and a transitional passage, yet with a certain special relation to Eteocles' earlier prayer.[102]

The play's structure, then, can be outlined as shown in figure 1. In view of the neatness of this structure, those troubled by the abrupt break at line 653 should not be too quick to criticize the play for lacking unity. The sudden change at that point is anything but a flaw in craftsmanship. I would agree with Solmsen that it results from the Erinys, as her operation, after a period of apparent quiescence, suddenly becomes manifest. The whole of the *Seven*, says Karl Reinhardt, follows the same pattern as individual scenes of the *Oresteia*. At first a person or event is viewed only in positive terms. But there is usually something drastically wrong, which breaks forth suddenly and despite all attempts to ignore it.[103] In the *Seven* the change, when it does come, is all the more startling and terrifying for the delay. And this kind of structure emphasizes that in spite of the most energetic and well-intentioned efforts to the contrary, *the curse will be fulfilled.*

Not only the sudden break, but the ring composition itself stresses the change. The portions of the play which follow the shield scene do not simply repeat their counterparts which precede it. The relation betweeen each pair of corresponding sections is that of mirror images. In the first epirrhematic scene, the chorus are in panic and Eteocles attempts to calm them. In the second, these roles are reversed: Eteocles is seized by a kind of mad desire, and the chorus, though

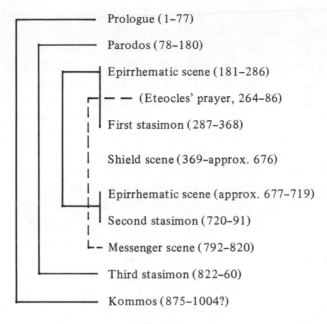

Prologue (1–77)

Parodos (78–180)

Epirrhematic scene (181–286)

— — (Eteocles' prayer, 264–86)

First stasimon (287–368)

Shield scene (369–approx. 676)

Epirrhematic scene (approx. 677–719)

Second stasimon (720–91)

Messenger scene (792–820)

Third stasimon (822–60)

Kommos (875–1004?)

FIGURE 1

themselves still agitated, try to dissuade him. Not only do they address him ominously as "child of Oedipus" at the beginning of each scene (lines 203, 677); but the similarity between lines 261 and 713 stresses the change in their relation to him. In the first stasimon, the chorus fear for the city and for themselves. In the second stasimon, the concern has largely shifted, and narrowed, from the city to its ruling family. Eteocles' prayer to the gods for victory is fulfilled, in the way described above, by the messenger's speech which announces the outcome of the battle in a manner Eteocles had not anticipated. Similarly, the chorus's generalized terror in the parodos is balanced by the lament over the curse's accomplishment in the third stasimon. Their dread has turned out to have been justified, though not by ruin of the city. The *kommos* at the end, aside from its verbal echo of the prologue as noted above, is the realization of a possibility voiced by Eteocles in lines 6–8, but under circumstances not contemplated there. Thus the tendency, as the play proceeds, is toward fulfillment, toward greater specificity as possibilities are eliminated in favor of the one inevitable result determined by the curse. And there is a consequent shift in emphasis and narrowing of focus from the city to the single house represented by the brothers. The fortunes of the city and of the family thus diverge.

The axis of this shift is, of course, the long shield scene. As I observed earlier, this scene portrays the process by which the burden of the conflict is transferred from the warring states to the single pair of opponents, Eteocles and Polynices. Some have found this central scene tedious, and improbable in the context of an impending assault. Not the least of these critics was Euripides. In his *Phoenissae*, Eteocles says to Creon of the Argive champions, "it would be an expenditure of a great deal of time to tell the name of each when the enemy has taken up position beneath the very walls."[104] This is apparently a criticism of Aeschylus. Instead, Euripides spends a great many lines on a messenger's speech describing the battle after it is over.[105] In Aeschylus's play, the corresponding messenger scene is remarkably brief—so short, in fact, that one writer postulates a giant lacuna where, he thinks, a similar description of the battle has dropped out of our text.[106] This suggestion does not do justice to the structure of the play; the messenger's report has a definite function, as we have seen, but that is not narration. Aeschylus composed a far more compact and forceful drama than Euripides. And since he threw the weight of it into the shield scene and reduced the messenger scene to the bare minimum necessary, we have to ask why.

The answer is not difficult. The battle is fought and won symbolically before the audience by means of the shield tokens. But that is not the complete answer. It must be added that the battle *in itself* does not matter very much, for it is the result—the outward manifestation only—of the curse. The battle merely provides the setting for the decisive duel between the two brothers. The Erinys contrives their meeting through the matching of heroes in the central scene. How she does so, according to a horribly consistent method of her own, will be discussed in a later chapter.[107]

SUMMARY AND CONCLUSIONS

The plot of the Theban trilogy was the effect of the curse on the family of Laius—the twisted tale of the births of his son and grandsons, and the destruction of all the members of that family. The trilogy was organized so that the three plays in turn represented the misfortunes of three successive generations. Possibly all three plays were constructed according to a common plan, though the state of the evidence leaves this uncertain. At any rate, in the *Seven* we can observe how the development of the plot is clarified by the structure. So long as the danger appears to come from an enemy attack on the city, no matter how grave it is, it can be met with the conventional resources of military measures and prayers to enlist divine aid. This is the evident situation in the part of the play which precedes the shield scene. After that scene, Eteocles is faced with a problem—no longer in his capacity as ruler but as an individual under a curse—and he is helpless against it. He can only let the situation take control of him.

The movement from the first section of the play to the third is not so much toward a change in circumstances as toward a recognition of the situation for what it really is. The relation between corresponding scenes and odes in these two sections stresses this new understanding. The shield scene gains particular emphasis from its position at the center of the framing sections. Although the curse is finally accomplished later by the brothers' mutual fratricide, in this scene it is already at work, paring away all other possibilities until, with the last set of speeches, the implications of the situation for himself and for his family become clear to Eteocles. This middle section of the play, then, not only provides a transition between the other two parts; it also presents the decisive moment of insight into what actually is happening.

This new knowledge must have had the startling quality of revelation, not only for Eteocles himself but also for the spectators. They would have known of the curse from the two preceding plays, and they may even have suspected that the danger was not so conveniently external as it appeared early in the *Seven*. They would also have recognized the result toward which the shield scene was leading. But only at the end of that scene does it become clear that the whole situation has been determined by the curse. Abruptly but unmistakably, events are seen to fit into an intelligible pattern.

The plan of the *Seven* seems to have been calculated to create this effect upon the audience, for it is clearly the way Aeschylus chose, above all other possible ways, to organize his plot. The structure thus gives to the plot the desired emphasis at each moment, and a comprehensible shape over all. This was not the function of the structure alone, however, but of the imagery and dramatic presentation as well.

2

Imagery I: The City

The imagery of the *Seven Against Thebes* has not received the systematic study it merits. A few themes and images have occasionally been pointed out, but rather sporadically, with little or no attempt made to relate them to one another.[1] The outstanding exception is the nautical imagery, on which no writer on the play can fail to comment. Most discussions of the imagery, in fact, begin and end with this,[2] and even its importance has been variously assessed. Of the writers who consider the nautical language basic to the *Seven*, van Nes and Cameron give it thorough treatment.[3] Cameron alone notices that it develops in the course of the play, along the lines to be indicated below. He also draws attention to several other important themes.

The discussion which follows here will include a number of themes and images which have never before been remarked, and will, in addition, attempt to demonstrate that there is a coherent pattern of interrelated imagery, nearly all of which is developed and modulated to emphasize the progress of the plot. A general view of the imagery may also shed light on individual passages which, in themselves, seem rather puzzling.

It has often been observed that the play has a double concern.[4] As the focus of the war narrows from the opposing armies to the fight between Eteocles and Polynices, so the attention of the play shifts from the city to the family. This movement is reflected in and reinforced by the development of the imagery. At the start of the play, when the curse is in the background (or has involved the whole city in a common danger in accordance with the oracle Laius received), Thebes and her ruling house, represented by Eteocles, are closely identified. Until the shield scene, the play's imagery refers to the city and the general threat of the war. It characterizes the life of the city, and the value and fragility of its qualities. In the shield scene, the great change takes place. Near the end of the scene, in a very striking

31

way, the imagery previously associated with the city is shifted to the family. Moreover, immediately afterwards, several other images, some of which were introduced earlier with only general reference, become prominent in connection with the two brothers and with the way the curse effects their ruin.[5] As the real meaning of the curse is revealed, the scope of the play narrows, and the imagery, at first almost free-floating, comes to be specifically applied to Eteocles and Polynices. In retrospect, its import appears to have been ominous for them all along.

Thus each time certain words, phrases, themes, and images recur in the *Seven,* they bear an important relation to the context. As the play progresses, moreover, this relation becomes clearer and alters in important ways.[6] It is therefore possible to speak of a structure of images and themes, and of their movement in the course of the play.

The images which at first have general reference to the city and its situation will be the subject of this chapter; those more closely associated with the brothers will be examined in the next.[7]

THE NAUTICAL IMAGERY

The language which depicts the city as a ship threatened by a violent storm at sea can justly be called the basic or unifying image of the play; the *Seven* is full of nautical terms from start to finish. But though this is a consistent image, it is not static.

At the very beginning, Eteocles introduces the two most important aspects of this image, when he characterizes the duties of the political leader (lines 2–3):

$$\text{ὅστις φυλάσσει πρᾶγος ἐν πρύμνῃ πόλεως}$$
$$\text{οἴακα νωμῶν, βλέφαρα μὴ κοιμῶν ὕπνῳ.}$$

The city has a stern and a tiller, and hence is a ship. And in the stern, handling the tiller, sits Eteocles. He is, then, in control of the city, and the responsibility for careful and vigilant guidance rests on him. This is a proper description of the position of the heir of the ruling house. But it is on precisely this point–on the legitimacy of Eteocles' control–that the questions of the play turn, just as one of the problems of the whole trilogy was the relation of the family to the state. Though the question at this point seems moot, it must have been fresh in the minds of the trilogy's original audience after the other two plays; as the *Seven* itself proceeds, this question will be found to have been, all along, very much alive. Thus the introduction of the idea of the helmsman, at the outset, is not haphazard. Aeschylus sustains this idea by using it twice more in the early part of the play. The spy compares Eteocles to a ship's οἰακοστρόφος in lines 62-63; and Eteocles himself draws a similar parallel in his efforts to pacify the chorus (lines 208-10). In each case, calm preparation and provident control are required of him if the city's safety is to be preserved.

Gradually, in the course of frequent repetition, Aeschylus fills in the important details of the image. The ship is in the midst of no easy voyage; it is being tossed by a storm which threatens to swamp it. The turbulent sea is the Argive army rushing fully armed to the attack, as the spy tells Eteocles (lines 59-61):

> ἐγγὺς γὰρ ἤδη πάνοπλος Ἀργείων στρατὸς
> χωρεῖ, κονίει, πεδία δ᾽ ἀργηστὴς ἀφρὸς
> χραίνει σταλαγμοῖς ἱππικῶν ἐκ πλευμόνων.

Here the plain before the city is the surface of the sea, for πεδία can be applied to either.[8] The foam on the agitated waves is represented literally by the foam from the horses' mouths. The whole army is a "wave on dry land," driven by the wind supplied by Ares, god of war (lines 63-64).

The details of this description are still tied rather closely to their literal counterparts. But when the terrified chorus use similar language, the only literal referent is the men of the assaulting army (lines 114-15):

> κῦμα περὶ πτόλιν δοχμολόφων ἀνδρῶν
> καχλάζει πνοαῖς Ἄρεος ὀρόμενον.

The wave is breaking around the city, again driven by the breath of Ares. But now the foam is represented by the tossing plumes on the invaders' helmets, and the sound of the rushing water is given by the onomatopoeic word καχλάζει. This is a splendid description, which conveys all the frightening sights and noises that attend the onset of the attackers.[9] Similar are the challenges which Capaneus hurls at Zeus—his κυμαίνοντ᾽ ἔπη (line 443), which Dumortier compares with the πόντον . . . κυμαίνοντα of *Iliad* 14.229.[10]

The plains before Thebes are in tumult with the advancing wave. The walls and towers of the city must be relied upon to keep it out. In the first explicit reference to these in the play, Eteocles uses terms which, as Tucker explains, "are accommodated to both a town and a ship" (lines 30–33).[11] In the same way, he tells the chorus to pray that the towers remain watertight against the enemy force (line 216): πύργον στέγειν εὔχεσθε πολέμιον δόρυ. The chorus themselves pick up this language a few lines later (line 234).

Thus the equation of city with ship is suggested and maintained in the early part of the play. Now let us see what Aeschylus does with it as the play develops. In a lengthy comparison during the shield scene (lines 602–608), Eteocles likens Amphiaraus's position in the Argive army to that of a pious man on a ship doomed by its evil crew or of a just man in a city of impious people. Although it uses the now familiar terms of ship and state, this passage differs significantly from those mentioned above. Here nautical language is not applied to a city. Ship and city are introduced paratactically and developed as separate but similar terms of comparison. For neither Thebes nor any other city is being described here, but a third element—the Argive army. Furthermore, in contrast to Thebes' position as it has been depicted up to this point, the ship and city to which the Argives are compared are threatened not from outside but by moral weakness within.

It is surprising to find nautical language used to describe the enemy, and to observe that the city has itself become a metaphor. Yet this can hardly be coincidence in view of the care and consistency with which Thebes has been identified with a ship. I would suggest that Aeschylus deliberately introduces a variation upon his imagery here to make us view the war from both sides and recognize the similarities between the Theban and Argive positions, and that he does so because the character of the war is now becoming more clearly defined. The situation is not, as it first appeared, simply one of a city in disarray attacked by a wholly unified aggressor. And even when we allow for the obvious differences between the two sides, this parallel remains: both the Argive army and Thebes are in danger, and this danger is highlighted in each case by internal disunity. Amphiaraus is at odds with the other Argives, and Eteocles with the chorus. Can we also detect a likeness between the city and the enemy in the nature and location of the danger? The moral position of Thebes as a whole is strong, but this claim cannot be made for its leader. Thus the city, like the enemy, is threatened from within by guilt, although in Thebes the taint is limited to the ruling house. We shall see later, in fact, that the speeches describing Amphiaraus, including the passage discussed here, have important implications for Eteocles' own situation.[12] At this point, we need only notice that the real conflict turns out to be inside his own curse-laden family.

This realization comes to Eteocles in the very next set of speeches, with the news that the attacker at the seventh gate will be his own brother. The spy closes his speech with a significant admonition (line 652): . . . σὺ δ' αὐτὸς γνῶθι ναυκληρεῖν πόλιν. Even if it were not repeated emphatically from two lines above, the imperative itself would indicate concern that Eteocles might relinquish control. Eteocles' speech which follows justifies this worry. Although, as he makes clear (lines 673-75), he is an appropriate opponent for Polynices in a military as well as a personal sense, in regard to his private fortunes he abandons the tiller (lines 689-91):

> ἐπεὶ τὸ πρᾶγμα κάρτ' ἐπισπέρχει θεός,
> ἴτω κατ' οὖρον, κῦμα Κωκυτοῦ λαχόν,
> Φοίβῳ στυγηθὲν πᾶν τὸ Λαΐου γένος.

As many have remarked, his attitude here contradicts his earlier words to the chorus (lines 208-10). The vessel is left to go with the wind. But the ship is now the family of Laius, the water that of Cocytus. And the wind? That is no longer Ares, but has become the *daimon* of the house (lines 705-708), the curse or the Erinys. Ares is still involved, but in a different manifestation—not as the god of war in general, but as the spirit of strife between the brothers.

This passage anticipates one of the most beautiful sections in the play, the lament in lines 854-60, where the boat is the one which crosses Acheron, rowed by the chorus's gestures of mourning, with the following wind of their cries, decked in black, a grim parody of the *Theoris* sacred to Apollo.[13] Here again the reference is solely to the brothers: the curse has done its work. The city, as represented by the chorus, is involved in the family's troubles no longer directly, through risk to its well-being, but sympathetically: it grieves.

Though nautical imagery refers to the family rather than the city in

lines 689–91, the shift in its application from the one to the other
is not complete until the second stasimon, when the chorus express
their fears in the light of the family's history (lines 758–65):[14]

> κακῶν δ᾽ ὥσπερ θάλασσα κῦμ᾽ ἄγει·
> τὸ μὲν πίτνον, ἄλλο δ᾽ ἀείρει
> τρίχαλον, ὃ καὶ περὶ πρύμναν πόλεως καχλάζει.
> μεταξὺ δ᾽ ἄλκαρ ὅδ᾽ ὀλίγῳ
> τείνει πύργος ἐν εὔρει.
> δέδοικα δὲ σὺν βασιλεῦσι
> μὴ πόλις δαμασθῇ.

Since this is a transitional passage between the stories of Laius and
Oedipus, the context suggests that the first line (758), with its image
of a "sea of troubles" driving waves of calamity, describes the experi-
ences of the family. But the following lines make it clear that the
chorus are also still concerned with the danger to the city posed by
the Argive attack. The words ἄλλο δ᾽ ἀείρει τρίχαλον continue
the sea imagery and refer to the problems afflicting the third generation of Laius's line. At the same time, with the relative clause in line
760, the phrase suddenly changes its reference and depicts the enemy
army rushing upon the city, in a return to the way nautical language
was used earlier in the play. There are reminiscences of previous
descriptions. Once again the city has a stern, and the wave foams
around it (καχλάζει, repeated from line 115). Against it the city can
interpose only a thin barrier, "a tower in width";[15] in the same way,
the city's walls and towers were earlier compared implicitly with the
sides of a ship.

Five years before, Aeschylus had used this same image of the "sea
of troubles" in the *Persians*.[16] There it had literal reference to the sea
battle of Salamis. In the present passage of the *Seven*, it also has a
literal counterpart—the attacking Argive army. The ease with which
this image passes from connection with the family into a description
of the city's peril emphasizes not only that the same danger threatens
both, but also that the enemy assault is itself a consequence and
manifestation of the curse.

Here, then, the vessel is at once the city and the family. The misdeeds of all three generations of the ruling house have endangered
Thebes, as Apollo's oracle implied. The last two lines of the passage

sum up this fact, but they also contain a shift in emphasis. Fitted
into the pattern of the past, the danger is now seen to arise from and
center on the family. No longer is the city in general faced with ruin,
but the family; the threat to the city is now that it might be involved
in the disaster of the house (δέδοικα δὲ σὺν βασιλεῦσι/μὴ πόλις
δαμασθῇ). A new distinction is felt between Thebes and her rulers.

In the following strophe, in fact, nautical language is applied to
individual men: when wealth grows too fat, it is necessary to jettison
some of the cargo (lines 769–71).[17] In the antistrophe, this statement
is brought to bear on the story of Oedipus, as the γάρ of line 772 indicates. It is now the individual, not the city, who is on a dangerous
course.[18] Aeschylus was to use the same figure, again with reference
to an individual case, in the *Agamemnon* (lines 1008–13).[19]

The messenger's news of the outcome of the battle, immediately
after this stasimon, makes the distinction complete. Lines 795–98 of
his first speech recapitulate much of the nautical language previously
applied to the city, but with this difference: the city's defense has
been successful and it is out of danger. Πόλις δ᾽ ἐν εὐδίᾳ—the storm
is over, the sky is clear, the sea is calm. Far different is the case of
the brothers. The daimon's gale has not veered to a gentle breeze (cf.
lines 705–708), and they have been swept away by their father's
curse (line 819).

Thus the application of the nautical imagery shrinks to the point
where, in lines 854–60, it refers exclusively to the brothers. This process begins in the shield scene and is continued in the following
epirrhematic scene and in the second stasimon. The same movement
can be clearly traced in two minor aspects of the same theme. In
line 283, when Eteocles says that he will select seven Theban champions to face the Argives, he calls them ἀντηρέται—"opposing row-
ers." Similarly, the spy urges him to select σοφούς τε κἀγαθοὺς
ἀντηρέτας to fight Amphiaraus (line 595). In the final lament, on the
other hand, the same term is applied to one of the brothers (line
992).

Secondly, near the end of their picture of the sack of a city, the
chorus describe how the "earth's bounty" is poured out in confusion:
ἐν ῥοθίοις φορεῖται (line 362). This phrase is interesting, for ῥόθιος
is commonly used of the noise of waves.[20] In the prologue, Eteocles says that he will be the object of the city's sorrow and resent-
ment if things go wrong, and he uses a word based on a similar root

(φροιμίοις πολυρρόθοις, line 7). Here too the sound of water is suggested.[21] Eteocles' prediction will come true, though in the form of disaster to himself and not to the city. Similarly, φορεῖται in line 362 can refer to an object swept along by the current. That is how the messenger uses the same verb in line 819, this time of the brothers carried away, clearly like a ship in distress, by their father's curse. And the latter line in turn recalls Eteocles' own phrase in line 690, ἴτω κατ᾽ οὖρον.

The nautical imagery makes vivid the urgency of the danger and the fragility of the city. The idea of a ship tossing amid angry waves gives an impression of imbalance, which the terrified women of the chorus visibly embody. The crisis has upset the normal equilibrium necessary to the survival of the city. Only a tower's width offers safety, just as a ship's sides are all that stand between what is inside the vessel and the raging waters without. The same applies to individual life. When this imagery shifts to Eteocles, it signifies the mental imbalance suggested by his words in the scene with the chorus in lines 677 ff. Human life, in the face of the gods' will and of daemonic powers, is fragile, readily upset by guilt. Here too, balance is necessary to safety (cf. lines 766–71).

Aeschylus did not originate the ship imagery. Archilochus and Alcaeus probably, and Theognis certainly, had used it, the last two to describe a city threatened by internal discord.[22] That may be, as has been claimed,[23] its final significance for Thebes in the *Seven*, but in the special and restricted sense which will be discussed in the next section. For the first half of the play, however, Aeschylus uses this imagery to describe a city under attack from outside. In this respect it must have had special meaning for the play's original audience. Not many years before, the city of Athens had literally been a ship, the wooden walls its defense.[24] Doubtless there were many, in that audience of 467 B.C., who could remember vividly the urgency of the Persian threat, and who knew what it was like when one's native city was sacked.

THE CITY'S WALLS: INSIDE AND OUTSIDE

The literal counterparts to the nautical imagery are the walls, gates, and towers of Thebes (lines 30–33). Though they are themselves invisible to the audience, repeated mention of them is important to

the setting of the play.[25] They are also the basis for another recurring
theme, for the walls divide the inhabitants of Thebes from the
attackers without (lines 762–63). The opposition between what is
inside the city and what is outside is a major preoccupation of the
Seven. One indication of this is Aeschylus's far more frequent use of
words for "inside" and "outside" in this play than in any of his
others.[26]

The Thebans are inside the walls; outside are the Argives—loud,
violent, and alien to the land. This distinction is made early in the
prologue, when Eteocles, urging the citizens to man the ramparts,
refers to the Argives as "strangers" (ἐπήλυδες, line 34—literally,
"those who have come in").[27] This seems to be a war of a familiar,
if grim, type: the defense of a city against a foreign invader, where
the consequence of defeat is the devastation envisioned in the first
stasimon. There is also a danger within Thebes—the chorus's panic,
which is verbally equated with the noise and disorder of the Argive
attack.[28] From Eteocles' standpoint, in Helen Bacon's words, "there
is a danger 'outside' which must not be let in, and a danger 'inside'
which must not be let out."[29]   Eteocles therefore admonishes the
chorus (lines 200–201):

$$\mu\acute{\epsilon}\lambda\epsilon\iota\ \gamma\grave{\alpha}\rho\ \grave{\alpha}\nu\delta\rho\acute{\iota}{-}\mu\grave{\eta}\ \gamma\upsilon\nu\grave{\eta}\ \beta\upsilon\lambda\epsilon\upsilon\acute{\epsilon}\tau\omega\ {-}$$
$$\tau\breve{\alpha}\xi\omega\vartheta\epsilon\nu\cdot\ \breve{\epsilon}\nu\delta\upsilon\nu\ \delta'\ \upsilon\breve{\upsilon}\sigma\alpha\ \mu\grave{\eta}\ \beta\lambda\acute{\alpha}\beta\eta\nu\ \tau\acute{\iota}\vartheta\epsilon\iota.$$

The emphatic placing and contrast of the adverbs assert the distinction between the woman's place inside the city, where the passive
virtue of refraining from harm is exercised, and the masculine sphere
of action outside.

Such appears to be the nature of the war through at least the
middle of the shield scene. As long as the struggle seems simply for
the purpose of repelling an aggressor and demands only the talents of
a good general, Eteocles can, for the most part, control the situation—and himself. But the reality is more complex; as it is revealed,
the boundary between the internal and the external becomes blurred.
For the real danger lies inside the city, in the ruling house. Its causes
are the curse and the resulting intrafamilial strife. Accordingly, in the
end the battle will be fought not only, and not principally, between
the opposing armies, but between the brothers, *within* the family.
The assumption that the threat is purely external, which guides

the action in the first half of the play, ultimately fails to repress this truth.

The ambiguity of two phrases early in the play hints at what will later become explicit. In lines 193–94, Eteocles accuses the chorus of aiding those outside, while "we are ruined by ourselves from within." He has in mind, of course, the unreliability of women (as he sees it). But his language (αὐτοὶ δ᾽ ὑπ᾽ αὐτῶν, and the change in subject and voice of the verb from the two preceding lines), though not inappropriate to the context, makes this statement strikingly applicable to Eteocles' own position as party to a fraternal quarrel. The spy's concluding words to Eteocles in the prologue raise a similar question (line 68): εἰδὼς τὰ τῶν θύραθεν ἀβλαβὴς ἔσῃ. The singular verb does not affect the accuracy of this as an assessment of the situation in a normal war. By obtaining intelligence of the enemy's plans, the commander, and through him the whole army and city, would be guarded from harm. But this is no normal war; and it is, after all, Eteocles whom the spy addresses. Knowledge of τὰ τῶν θύραθεν is precisely what brings Eteocles face to face with his own brother in the course of the shield scene, though at the same time it does preserve the city.

From this point of view, Eteocles' words about the Sphinx on Parthenopaeus's shield are paradoxical (lines 558–60):[30]

> οὐδ᾽ εἰσαμεῖψαι τεῖχος ἐχθίστου δάκους
> εἰκὼ φέροντα πολεμίας ἐπ᾽ ἀσπίδος
> ἔξωθεν εἴσω . . .

The last two words, emphatically placed as before (line 201), insist on the difference between inside and out, and reflect a continued assumption that danger from without threatens to burst into the city. But they also invite the audience, who presumably would be alert to the discrepancy from having just seen the first two plays, to reflect on what is being ignored. For there is really no question of Parthenopaeus's introducing the Sphinx into the city. She afflicted Thebes long before the Argive attack; and in the version of the myth followed by Aeschylus her presence may have been a consequence of guilt in the ruling family.[31] If so, Parthenopaeus's shield token is a reminder that the invasion, like the Sphinx before, has been brought on the city by the house of Laius and is but the latest stage in the operation of the curse. That Parthenopaeus will be stopped before he can bring the Sphinx's image within the walls (lines 560–61) is consistent with the way Thebes finally is relieved of the danger posed by her rulers.[32]

This passage adumbrates the position of Eteocles and Polynices themselves. In their case too, what appears external turns out, fatally, to be internal. The arbiter who divides their inheritance is to be a foreigner from Scythia (line 728). But that means that he is the iron of their weapons, and hence is Ares, overseer of their duel, all too truly an insider (for example, lines 940–46). Thus the concepts of "inside" and "outside" draw attention to the contrast between the apparent and the real situation and then, by their realignment, locate the danger more precisely. The play moves from an early opposition between the citizens within the walls and the enemy without (though with indications even there that this is not the entire truth) through the shield scene, where this distinction becomes questionable, to the whole conflict's final concentration within the family.

There is no civil discord in the city, in the sense that might have been expected when two heirs to the power quarreled. No rival factions group themselves around Eteocles and Polynices. It is true that the chorus's panic threatens to create confusion for a time; but as the shield scene shows, Thebes can find capable defenders. The only significant inner disharmony is between Eteocles and the chorus, aggravated by Eteocles' condemnation of women, which in its extremity matches the maidens' fear. That the ruler is in conflict with his citizens is an indication of his family's peculiar position in Thebes.

Each generation of this family, in fact, has been at once of the city and alien. The confusion between the internal and external which runs through the *Seven* stems from this ambiguous history, and may thus have been a theme of the whole trilogy.[33] Laius was a Theban, but he returned from exile to assume power, and he brought with him the *miasma* of a curse, which perhaps was manifested later in the Sphinx. Oedipus's case was just the opposite. An apparent foreigner who had rescued the city from the Sphinx, he was revealed as a Theban who disrupted the inner structure of his family by marrying his mother. Polynices is a member of the attacking force. As one of the seven enemy leaders, he acts like an outsider. While the war is treated as an external affair, his presence is not even mentioned. He is first named, in the extant play, only late in the shield scene (line

577), just before his personal dispute with Eteocles comes to a head, and—significantly—when Amphiaraus is reported as chastising him for invading his native land. He is as much an insider as his brother. Eteocles himself, ostensibly the city's defender, is at odds with the chorus, participated in the quarrel which brought on the invasion in the first place, and is heir, with Polynices, to the family curse. One of the paradoxes of the *Seven* is that at first the city as a whole seems to be in danger, but not Eteocles personally, while at the end of the shield scene these positions are reversed. The family, as a line which should not have been continued, is an excrescence on the city; and just as the source of the danger is found to be not external but internal, so the real disharmony within Thebes is not between male and female, responsible and irresponsible citizens, but between the city and its ruling house.

The ambivalence of the family's position makes it fitting that the decisive fight should occur just on the dividing line between inside and outside, at the seventh gate. At line 277, Eteocles promises the gods that, if victorious, he will erect a $\tau\rho\sigma\pi\alpha\hat{\iota}\sigma\nu$ in their honor. This trophy, as the name implies, was set up by the victors in a battle at the point where the defeated army turned in retreat. The chorus suggest to Eteocles (line 706) that the daimon might *turn* eventually and blow more gently ($\lambda\dot{\eta}\mu\alpha\tau\sigma\varsigma \ldots \tau\rho\sigma\pi\alpha\dot{\iota}\alpha \,\chi\rho\sigma\nu\dot{\iota}\alpha$). But it does not. The curses rout the family instead ($\tau\epsilon\tau\rho\alpha\mu\mu\acute{\epsilon}\nu\sigma\upsilon \,\pi\alpha\nu\tau\rho\acute{\sigma}\pi\omega \,\varphi\upsilon\gamma\hat{q}$ $\gamma\acute{\epsilon}\nu\sigma\upsilon\varsigma$); and while the curses raise a piercing victory-cry, a $\tau\rho\sigma\pi\alpha\hat{\iota}\sigma\nu$ is erected to Atê in the gate (lines 954–56), where the brothers have killed each other, where inside and outside meet.

Earth Imagery and Related Themes: Plants and Crops, the Family, and the Ages of Man

One aspect of the city is its walls and towers, but the *polis* also comprises the land which surrounds the walls and on which they stand. The earth is a rich source of imagery in the *Seven,* and with it several other themes are so closely connected that they cannot be considered in isolation.

Eteocles clearly expresses the Thebans' relationship with the earth in the prologue when, in urging them to defend their city, he invokes its most precious facets, among them (line 16): $\tau\acute{\epsilon}\kappa\nu\sigma\iota\varsigma \,\tau\epsilon, \,\Gamma\hat{\eta} \,\tau\epsilon$ $\mu\eta\tau\rho\acute{\iota}, \,\varphi\iota\lambda\tau\acute{\alpha}\tau\eta \,\tau\rho\sigma\varphi\hat{\omega}$. The land is the citizens' mother and nurse.

Probably φιλτάτη implies not only affection but also family relationship. Eteocles appeals to the same feelings of filial duty when he says that Melanippus, whom he sends against Tydeus, will "ward off the enemy spear from the mother who gave him birth" (line 416). Having borne these children, the earth nourishes them through her fruitfulness. This generous profusion is the basis of the chorus's appeal to the gods near the beginning of the first stasimon (lines 304-11) and is summed up by their reference to the earth's gift near its end (line 361).

In this earth the city is rooted, like a plant. Eteocles' own words suggest this, when he prays to the Erinys not to uproot it (lines 71-72). And the chorus give at least an idea of its deep foundations when they say (line 247): στένει πόλισμα γῆθεν, ὡς κυκλουμένων. The Thebans themselves are like plants (line 12). In fact, they are literally rooted in the soil, for their ancestors were the *Spartoi,* "the sown ones."[34] Melanippus is a direct descendant of these mythological forebears (lines 412-13):

σπαρτῶν δ' ἀπ' ἀνδρῶν, ὧν "Αρης ἐφείσατο,
ῥίζωμ' ἀνεῖται, κάρτα δ' ἔστ' ἐγχώριος.

The earth is what makes possible the rhythm of life. On it, men are nurtured, mature, and grow old. It is natural that Thebes should possess citizens of all ages—those too young to fight, those in their prime, and the old. Eteocles addresses these three ages in the prologue (lines 10-13).[35] The earth undertook the toil of raising them, he continues (lines 17-20), so that they might grow to defend her in repayment. Basic to this cycle of life is the family, which defines the position and duties of the three age groups, and by which men continue their line. So Eteocles urges the citizens to protect their children (line 16) in addition to the earth and the altars of the gods.

Thus Aeschylus defines, through his language in the early part of the play, the natural cycle which gives stability to life in a city and binds men, through ties of kindred affection, to a particular place. It would be difficult to find a deeper appreciation of the land and man's relations with it. The nearest parallels are the great choral benedictions on Argos and Athens in the *Suppliants* and the *Eumenides.*[36] They contain prayers for fertility, for the flourishing of crops and families, and for protection against war. In particular, the chorus in the *Eumenides* pray that *stasis* be averted:[37]

> τὰν δ᾽ ἄπληστον κακῶν
>   μήποτ᾽ ἐν πόλει στάσιν
> τᾷδ᾽ ἐπεύχομαι βρέμειν,
> μηδὲ πιοῦσα κόνις μέλαν αἷμα πολιτᾶν
> δι᾽ ὀργὰν ποινὰς
> ἀντιφόνους Ἄτας
> ἀρπαλίσαι πόλεως ...

The situation in Thebes is not quite the same as that envisioned in this passage, since there is no strife between factions of citizens. But there is enmity within the ruling house, and the resulting war has threatened the city's life. When the chorus of the *Seven* contemplate the impending duel of the brothers, they use the same figure—the earth drinking blood shed in murder (lines 734–39):

> ἐπεὶ δ᾽ ἂν αὐτοκτόνως
> αὐτοδάικτοι θάνω-
> σι, καὶ γαῖα κόνις
> πίῃ μελαμπαγὲς αἷμα φοίνιον,
> τίς ἂν καθαρμοὺς πόροι,
> τίς ἂν σφε λούσειεν; ...

Aeschylus seems to have had a consistent vision of prosperous life in a polis which is in harmony with its land. It is what John Jones terms "the Aeschylean norm," and it is delineated in the *Oresteia*, he says, by stress brought on it through "aberration."[38] The same is true in the *Seven*. All the richness of the city's life is asserted in the face of the imminent threat. The glimpses of it which Aeschylus gives show what is at stake, and when Thebes is out of danger her life is, by implication, restored. Restored and strengthened, because with the death of the brothers and the end of the guilt-laden family, the internal rift is healed.

The war which upsets this balance is the fault of the brothers. Although Eteocles may seem to participate in this vision of ordered life when he appeals to it in the prologue, the situation of his family actually cuts him off from it. His isolation from it, along with that of

Polynices, comes to be stressed through the imagery in the course of the play, beginning in the shield scene.

The Argive army, which the brothers' quarrel has brought against the city, is alien to the land. That is the clear impression given in the early part of the play by both the imagery and the dramatic presentation.[39] In particular, the kind of imagery under discussion here sets the Argives off as intruders. The entire first stasimon, especially such lines as 360–62, has this effect. Also, in the shield scene, the figure of Parthenopaeus blurs the distinction between the ages characteristic of the city: he is an ἀνδρόπαις ἀνήρ (lines 533–35). Lasthenes, by contrast, who is sent to oppose Amphiaraus (line 622), maintains the physical distinction between the ages but possesses the peculiar excellences of both the old and the young. Parthenopaeus does not conform to the normal cycle of the individual's life.

His status in relation to the city is, however, ambiguous. Just as the Thebans are sprung from their earth, Parthenopaeus himself is like a plant (βλάστημα, line 533). He has his own roots in the soil of another place. And as a metic he is repaying to Argos his debt of nurture (line 548), just as the Thebans do with regard to their land. In this sense, he is a formidable enemy; for while Thebes can find, in her close relations with her soil, resources against the Argives generally, these will be less effective against Parthenopaeus, who has his own special bond with Argos and Arcadia.

Amphiaraus also occupies a special position.[40] The Argive Seven swear that if they do not sack Thebes, they will "turn the earth to mud with their gore" (line 48). Amphiaraus, on the contrary, who knows that he will be swallowed up in the earth, says that he will "enrich the land" with his prophetic art (lines 587–88). His wisdom is described in terms of crops (lines 593–94), as is Apollo's a little later (line 618). Eteocles uses the same language in his reply to the spy's description of Amphiarus, but in regard to the crop of Atê and in lines with a very clear import for himself (lines 600–601).[41]

Parthenopaeus pays his debt to his adopted Argos; the brothers endanger their native land. Amphiaraus, an outsider, will enrich the soil; Polynices violates his maternal earth, and Eteocles shares his guilt. Once again the boundary between inside and outside has broken down. Amphiaraus himself recognizes the irony of his position, for he prophesies his own fate immediately after reproaching

Polynices for attacking his native city, with all that that implies (lines 580-86). He concludes his rebuke with the question:

> πατρίς τε γαῖα σῆς ὑπὸ σπουδῆς δορὶ
> ἀλοῦσα πῶς σοι ξύμμαχος γενήσεται;

In the *Persians*, Darius warns against future expeditions against the Greeks (line 792): αὐτὴ γὰρ ἡ γῆ ξύμμαχος κείνοις πέλει. Evidently the land itself offers resources to its defenders. Polynices will fail for this reason. But neither will Eteocles triumph. Like the Argives except Parthenopaeus and Amphiaraus, the brothers do not share in the bond which unites a man with the soil that nurtured him.

The passages just mentioned are hints, given in the shield scene, of the brothers' true situation. They look ahead, ominously, to what will happen. Beginning with Eteocles' outburst (lines 653 ff.), the imagery we have been examining occurs often. It stresses the abnormality of the relationships within Laius's family and of that family's position regarding the earth. Eteocles' tirade against his brother contains this remarkable sentence (lines 664-69):

> ἀλλ᾽ οὔτε νιν φυγόντα μητρόθεν σκότον,
> οὔτ᾽ ἐν τροφαῖσιν, οὔτ᾽ ἐφηβήσαντά πω,
> οὔτ᾽ ἐν γενείου ξυλλογῇ τριχώματος,
> Δίκη προσεῖδε καὶ κατηξιώσατο ·
> οὐδ᾽ ἐν πατρῴας μὴν κακουχίᾳ
> οἶμαί νιν αὐτῷ νῦν παραστατεῖν πέλας.

It is interesting that the stages of Polynices' life, from his birth to the present moment, should be enumerated. One naturally thinks of lines 10-20 of the prologue, and Aeschylus must have intended a contrast between the two passages. Polynices' life has evidently not followed the normal rhythm of receiving the earth's favors and repaying the debt. It has not been attended by justice; instead, he is now harming the land (line 678).

The phrase φυγόντα μητρόθεν σκότον is arresting. The darkness is that of the womb, but who is the mother? It is surprising that she is never named in the whole of the *Seven*, although Homer knew a name for her.[42] Aeschylus seems to have kept her anonymous deliberately, to maintain the ambiguity between the physical mother of both Oedipus and his sons and the earth mother. In the sixth pair of speeches, Amphiaraus is reported to have described Polynices' attack on Thebes in language which suggests violence to his family as well as to his native land (lines 582–84):

> . . . πόλιν πατρῴαν καὶ θεοὺς τοὺς ἐγγενεῖς
> πορθεῖν, στράτευμ᾽ ἐπακτὸν ἐμβεβληκότα;
> μητρός τε πηγὴν τίς κατασβέσει δίκη;

There follows a reference to the earth as πατρίς . . . γαῖα (line 585, quoted earlier). The spring, the source of Polynices' life (here naturally associated with the earth), is the mother whom he threatens to make barren.[43] But the land and the city belong to the father. Oedipus himself, though unknowingly, violated his mother and displaced his father Laius. The position of Eteocles and Polynices is parallel to his, for in quarreling over possession of Thebes, they are offering violence to the mother and seeking to replace their father in turn.[44] There is thus a suggestion that the brothers are not only each other's rivals over power and wealth, but sexual rivals of Oedipus as well, even though he is dead.[45] When they are buried, they will be "an affliction bedded beside their father"—πῆμα πατρὶ πάρευνον (line 1004). The phrase neatly conveys their position in this confused family.[46] Moreover, though each finally gains a share in the mother, they enjoy neither a productive sexual relationship nor material possessions. The brothers, below the ground, will have unplumbed wealth beneath them (lines 949–50), but will be "without a portion of the wide plains" (line 732). Of these, they will get only what is needed to bury them (lines 731, 818). So, having left the mother's darkness as products of incest, they return to it, again unnaturally, in mutual fratricide.

Thus the earth, which is the mother and nurse of all the Thebans, comes to be identified with the mother of Eteocles and Polynices to show how their existence is a perversion of the normal pattern of life. Aeschylus uses the related plant-and-crop language in precisely the same way: the brothers are depicted as plants, but unlike the Thebans they do not flourish. Though Oedipus's union with his mother is likened to the sowing of a field (lines 753–56), he "endured a bloody root." Contrast the case of Melanippus, cited above. The brothers return in death to the gloom of the lower world (lines 854–

60), the "all-receiving and invisible land." Here πάνδοκον recalls
πανδοκοῦσα in line 18, where it described the earth as nurse and
mother.[47] In the earlier line, the earth undertook all the toil of nurture, so that the citizens might grow; but she engulfs the brothers.
There is no idea of fruitfulness here.

The fratricide is viewed as overturning nature. The chorus's last
words to Eteocles are (line 718): ἀλλ᾽ αὐτάδελφον αἷμα δρέψασθαι
θέλεις; Δρέπεσθαι signifies the opposite of sowing and nurturing
plants—cutting off their fruit to enjoy it. But what Eteocles plucks
will be his own brother's blood. The lawless bloodshed for which he
longs, the chorus admonish him, is "of bitter fruit" (πικρόκαρπον,
line 693). Καρπὸς οὐ κομιστέος—the involuntary hint given by Eteocles himself in lines 600–601 becomes explicit here.

Perhaps the sharpest contrast in the play between the brothers
and the city is in respect to the family (in a human sense, and aside
from its associations with the earth and plants). The line of Laius is
marked by confusion between the generations, similar to the mixture
of ages noted above. The relations between its individual members
are unnatural. Oedipus murdered his father; the paradox of his
marriage to his own mother is vividly expressed by the chorus (lines
750–57). Their sons kill each other. The mother is called by the
chorus (lines 926–32) the most miserable of all women. The brothers
themselves die childless (line 828). The normal cycle of family life
is forbidden to this race.

The word φίλος, applied in line 16 to the earth mother and indicating kinship, has already been noted. It recurs in the same sense
in line 695: φίλου γὰρ ἐχθρά μοι πατρὸς μέλαιν᾽ Ἀρά. . . . The
juxtaposition of the first two adjectives draws attention to the
incongruity of a father cursing his own sons. Oedipus's Erinys is
"house-destroying" (line 720), the strife through which she works a
"child-slayer" (line 726). In the same way, the paradox of the
mutual murder is expressed in line 971: each brother died at the
hands of a close relative (φίλος). The brothers are "of the same seed"
(ὁμόσποροι, lines 804, 932–33); they strike one another through
"sides sharing in the same entrails" (lines 889–90);[48] and their kindred blood mingles on the ground, now literally united (lines 937–
40). If Melanippus is "particularly native" to Thebes (line 413:
κάρτα δ᾽ ἔστ᾽ ἐγχώριος), the brothers, in death, are "especially of
the same blood" (κάρτα δ᾽ εἰσ᾽ ὅμαιμοι, line 940).

When the messenger appears after the battle to announce the safety of the city's ship, he greets the chorus as παῖδες μητέρων τεθραμμέναι (line 792).[49] Like the nautical imagery in the same scene, this seems to contrast the city and the race of Laius. The maidens belong to normal families, the relations of which follow the usual peaceful and productive pattern. What the messenger tells them is, in effect, that the line which endangered the city by its very existence is now extinct. The rhythm of life outside that particular family can continue undisturbed. The maidens, products of families which have flourished in the usual way, can have normal marriages themselves, for their earlier fears of a captive concubine's life, expressed in the first stasimon (lines 332–35, 363–68), have not been fulfilled.

In the light of this emphasis on the family, Eteocles' attitude in his earlier scene with the chorus becomes intelligible. There is undeniably a danger that the maidens' panic will infect the whole city. But Eteocles' remonstrances take the form of a sweeping denunciation of women in general (lines 187 ff.). Not for him the normal relations between male and female; and his words here may be meant to indicate early in the play that he stands outside the typical pattern of life, despite his appeal to it in the prologue. The same idea may be hinted at in his mixture of genders in line 197. The whole passage, as was remarked earlier,[50] gives evidence of a sexual disturbance which seems a symptom of the curse on Laius's family.

We might plausibly connect several other aspects of the earth imagery with prior events in the myth and in the trilogy. The theme of nurture may reflect problems within the family. The question of Oedipus's nurture was vexed, and his survival of the attempt to expose him was crucial to fulfilling the curse. Whatever the circumstances which provoked his own curse on his sons, they must have involved a similar problem.[51] *Trophê* would thus have been a natural point on which to contrast the city and the family in the *Seven*. And when we recall on the one hand the earth's figurative role there as nurse of the Thebans, and on the other the dreadful ambiguity in the brothers' relation to the earth, we can judge how skillfully Aeschylus transmuted the literal events of his story into imagery.

The theme of the ages of man must stem in the same way from the dislocations within the family. But it can be linked specifically with the riddle of the Sphinx, which tied the stages of human life to the natural rhythm of the day. Oedipus solved the riddle, but by marrying his mother he transgressed the proper boundaries between generations. Similarly, Eteocles recognizes this distinction in the prologue (lines 10–13), but is himself involved in the guilt which blurs it. Parthenopaeus, too, who embodies that confusion, bears on his shield the image of the Sphinx. In contradiction to the wisdom of her riddle, that monster, herself perhaps a manifestation of the family's guilt, was engaged in cutting men's lives short.[52]

By thus evoking earlier stages in the history of this tormented family, the imagery implies that the past heavily influences the present and is decisive in shaping the future. This order is made explicit in the second stasimon, when the chorus perceive it with frightful clarity at the moment of crisis for the third generation.

THE THEME OF BLOOD

One other persistent theme of the play ought to be mentioned here: the theme of blood. It is closely related to that of the family, though it is more relevant to the brothers themselves than to the city. Most of the occurrences of this theme have been noted in the preceding pages, but its development should be sketched. At first, blood is a feature of the war generally. The Argive Seven plunge their hands into a bull's blood and vow either to sack the city or to spill their own blood (lines 42–48). Blood is prominent in the destruction of the city contemplated by the chorus in the first stasimon (lines 348, 351). During the shield scene the chorus fear that they will see the "bloody fates" of their φίλοι (lines 419–21). They have, of course, general slaughter in mind, but that is just what they will see in the case of Eteocles and Polynices. The transition of this theme from the city to the brothers comes when the chorus urge Eteocles not to go to the seventh gate (lines 679–80):

ἀλλ' ἄνδρας 'Αργείοισι Καδμείους ἅλις
ἐς χείρας ἐλθεῖν· αἷμα γὰρ καθάρσιον.

Whatever the exact meaning of the last phrase, there is a clear contrast between the αἷμα of 680 and the blood shed in fratricide, for the chorus continue (lines 681–82):

ἀνδροῖν δ' ὁμαίμοιν θάνατος ὧδ' αὐτοκτόνος—

οὐκ ἔστι γῆρας τοῦδε τοῦ μιάσματος.

This kind of bloodshed is unlawful (line 694). There follow, later on, the references to the "bloody root" which grew from Oedipus's sowing and to the brothers' blood spilled and mingled on the ground. Blood is common to the members of a family: they are ὅμαιμοι. But in the blood of this family runs a curse. If the *Laius* contained a description of Oedipus tasting his father's blood, then this theme may have run through the whole trilogy.[53]

The Gods

The city's ties with the land are important, but its relations with its gods are basic to its existence. In this case too, Aeschylus presents a picture of a normal pattern of life, from which the ruling family is excluded and which it threatens to overturn. Eteocles invokes this relationship in urging the citizens to defend the altars of their gods (lines 14–15):

πόλει τ' ἀρήγειν καὶ θεῶν ἐγχωρίων
βωμοῖσι, τιμὰς μὴ 'ξαλειφθῆναί ποτε . . .

The gods are "native"; the implication is that Thebes has a special claim on their protection. The chorus therefore beg them for help in the parodos and first stasimon. One of the pairs of gods to whom the chorus appeal in lines 109–50 is especially "native," Ares and Aphrodite, parents of Harmonia and so the divine ancestors of the Theban race (lines 135–40). Thus the chorus summon up the whole mythical past of the city as a basis for their prayers.

What binds the gods to the city and the city to the gods is a systematic interchange between them. This is clearly expressed by Eteocles at the end of his prayer in the prologue (lines 76–77):

γένεσθε δ' ἀλκή· ξυνὰ δ' ἐλπίζω λέγειν·
πόλις γὰρ εὖ πράσσουσα δαίμονας τίει.

This has sometimes been understood as a mark of Eteocles' cynicism in religious matters. But such a view ignores the fact that the chorus end their own pleas in the parodos by reminding the gods of sacrifices received from the city (lines 179–80). Similarly, in the first stasimon, they claim that the gods could not depart to a better land than Thebes (lines 304–11) and promise them future honors in return for their aid (lines 312–17). Sacrifices matter to the gods; the idea is at least as old as Homer. In the *Iliad*, Zeus grants Troy's destruction to Hera only reluctantly. The Trojans are dear to him, he says, for they have never failed to honor him by sacrifice.[54] In the *Seven* this relation, systematized by ritual, is yet another sign of the "norm" which the war threatens to disrupt.[55] The gory sacrifices performed by the Argives (lines 42 ff.) express a distorted version of this norm. Their gods are Ares, Enyo, and Phobos (line 45). Moreover, Parthenopaeus reveres his spear more than a god (lines 529–30); and, of course, the Argives' boasts, detailed in the shield scene, are hybristic.

Is Eteocles in any way impious? Golden, for example, considers his religious outlook "highly pragmatic. . . . He is able to manipulate all of the doctrines of the conventional religion to suit his purposes and will."[56] Certainly his relations with the gods are uneasy, but the case does not appear that simple. His words early in the play seem to indicate that passive trust in the gods is not enough to meet the present situation; military steps are also necessary. At the same time, Eteocles recognizes the limits of human endeavors, conceding that the final outcome will be decided by the gods.[57] Yet the first episode, in its total effect, does tend to isolate Eteocles from the usual relationship between men and gods. As in the case of the earth, he apparently understands its value, but something prevents him from engaging in it fully. That can only be the curse. Rather than insist on a characterization of Eteocles, however, we ought perhaps to consider themes in the play which are associated with the gods.

The ambiguity of Eteocles' position is clearly brought out in the repetition of the word $\tau\epsilon\lambda\epsilon\hat{\iota}\nu$. Like $\kappa\rho\alpha\acute{\iota}\nu\epsilon\iota\nu$, it is a favorite word with Aeschylus and is always significant when he employs it in reference to the gods, particularly to Zeus.[58] In the *Seven*, it is first used in the prologue, when Eteocles encourages the Thebans (line 35: $\epsilon\mathring{\upsilon}\ \tau\epsilon\lambda\epsilon\hat{\iota}\ \vartheta\epsilon\acute{o}\varsigma.$). From there, it can be traced through the chorus's fearful doubts, prompted by the war, in the parodos (line 157) to a similar outburst of fright in the second stasimon; but here they fear that the Erinys will "accomplish" the curses of Oedipus (lines 724, 791; cf. 655). Finally, after news of the battle, the chorus lament the completion of the curse (lines 832–33). In this respect as in others, the play moves from the general to the specific, as the conclusion to be feared becomes no longer that of the war (for the gods do protect the city) but that of the curse which ruins the house.

A more direct statement of Eteocles' situation with regard to the gods is given in his prayer in lines 69 ff. There he appeals not only to Zeus, Earth, and the gods of the city, but also to the curse and his father's Erinys. This is in accord with his double role as political leader and accursed individual, and at this point in the play both aspects seem fused. But then he asks, "do not uproot the city at least. . ."[59] Is a distinction being made here between Eteocles and the city? Perhaps, instead, a distinction is being blurred, which only later becomes prominent. The curse at this point is threatening the whole city; private and civic are identified, and that may be why the curse is asked, along with the other gods, not to destroy the city. In the last pair of speeches in the shield scene, when it is becoming evident that the real conflict is the personal quarrel, a prayer of Polynices is reported, which forms an important contrast to Eteocles' earlier one (lines 639–41):

> τοιαῦτ' αὐτεῖ καὶ θεοὺς γενεθλίους
> καλεῖ πατρῴας γῆς ἐποπτῆρας λιτῶν
> τῶν ὧν γενέσθαι πάγχυ Πολυνείκους βία.

Polynices calls upon the native gods of Thebes, much as Eteocles does. That is probably intended as a mark of piety; but the phrase θεοὺς γενεθλίους . . . πατρῴας γῆς inevitably evokes the curse and the Erinys, the family's own divinities.[60] Thus Polynices implicitly juxtaposes civic and individual gods as Eteocles did explicitly; but he does so to plead his case against his brother, not (like Eteocles) in the city's behalf. This is a mark of how the scope of the war has shrunk; Thebes' involvement in the conflict is no longer the central concern, even though Polynices prays as a Theban. The incongruity of his invocation of the city's gods when he is the aggressor only draws attention to the fact that the actual issue is between the two brothers. Thus Polynices' prayer seems to balance and shed light on the earlier one of Eteocles.

It is right at the break in the play, when Eteocles has learned who his opponent at the seventh gate will be, that the family's alienation from the gods becomes explicit,[61] and the reason is the curse (lines 653–55):

> ὦ θεομανές τε καὶ θεῶν μέγα στύγος,
> ὦ πανδάκρυτον ἀμὸν Οἰδίπου γένος ·
> ὤμοι, πατρὸς δὴ νῦν ἀραὶ τελεσφόροι.

In the scene which follows, the chorus suggest to Eteocles that the curse can be appeased with sacrifice (lines 699–701). Wilamowitz dismisses this idea as "die Gesinnung des Ablasskrämers."[62] But sacrifice is the expression of the city's relations with the gods, and on it they have based their prayers for safety. Eteocles rejects this course, however; the entire family is so deeply enmeshed in the curse that there is no way out. The gods, he has said (lines 217–18), leave a captured city. Though they will not depart from Thebes, they have abandoned his family (lines 702–704):

> θεοῖς μὲν ἤδη πως παρημελήμεθα,
> χάρις δ' ἀφ' ἡμῶν ὀλομένων θαυμάζεται ·
> τί οὖν ἔτ' ἂν σαίνοιμεν ὀλέθριον μόρον;

This is the rhetoric of desperation; the only favor the gods will accept from the family is its obliteration. The contrast with the city is sharply drawn.

If the city has its particular gods, so does the family. Apart from the Erinys, there are two gods with whom the family has a special relationship, and it is a vexed one. First there is Apollo. In line 691, the race of Laius is said to be "hated by Phoebus." As argued above, this is not because of Apollo's spite against Laius. In this line, στυγηθέν recalls μέγα στύγος of line 653. The cursed family is hateful to all the gods, and to Apollo in particular; the nature of its fate is alien to his worship (for the contrast, cf. lines 854–60). In addition, he watches over the fulfillment of his oracle. His prophecies will bear fruit, not only in the case of Amphiaraus (line 618), but in regard to this family as well. The fatal battle takes place at the seventh gate under Apollo's supervision, and the number is appropriate, as line 800 indicates, for it is specially associated with the god. The Medicean scholiast explains that Apollo was born on the seventh day of the month. In fact, by Aeschylus's time consultations at Delphi took place regularly on the seventh of each month of the oracle's operation, to commemorate that event.[63]

The other god whose position in the *Seven* is ambiguous is, of course, Ares. In terms of the war itself he has a double aspect. On the one hand he is the terrifying spirit of battle, throwing everything into confusion, the embodiment of imbalance and the particular deity of the Argives. They swear their oath by him (line 45). His blast drives the wave of Argives against Thebes (lines 63–64, 115). Hippomedon, like a Bacchant, is ἔνθεος Ἄρει (line 497). And when a city is sacked, it is Ares who "pollutes reverence" (line 344). On the other hand, he is the ancestor of the Thebans, παλαίχθων (line 104), who once loved the city well (line 107) and to whom the chorus particularly appeal. It is symptomatic that these two facets of the god appear side by side in the parodos. To the Argives' Ares the city opposes its own special deity.

But Ares also appears in a third guise. In regard to the family, he is neither external threat nor beneficent ancestor, but the personification of internal division—literal division, for he is the arbiter of the brothers' dispute. The *Seven*, then, is a "drama full of Ares" in several senses, and Benardete only slightly exaggerates when he says that "*the* question" of the play is "τί ἐστιν Ἄρης;"[64]

The importance of Ares furnishes an example of how the various themes in the *Seven* are related to each other. In this case, the theme of the gods and the nautical imagery overlap. Early in the play, Ares is the source of the wind which hurls the wave of the enemy upon the city. Later, the wind which sweeps away the vessel of the family is its daimon (lines 705–708) or Oedipus's imprecations (line 819). Thus nautical language is applied to the family just as its true relations with the gods are made explicit. Ares himself disappears as the cause of the wind (that is, as the deity of warfare in general), but later reappears in a more specific capacity as the arbiter between the brothers. A third image, that of the lot, is thus brought into alignment with the other two.

LANGUAGE OF DEBT AND COMMERCE

The reciprocal relationship with its gods is one facet of the city's balanced life. It has a similar relationship with the earth. The latter is expressed at the beginning of the *Seven* in terms of a debt. The

earth, says Eteocles, brought up the Thebans (line 20):[65] πιστοί
ϑ᾽ ὅπως γένοισϑε πρὸς χρέος τόδε. Here commercial language is an
expression of the city's way of life; but it comes to have a more
specific application to the fate of the brothers.

It is used in the shield scene in connection with the war. The
Theban champions are called "guarantors of a debt" (φερέγγυοι)
who "stand before" the city to protect it (lines 396, 449, 470). They
are faithful to the obligation expressed in the prologue. Parthenopaeus, by contrast, is repaying his own debt of nurture to Argos (line
548) and is no petty retailer of war (lines 545–46).

Eteocles turns the boasts of Tydeus and Capaneus to advantage
(line 437): καὶ τῷδε κέρδει κέρδος ἄλλο τίκτεται. This line evidently means that in Capaneus's case (καὶ τῷδε) new profit (κέρδος
ἄλλο—Capaneus's arrogance, which will anger Zeus) is being added
with interest to the profit already in hand (κέρδει—Tydeus's boasts,
which will be self-destructive).[66] Eteocles is triumphant. The situation is different when he follows his exclamations over the fate of
his family with the words (line 656–57):

ἀλλ᾽ οὔτε κλαίειν οὔτ᾽ ὀδύρεσθαι πρέπει,
μὴ καὶ τεκνωθῇ δυσφορώτερος γόος.

There is no longer any question of profit, but of interest accruing in
the form of a still more serious cause for lamentation[67]—as in fact
happens with his own and Polynices' deaths. In the subsequent
exchange with the chorus, however, Eteocles does mention gain, and
his language stands the whole notion of profit on its head. The curse
sits near him (line 697): λέγουσα κέρδος πρότερον ὑστέρου μόρου.
Winnington-Ingram plausibly suggests that κέρδος here should be
connected with the same word in line 684 (μόνον γὰρ κέρδος ἐν
τεθνηκόσι), and that both refer to killing Polynices.[68] "Kill him and
then die"—it is a ghastly reciprocity.

The only gain the brothers can expect, then, is each other's murder,
for as members of Laius's family they have been under an obligation
to the curse. The development of commercial language culminates
when, after the death of the brothers, the chorus observe that
Oedipus's curse has exacted payment of the debt owed it, and the
influence of Laius's transgression is felt in the background (lines
840–42):

ἐξέπραξεν, οὐδ᾽ ἀπεῖπεν
πατρόθεν εὐκταία φάτις·
βουλαὶ δ᾽ ἄπιστοι Λαίου διήρκεσαν.

The curse is the creditor, to whom the brothers' destruction has been due.[69] It has shaped events, and any hope for gain on their part has been illusory.

But what of the city? Its guarantors have discharged their function faithfully, and it has not been ruined.[70] When he announces Thebes' victory, the messenger's repetition of the commercial language associated with the champions contrasts sharply with the application of such language to the brothers' fate (line 797–98):

στέγει δὲ πύργος, καὶ πύλας φερεγγύοις
ἐφραξάμεσθα μονομάχοισι προστάταις.

THEMES ASSOCIATED WITH THE WAR

The themes used to characterize the war can be treated more summarily. As the scope of the war narrows, they gradually focus on the brothers and on the final result of the play. But at first they are associated with the Argive army and with the reaction its attack provokes in the city.

From start to finish, the *Seven* is pervaded by discordant and terrible noise. There is, first, the sound of the Argives as they advance—the clatter of their weapons, for example (κτύπος, lines 83, 100, 103; cf. 160), or the neighing of their horses (line 245). Eteoclus shouts (βοᾷ) his boast, silently but unmistakably, in the letters on his shield (line 468). Between the two extremes that these examples represent lie many other harsh noises which issue from the Argives and create an impression of terrifying force.[71] There is a corresponding confusion within the city, and the sounds of the maidens' panic answer those made by the enemy. Their first word in the parodos is θρεῦμαι (line 78), and the dochmiacs there provide a fitting and impressive medium for their cries of terror. These shrieks are, without question, dangerous to the city. But it is interesting too that the sounds both outside and within the city combine to give a total picture of the confusion wrought by war. Then, when the conflict narrows to the fight between the brothers, the sounds of war give way to those of lamentation.

Perhaps the following pair of passages illustrates this best. The city, threatened by the enemy, groans from its roots in the earth (line 247): στένει πόλισμα γῆθεν, ὡς κυκλουμένων. But after the brothers' mutual murder, the city, the towers, and the plain groan again—now not in confusion or terror, but in sorrow (lines 900–902):

> διήκει δὲ καὶ πόλιν στόνος,
> στένουσι πύργοι, στένει
> πέδον φίλανδρον . . .

Similarly, the chorus's ὀξύγοοι λιταί to the gods (line 320) are replaced by the γόοι of grief at the end (lines 854 ff., 917–18, 964, 967).

In this play, Aeschylus often represents the sounds in terms of music. Haldane describes well his general use of this imagery:

> Thus Aeschylus found in the various types of music and song practised in his day a convenient set of symbols, the significance of which would be immediately apparent to his audience. Around each clustered associations of occasion, atmosphere, and emotion which could be counted upon to awaken a definite, predetermined response. With skillful manipulation such images could be used to focus a climax, to highlight a moment of conflict or irony or, linked together from scene to scene, to underline the pattern of a drama.[72]

This is certainly what he does in the *Seven*. The Argives have on their horses and chariots noise-making devices which produce a grotesque distortion of music and which are themselves described as musical instruments (lines 122–23, 205–207, 463–64). The chorus's songs are anything but harmonious (cf. διερροθήσατε in line 192). Eteocles tries to induce them to sing the paean instead, the auspicious song chanted by Greek custom before a battle (lines 267–70). But just as his own well-omened words in the shield scene issue in the fulfillment of the curse, so in the end music is again distorted. The chorus sing a lament over the brothers, and the curse raises its own shrill song of victory (lines 953–55).

Related to the music is a strain of Dionysiac language in the play. The chorus depict their dirge in lines 835–39 as a Dionysiac song; it is actually an inversion of that cheerful music.[73] Earlier in the play there are also traces of the Dionysiac. Hippomedon revels like a Bacchant, but he is inspired with Ares (lines 497–98). Similarly, the chorus describe the noise of the Argives in words that are appropriate to Dionysus. Βρέμειν and βρόμος occur several times (lines 85–86, 213; cf. 463–64,[74] 476). One of the titles of Dionysus was *Bromios*. They speak of the ὄτοβος of the Argive chariots (lines 151, 204–205; cf. the syrinxes of line 206); the word is not inappropriate to the music of a flute.[75] There is also a suggestion in line 214 that the chorus are like maenads (ἤρθην φόβῳ, in close association with βρόμος, line 213); what goads them, however, is not ecstasy but terror.[76]

This language is part of the more comprehensive theme of madness. The latter is used in the play to link all the stages of the family curse. It has been remarked already that Laius's error was due to atê resulting from the curse.[77] Oedipus in turn was in a rage when he cursed Eteocles and Polynices; he was βλαψίφρων (line 725), and he uttered the curse μαινομένᾳ κραδίᾳ (line 781). In the third generation the curse has brought on the war; the Argives boast μαινομένᾳ φρενί (line 484). And in the ending of the quarrel, the brothers kill one another ἔριδι μαινομένᾳ (line 935). Eteocles refers to the letters on Polynices' shield with scornful alliteration (line 661): ἐπ' ἀσπίδος φλύοντα σὺν φοίτῳ φρενῶν. And he describes his brother as a φὼς πάντολμος φρένας (line 671). The chorus term his own determination to fight Polynices an irrational desire, a product of atê (lines 686–88, 692, 698).[78] It is, therefore, no accident that the iron which is to be the arbiter between the brothers is called ὠμόφρων (line 730; cf. lines 536–37). The madness of war is but an external sign of a mental imbalance within this family which has infected the whole city. Finally, in the parodos the "spear-shaken *aether*" rages with the violence of war (ἐπιμαίνεται, line 155), but at the end of the play the chorus's hearts rave with grief (μαίνεται γόοισι φρήν, line 967). This contrast marks the shift from general warfare to the curse's particular result.[79]

DIVINATION AND PROPHECY

The outcome of the war cannot be foreseen. But from the beginning of the play there is what seems to be an effort either to predict or to shape its course. Various forms of divination, for example, are mentioned.[80] In the prologue there is the seer with his ornithomancy, who has informed Eteocles that the Argives are planning an attack (lines 24–29). There is a sort of retrospective oneiromancy, as Eteocles realizes, in the light of his new situation, the truth of some dreams he has had (lines 710–11). The mention of Ares' dice (line 414) may be a reference to cleromancy; as will be argued in the next chapter, the lot plays an important role in the *Seven*.

Finally, cledonomancy, the gathering of omens from chance utterances, is prominent, especially in the shield scene. Words in the play are effective, as Cameron says, "in the need for silence at solemn moments so as to avoid ill-omened chance utterance, in the manipulation of chance utterances to the advantage of the one who accepts them, in cursing, and in the invocation or acceptance of the omen implicit in a name."[81] Names are particularly important. There is a consistent feeling that a name ought to reveal something about its bearer. This is a common Greek belief. But against this background there is special point when Amphiaraus emphasizes the component parts of the name Polynices (lines 577–79), or when the chorus play on the names of both brothers (lines 829–31; the lacuna does not obscure the sense).[82]

Divination and attention to words are not, however, the only means in the play of straining toward the future. At several points, alternatives are posed which give what seem in each case the likely results of the action. These shift somewhat and become more specific as possibilities are gradually eliminated and the play moves toward *the* final outcome. Eteocles utters the first pair of choices in the prologue (lines 4–9). Both of these possibilities come true in the end, though neither is an accurate forecast in itself. The outcome is really a third possibility not contemplated at the beginning of the play. Thebes *does* fare well, and at the same time Eteocles *is* "hymned"—in mourning.

The Argives are more accurate when they vow either to sack the city or to spill their blood (lines 46–48). The latter is what happens. Similarly, the second term of Eteocles' prediction in lines 477–79 is fulfilled in the event. Both of these examples refer to the war, and Thebes' survival can be in no serious doubt after the fourth pair of speeches in the shield scene. But as the play moves to its climax

and the focus shifts to the brothers, Polynices utters his own oath
(lines 636–38):

> σοὶ ξυμφέρεσθαι καὶ κτανὼν θανεῖν πέλας,
> ἢ ζῶντ᾽, ἀτιμαστῆρα τὼς ἀνδρηλάτην,
> φυγῇ τὸν αὐτὸν τόνδε τείσασθαι τρόπον.

This is devastating accuracy. The natural alternatives would be "to
drive you out or die in the attempt." Polynices, it seems, has slipped
into a way of speaking which will turn out to have been prophetic.

The concern throughout the play with divining the future culminates in line 808, where the chorus, anticipating the news they are
about to hear, exclaim, μάντις εἰμὶ τῶν κακῶν. Thus prophecy has
focused on the specific horror of the result. Similarly, the Erinys of
Oedipus has a particular kind of foresight, for a little earlier (line
722) she was called κακόμαντις. Like Apollo's oracle, the Erinys
possesses her own logic, which is unimpeachable, though most easily
followed in hindsight. Her inexorable procedure according to this
logic is reflected in the imagery of allotment, which will be examined next.

3

Imagery II: The Family

The themes and images in the *Seven* which are at first associated with the city and with the war in general gradually attain, as we have seen, greater specificity as they focus on Eteocles and Polynices and on their quarrel. The phases in the development of the imagery mark the stages in the progress of the play toward its final result. A few other images undergo a similar development. These, however, receive stronger emphasis at the end of the play than at the beginning, and seem connected more closely with the brothers themselves than with the city. They cluster around the idea of the lot.

Language of allotment occurs regularly, in various contexts, throughout the *Seven*. Its development as a theme will be outlined later in this chapter. Of final importance to the play is its use to describe the brothers' duel and mutual fratricide at the seventh gate. Such language first appears in this connection, in an explicit and sustained way, at the beginning of the second stasimon (lines 720–33). Thereafter it furnishes the basic imagery of the choral lament, from line 822 onward. This imagery seems closely related to—indeed, may have originated in—the terms of Oedipus's curse on his sons, given, apparently, in lines 788–90:

$$\ldots\, \kappa\alpha\acute{\iota}\, \sigma\varphi\epsilon\, \sigma\iota\delta\alpha\rho\sigma\nu\acute{o}\mu\omega$$
$$\delta\iota\grave{\alpha}\, \chi\epsilon\rho\acute{\iota}\, \pi\sigma\tau\epsilon\, \lambda\alpha\chi\epsilon\hat{\iota}\nu$$
$$\kappa\tau\acute{\eta}\mu\alpha\tau\alpha.$$

Here $\delta\iota\alpha\lambda\alpha\chi\epsilon\hat{\iota}\nu$ seems to signify not simply "share" but literally "divide by casting lots." From the iron which the brothers' hands are to wield evidently comes, moreover, the picture of the iron dealing out the lots as arbiter between them (for example, lines 727 ff.). Thus the wording of the curse apparently implies that the brothers normally would be expected to cast lots peacefully to divide the possessions they inherit, but that they are doomed instead to share their patrimony by hostile means. There would then be a bitter paradox in the use of language usually associated with a peaceful procedure to describe the violent enmity which is the fate of the sons of Oedipus. Its similar use in the final lament would signify the literal fulfillment of the curse: the brothers do, in fact, share their inheritance by the sword.

The Lot and Greek Systems of Inheritance

If the lot imagery late in the *Seven* has the effect indicated above, an audience of the fifth century B.C. must have been familiar with a custom whereby two or more heirs would divide their patrimony into equal parts and cast lots for the shares, with the whole procedure supervised by an arbiter in case of disagreement. Before considering that imagery itself, therefore, we must ask whether, and if so, in what form, Aeschylus's contemporaries would have known of such a practice. This inquiry is particularly necessary because the issue of inheritance in the play has been given a different interpretation from that adopted here.[1]

Myth and literature provide many examples of the apportionment of possessions by lot. The archetype of these is the famous story of how the sons of Kronos shared the territory they had wrested from their father. In the *Iliad*, Poseidon relates that he and his brothers Zeus and Hades divided the world into three portions and then drew lots to determine which part each was to receive ($\pi\alpha\lambda\lambda o\mu\acute{e}v\omega v$; note how $\lambda\alpha\gamma\chi\acute{a}v\epsilon\iota\nu$ occurs in three successive lines).[2] This sounds very much like the system I would postulate for the *Seven*. Though later writers assume that Zeus drew the choicest portion,[3] Poseidon insists that the shares were equal. He uses the story, in fact, to justify defiance of Zeus's command to leave the battle at Troy. Concerning this passage H. J. Rose remarks:

> The absence here of any notion of primogeniture, the exclusion of the sisters from the division, and the retention of a sort of glorified equivalent of the paternal hearth and the land immediately around it [i.e., earth and Olympus, which remained common property] are all quite in accord with early Greek law.
> . . . Nor need we hesitate to press the comparison because Kronos was not supposed to be dead. . . . His position . . . is exactly that

of the aged father of a Homeric chieftain, Laertes for instance in the *Odyssey*, who has retired from active control of his kingdom or barony. As might be expected from the age of the legend, the characters in it behave precisely like rather primitive Greeks.[4]

Hesiod, for whom Zeus's supremacy is more definite than in the *Iliad*, tells in several passages of the *Theogony* how Zeus apportioned their τιμαί to the other gods.[5] But he speaks as if the Titans, and also Aphrodite, received their τιμαί by lot.[6] In these passages, τιμαί refers more to privileges than to physical provinces. But the connection between the two is very close, and this division is at least analogous to the one made by the sons of Kronos.

Allotment is also employed by humans. In the *Odyssey*, during the fictitious account of his history which he gives to Eumaus, Odysseus relates how his half-brothers shared their inheritance and gave him only a pittance because he was illegitimate. They divided the property, he says, and cast lots for the portions.[7] Similarly, just after recounting the gods' division of the world by lot in his *Seventh Olympian*, Pindar says that the three sons of Helios shared Rhodes, which their father had received (somewhat irregularly).[8] There the word μοίρας may well imply the sons' use of the lot also. In both of these cases, human practice is apparently conceived as mirroring the divine precedent.

Another instance from myth is the story of the Heracleidae. According to Apollodorus, they drew lots for the Peloponnesus (their inheritance, in a sense, from Heracles) after regaining control of it. They divided the territory into three parts and agreed that the one whose lot came up first got Argos, the one who placed second, Lacedaemon, and the third, Messene.[9] These regions cannot have been ranked in descending order of value, however, but must have been equivalent, since Cresphontes particularly wanted Messene. Pausanias tells the story with some alterations.[10] In his version Cresphontes, in his desire for Messene, demanded priority on the basis of age over the sons of his younger brother Aristodemus (now dead). His claim was disputed and they resorted to allotment. In both accounts, though in different ways, the outcome was affected by prior tampering with the lots. This division of the Peloponnesus by lot was known in the fifth century; Euripides recounted it in a lost play.[11]

From such stories as these, equal division of inheritance and use of allotment to forestall or settle quarrels must have been widely familiar. As for arbitration, it was employed frequently in the fourth century B.C., and probably also in the fifth, in both civil and private disputes, as we shall see.[12] The above examples are thus sufficient to show that Aeschylus could rely on his audience to be fully aware of the incongruity when he applied terms of allotment and related procedures to the brothers' fratricide. Still, one would like to know whether the practice Aeschylus evoked was known to the spectators from their daily lives also—whether, that is, equal sharing among heirs, by lot if necessary, was common at that time. I believe that a strong argument can be made that it was, even though nothing is known about laws of inheritance in the fifth century B.C.

The one piece of clear evidence from antiquity for such a use of allotment is late. Plutarch recommends that brothers, to avoid ill feelings, by themselves or in the presence of a common friend, divide their inheritance by "the lots of justice" (quoting Plato).[13] The context and Plutarch's language indicate that equality of division was a problem and that quarrels were common. Moreover, the "mutual friend" sounds very much like an arbiter should the need for one arise. We cannot, of course, infer fifth-century practice from this passage.[14] Yet it seems significant that the Platonic phrase which Plutarch cites is from a passage in the *Critias* (109b–d) which tells the story of the allotment of the world among the sons of Kronos. The allusion indicates a continuity in conception from early myth to a human institution of late antiquity.[15]

In the fourth century B.C., disputes over patrimony occurred frequently and provided considerable business for the orators. The extant speeches thus give a fair amount of information on contemporary Attic laws of inheritance. Most importantly, we know that by Isaeus's time the law required that all legitimate male offspring receive an equal share of their father's property (ἅπαντας τοὺς γνησίους ἰσομοίρους εἶναι τῶν πατρῴων).[16] This is reminiscent of the *Odyssey* passage cited above, in which the legitimate sons shared the patrimony and though the illegitimate son received something, that was very little. Here, then, is another link between law and a method reflected in literature centuries earlier.

In Isaeus's phrasing, ἰσομοίρους may imply use of the lot, but that is uncertain. In a law quoted by Demosthenes, however, which gives the order of heirs in cases where neither male children nor a will existed, the phrase μοῖραν λαγχάνειν occurs, followed by λαγχάνειν in the next sentence.[17] This at least strongly suggests allotment. Similarly, we find in Isaeus a case in which the heirs had divided the property amicably twelve years before. Isaeus speaks of their shares as ἃ ἔλαχε.[18]

In the fourth century B.C., a father could prevent quarrels by dividing his property equally among his sons during his lifetime or by will. If he did not do so, on his death the heirs could hold the property in joint ownership, or they could split it into equal parts and assign the shares by lot or by mutual agreement. If, however, they could not concur on an equal division, they would employ an arbiter. A legal procedure is known which sheds light on the latter case. When one of the joint owners of property wanted to divide it, the archon would be asked to appoint an arbiter (δατητής) in an action called εἰς δατητῶν αἵρεσιν. The co-owners could contest the motion, but if it was successful the archon would make the selection. This much we know from Aristotle, who mentions this action in a list of the duties of the eponymous archon.[19] Apparently the arbiter would then evaluate the property and form equal shares, and the claimants would cast lots for them under his supervision.[20]

Although the details of this action are not certainly known, some guesses can be made. According to the sources the suit was brought in cases where one owner wanted to divide the property and the others did not. It is reasonable, however, to infer from the name of the process ("action for the purpose of choosing arbiters") that it was also used when the owners could not agree on an equitable formation of shares. In the second place, this action could apply to a variety of cases, but it probably originated in the division of inheritance.[21] Finally, evidence is again lacking for the fifth century B.C. Since Aristotle alludes to the procedure in the fourth century, however, and the *Seven* mentions arbitration and allotment in connection with the sharing of patrimony, we may justly suppose that the practice was current in the earlier period too, whether or not it was formalized in law. In this connection, it is important to remember how pervasive the lot was in Greek life. In Athens in particular it was commonly employed in politics and the law courts. Recourse to the lot would have been natural to settle disputes or, in general, whenever absolute equality was desired in sharing anything, whether meat at a banquet or property.

This conclusion assumes that equal division of patrimony was the rule in the fifth as well as the fourth century B.C. Cameron takes a different view and raises points about the nature of inheritance and land tenure which, if valid, would rule out that assumption.[22] These must therefore be considered.

Cameron argues against the authenticity of the ending of the play by interpreting ἐπιγόνοις in line 903 as "younger sons" rather than as a reference to the Epigoni. This meaning would be appropriate, he says, if a system of primogeniture prevailed in early Greece whereby the younger, noninheriting sons would emigrate. That, he claims, is implied by Hellanicus's version of the brothers' quarrel, according to which Eteocles gave Polynices his choice of the rule over Thebes or the chiton and necklace of Harmonia. Polynices chose the latter and departed to Argos. Cameron then gives an interpretation of the lot imagery in the *Seven* different from the one above, and speculates that it reflects a recent change from primogeniture to equal division, with Eteocles defending the former and Polynices trying to institute the latter.

This view involves a number of difficulties.[23] Most pertinent is Cameron's statement, "It is generally agreed that before the fifth century, and even into the fifth century, land was inalienable and indivisible." Land is thought to have been inalienable in Athens before Solon, and it certainly could be mortgaged and sold in the fourth century B.C. But there is no agreement on when the shift to alienability occurred. Fine has argued for the time of the Peloponnesian War.[24] The arguments for putting the change in the period after Solon's reforms seem more compelling, however.[25] The original purpose of inalienability was probably to maintain each family's parcel of land intact and so (in Woodhouse's words) "to keep the number of households constituting the state at a constant figure as far as possible, and on a fairly even footing in respect of property by preventing the concentration of family lots in a few hands through sale, bequest, or gift."[26] One may wonder how weighty this object had become in post-Solonian Athens, with its growing commercialism and the gradual waning in importance of the extended family or *genos*. Sparta, Corinth, and (perhaps) Thebes, where land was inalienable until relatively late, are not valid parallels for Athens of the fifth century B.C. at any rate, since they were aristocratic societies. Conceivably, as Cameron says, "the equal division of land among several heirs would . . . result in atomizing the parcel [of land] into smaller and smaller holdings." It is, however, easy to imagine how subdivision of a small plot could have been avoided if necessary. The heirs might hold it in common, for instance—this was always an option—or the land might be one share, with the other share or shares composed of movable property. This would be at the discretion of the heirs and not a matter of law. A far more serious danger was the accumulation of large holdings by a few wealthy men. Against this tendency equal division among heirs would have acted as a brake.[27]

The most likely conclusions about land tenure in fifth-century Athens, then, indicate equal sharing of inheritance. Furthermore, it is doubtful that primogeniture was ever practiced in Greece.[28] Such faint and scattered traces as there may be of the eldest son's receiving certain privileges do not support such a system. Nor do the myths which Cameron cites.[29] Consider, for instance, the version attributed to Hellanicus of the settlement between the sons of Oedipus. Eteocles split the inheritance into two shares. One was the land which would have gone with the kingship—that is, the immovable property. The other was composed of the movable possessions. That Polynices emigrated upon selecting the latter implies nothing about customary practice, as Cameron claims; it was simply a device for leaving Eteocles in peaceful occupation of the royal power. The interesting feature of this story, however, is that Eteocles formed the portions and gave Polynices his choice. Therefore the shares must have been equal. This method of amicable settlement, which avoided arbitration and allotment and yet ensured fair distribution, was actually employed in the fourth century B.C.[30] Thus, though I doubt that Aeschylus used the same form of the story in the Theban trilogy, Hellanicus's version may be taken as evidence for equal division in the fifth century.

From the Homeric epic through Plutarch, then, there are persistent indications of impartial distribution of patrimony among legitimate sons, often by lot, and the use of arbitration and allotment to resolve any disagreements. In Athens, such a method would have arisen, if not earlier, at least when land became alienable—that is,

most likely before the fifth century B.C. But our case need not rest
on this last point. Parallels in myth and other literature are adequate
proof that this system of inheritance would be intelligible to the
Seven's audience. At the same time, it is quite likely that with his
lot imagery Aeschylus was playing on actual contemporary practice.

LOT IMAGERY IN THE PLAY: A GENERAL VIEW

The fundamental importance to the *Seven* of imagery based on the
lot has often been overlooked. In a recent article, however, Anne
Burnett notes the frequent occurrence of this imagery and suggests
that it clusters around two earlier events: Oedipus's curse, which
threatened his sons with a hostile division of their inheritance, and a
dream of Eteocles (lines 710–11) which seemed to hold out promise
of a peaceful settlement under the guidance of a foreign arbiter.
Only at the end of the shield scene are both understood to point to
the brothers' death.[31] This is an elegant sorting out of the lot imagery,
and in the absence of the trilogy's other plays it is probably as much
as can be done in this direction. I shall confine my discussion to the
function of this imagery in the *Seven* itself; but the background to it
may be as Burnett believes.

Borecký also makes some helpful observations on the language of
allotment in the play.[32] At least until the end of the fifth century B.C.,
he argues, λαγχάνειν and its compounds and cognates do not mean
simply "obtain," but always carry something of their original,
literal reference to the casting of lots. He divides the occurrences of
these words into three groups: (1) the literal process of allotment;
(2) the "primitive Verteilung"—the method, originally by lot, of
dividing land, booty, or meat at meals and sacrifices (and also, he
maintains, inheritance); and (3) in connection with fate and death,
which the Greeks had always conceived as a lot which befell a man
or was apportioned to him by a higher power. All three, Borecký
points out, are represented in the *Seven*: (1) the Argive chiefs literally cast lots to determine which gate of the city each should attack;
(2) the brothers' division of their patrimony is described in terms of
allotment; and (3) in the end this process leads to their deaths, and
they obtain not shares of all the Theban soil, but only as much land
as is needed to bury them.

A passage in the choral lament near the end of the play, where the

lot and the other themes related to it converge, will show the significance and complexity of this image (lines 906-14):³³

> ἐμοιράσαντο δ᾽ ὀξυκάρδιοι
> κτήμαϑ᾽, ὥστ᾽ ἴσον λαχεῖν.
> διαλλακτῆρι δ᾽ οὐκ
> ἀμεμφεία φίλοις,
> οὐδ᾽ ἐπίχαρις Ἄρης.
>
> σιδηρόπληκτοι μὲν ὧδ᾽ ἔχουσιν   [στρ.
> σιδηρόπληκτοι δὲ τοὺς μένουσι—
> ταχ᾽ ἄν τις εἴποι, τίνες;
> τάφων πατρῴων λαχαί.

The brothers have divided the possessions equally; the idea of division, as we shall see, runs through the latter part of the play. But
ὀξυκάρδιοι is incongruous when juxtaposed with terms which would
normally denote a peaceful settlement, and it thus points to the
ambiguity of these terms. Basic to the word for "divide" used here,
ἐμοιράσαντο, is *moira*—not merely "portion" but "fate." Similarly,
the phrase ὥστ᾽ ἴσον λαχεῖν signifies that the brothers have been
allotted equal shares not of property but of death. This meaning is
unmistakable since their fate has been described in the lines just
before this passage (especially line 905: ϑανάτου τέλος).³⁴

The object of an arbiter was to prevent or to resolve disputes.
But the arbiter in *this* apportionment has been Ares, who has come
to embody the brothers' hostility and who has been associated with
the iron of their swords. The mediator gets no thanks; he has been
all too impartial. Ares' name leads naturally to the thought of iron.
The last four lines pose and then answer a grim riddle. The brothers
lie smitten by iron; and there await them, as their portions of land,
iron-struck—"shares in their father's grave."³⁵ Allotment and violence
are again yoked together. Moreover, if the scholiast is right, λαχαί
in line 914 refers not only to shares obtained by lot but also to
the digging of the grave. The pun would further associate the lot
with death. But even without the pun the line has the same effect,
since it recalls what has been said before (for example, lines 732-
33): that the only land the brothers get is that required for their
burial. The normal intention of the lot has thus been defeated,

and the Erinys has twisted the whole process to her own ends.

In the above passage, then, we can distinguish four main themes: the lot, arbitration by the iron and Ares, division, and moira. This example well illustrates their close interrelationship. We can now examine each of them individually as it occurs in the course of the play.

THE LOT AS A THEME IN THE *SEVEN*

The lot is introduced in the prologue as a literal procedure, when the spy tells Etcocles that he left the Argive chiefs casting lots to determine the order of their attack on the city (lines 55–56). There are subsequent references to the enemy's allotment in the parodos (lines 124–26) and in the shield scene (lines 375–76, 423, 451, 457–60).[36]

The method used in this drawing of lots is familiar from Homer. In Book 7 of the *Iliad* (lines 161–205), for instance, a Greek champion is selected to oppose Hector in single combat. Each of the nine candidates marks his own κλῆρος or lot to distinguish it from the others and puts it into Agamemnon's helmet (lines 175–76). Nestor then shakes the helmet, and the first lot to "jump out" is that of Ajax (lines 181–83).[37] In the *Seven,* this method is referred to explicitly in line 459.

The figurative lot, by which the brothers divide their patrimony, first receives detailed treatment in the second stasimon. There the chorus, speaking of Oedipus's curse on his sons, picture the Chalybian stranger "distributing the lots" and assigning the brothers as much earth to dwell in as the dead need (lines 727–33). The word used here for the casting of the lots is διαπήλας, from πάλλειν. It and κλήρους (line 727) recall terms used of the Argive lot. Related words (κληρουμένους and πάλῳ), for example, are employed in line 55.

After the battle, the messenger recapitulates the allotment theme in announcing the brothers' death (lines 816–19). The chorus's fears have been fulfilled; so have the terms of the curse, in an almost literal sense. In the final lament, the chorus also speak of the brothers' division of their patrimony as a lot, but they now associate it with their final portion—their death (lines 907–14, 947–50).

It should be clear from the summary just given that the Argive lot is prominent in the play from the prologue through about the middle of the shield scene, and that in the latter part of the play the lot is used frequently as an image for the brothers' combat and death. These two aspects of the lot are closely related. The emphasis shifts from one to the other, and the transition is made in the central scene. It will be argued later that the shield scene represents the consummation of the allotment process. Here it will be sufficient to remark that Polynices' position at the seventh gate has been directly fixed by lot, and that on the other side Eteocles is the only one of the seven Theban champions left to oppose him, the others having been matched with the appropriate Argive opponents at the six remaining gates. It is this final pairing that makes possible the other lot under the supervision of the iron. Thus by implication Aeschylus seems to relate the two types of draw, and it can therefore be claimed that the lot develops as a theme. At first it is connected with the war; but as the scope of both the war and the curse shrinks through the shield scene to the brothers, so the lot becomes the image for their individual quarrel. Its reference narrows, in a movement parallel to that of all the other themes of the play. The transition occurs with the word λαχόν in line 690, in the very passage which marks the shift in application of the nautical imagery from the city to the family.[38]

ARBITRATION

The theme of the iron as arbiter between the brothers does not develop over the course of the play. Instead it is introduced at the climax, as the implications of the curse become evident, and occurs from then on as part of the lot imagery.

In the iron of the brothers' swords, the whole idea of arbitration is turned inside out, for this mediator is an emblem of the curse. The iron is identified with the Erinys in the first strophic pair of the second stasimon (lines 720–33). As Fraenkel points out, the two stanzas have a similar construction.[39] Both contain riddles; each begins by describing the nature of its subject, naming it directly only in the fourth line, while the last three lines state its effects. The key to each riddle ('Eρινύν, σίδαρος) is given in the same metrical position in its stanza. Again, almost immediately before this ode, Eteocles, fully armed and determined to fight his brother, speaks of himself as if he were an iron sword (line 715): τεϑηγμένον τοί μ᾿ οὐκ ἀπαμβλυνεῖς λόγῳ. Later, the chorus, who have dreaded and then heard definite news of the curse's accomplishment, echo his language in a reference to the oracle Laius received (line 844). Behind the iron, then, stands the horror of each stage in the family's history.

With the figure of iron, Aeschylus distorts several similar and often overlapping uses of arbitration. One was political mediation. From the archaic period on, states often enlisted foreigners to act as arbiters of internal disputes between rival factions.[40] But, as Engelmann notes, an arbiter was usually sought from a friendly state; in this play, he is a barbarian. Moreover, he continues, it was customary to give profuse thanks and even civic honors to an arbiter who had performed his function well, but here the mediator, though completely fair, gets no thanks (lines 908–10, 941–46).[41]

There are, however, further nuances. The mediator is not only iron, the Scythian stranger, but also Ares. The identification of the two is natural and may refer particularly to the fact that the Scythians worshipped Ares in the form of an iron sword.[42] But by this point in the play Ares embodies the hostility between the brothers and is, unlike the iron, not a foreigner at all. This, as previously noted, is an example of the confusion between internal and external evident elsewhere in the play as well.[43]

Arbitration was also regularly employed in cases of individual disagreement. It is to this private form of the practice that Aeschylus alludes in a passage in which he also equates the iron and Ares (lines 941–45):[44]

> πικρὸς λυτὴρ νεικέων ὁ πόντιος
> ξεῖνος ἐκ πυρὸς συθείς
> θηκτὸς σίδαρος · πικρὸς δὲ χρημάτων
> ἴσος δατητὰς ''Αρης ἀρὰν πατρῴ-
> αν τιθεὶς ἀλαθῆ.

It is incongruous to call the iron a "resolver of quarrels." It is no less so to term Ares a δατητάς (*datetês*), since, as explained earlier, this word was regularly applied to legally appointed arbiters of disputes over property.[45] Here is a striking instance of the way in which Aeschylus uses the system of equitable distribution to describe the very enmity it was designed to prevent.

In addition to the *datetai*, there was another class of arbiters in

Athens, called *diaitetai.* Of these there were two kinds.[46] First, there was a board of public arbiters selected annually by lot from men over sixty years of age.[47] They were thus called κληρωτοὶ διαιτηταί, and they had jurisdiction in private legal actions. One of them was chosen by lot to hear each case before formal judgment, and his decision, if the arbitration was successful, had to be submitted to the competent magistrate for ratification. Even then, the decision could be appealed. Private diaitetai were somewhat different. At any point in a private case, the parties could agree to submit the matter to one or more arbitrators of their own choosing, not neces-sarily from the public board. These were called αἱρετοὶ διαιτηταί, and the agreement an ἐπιτροπή.[48] The essential point about both kinds of diaitetai is that their task was principally informal, intended to accomplish not so much a legal judgment of the case as a recon-ciliation of the two parties.[49] For this reason, they were known as διαλλακταί, "reconcilers," and the verbs διαλλάττειν and ἀπαλ-λάττειν occur frequently in connection with their activities.[50]

The law establishing the diaitetai was probably passed soon after 403 B.C. by the restored democracy. But the practice of arbitration was clearly much older, and the law simply regularized it.[51] Plutarch, for instance, relates a slander of Themistocles against Aristeides, that he was usurping the function of the law courts "by deciding and judging all matters" (τῷ κρίνειν ἅπαντα καὶ δικάζειν) and so imper-ceptibly accumulating the powers of a monarch.[52] This activity, in all likelihood, was informal arbitration. Moreover, the same language is used of arbiters in the fifth century B.C. as was later applied to the diaitetai, including the latter term itself. Herodotus, for example, tells how Periander mediated between (κατήλλαξε) Athens and Mytilene in their dispute over Sigeum: τούτῳ γὰρ διαιτητῇ ἐπε-τράποντο.[53]

It is probably to this more or less formal function of the diaitetes that Aeschylus alludes when he calls the iron a "settler of quarrels" (line 941), terms Ares a "reconciler" (διαλλακτήρ, line 908), and says that the brothers have been "conciliated with the aid of iron" (διήλλαχθε, lines 884–85; cf. 767). He is constructing a deliberate paradox in the notion of Ares (or iron) as a mediator who, though impartial, receives no gratitude for his services. Finally, however, the god does accomplish a reconciliation of sorts when the brothers are united in death, and an end to strife when the family is obliterated.[54]

DIVISION

The purpose of the lot should be to apportion the property; indeed, the word for "arbiter" used in the *Seven,* δατητής (line 945), literally means "one who divides." Aeschylus touches frequently on the idea of division in the latter part of the play. Like the iron, this theme is not developed gradually but appears and recurs in connection with the brothers. It is used in an ambiguous way which emphasizes, like the idea of the arbiter, that Aeschylus is depicting no ordinary lot which results in an amicable settlement.

The theme of division is introduced near the end of Eteocles' second scene with the chorus, when he exclaims on the fatal truth of the dreams, "dividers of my father's possessions" (δατήριοι, line 711). We might note that at this point in the play, just before the image of allotment appears in its entirety in the second stasimon (lines 727–33), three of its components occur separately for the first time: the lot itself, now applied to the family (line 690), the iron in the person of Eteocles (line 715), and division, foretold in dreams. This fact, far from accidental, is one more indication of the shift in the play which is stressed both structurally and thematically. When these images are gathered together in the ode which follows, the lot is applied more particularly to the present generation, the iron is transferred from Eteocles himself to the arbiter between him and his brother, and division occurs in fulfillment of the dreams, though now the iron is a "divider of property" (κτεάνων χρηματοδαίτας, line 729). Thus Aeschylus points these themes toward the final outcome.

A literal division does in fact take place, though not in the sense contemplated in the lot procedure. The chorus express their fear of the consequences if the brothers die "self-divided" (αὐτοδάικτοι, line 735).[55] That is what happens when they kill each other and perish διατομαῖς οὐ φίλαις (line 934), by a blow that pierces both the house and their bodies (lines 895–96). This wound finds its counterpart in the lament that rends the city, for the chorus continue, after the last passage cited, διήκει δὲ καὶ πόλιν στόνος (line 900). Their cry of grief is "piercing" (δαϊκτήρ, line 916) and "heart-rending" (δαϊόφρων, line 918). There is possibly an echo of these words in δαΐ a few lines later (line 925), though it means "battle" and is from a different root. The wordplay would stress that this division has been hostile.

For the brothers have not succeeded in sharing the earth between them. Their wealth in land will be beneath their bodies; the Theban plains will remain whole (lines 731–33, 816–19, 947–50). Nor is there any distinction in their fates. Just as their blood mingles on the ground, so they receive an equal portion (line 908). Their double-ness is stressed (lines 849–50, 972), but that is simply a way of seeing them as a unit, an equal pair. The dual case, often applied to them after their fate has become known (from the messenger's speech on),[56] has the same effect. They are two, but spoken of together.

MOIRA AND DEATH

For the brothers, then, there is no division of land, but only death. The double meaning of the word μοῖρα points to the same conclusion. As in line 907 (discussed earlier), the word occurs in conjunction with λαγχάνειν in line 947:[57]

$$\text{ἔχουσι. μοῖραν λαχόντες ὦ μέλεοι}$$
$$\text{διοδότων ἀχθέων,}$$
$$\text{ὑπὸ δὲ σώματι γᾶς}$$
$$\text{πλοῦτος ἄβυσσος ἔσται.}$$

The brothers have received by lot a portion of "god-given (sor-rows?)," god-given because the gods ultimately guide the results of allotment.[58] Their shares in land will consist of "boundless wealth beneath their bodies"—a variation on a now familiar idea. But this ironic reference to their burial makes explicit the other sense of moira, the portion of death.

In the refrain of the final stages of the lament (lines 975, 986), moira is personified as the goddess "whose gifts are heavy" and invoked along with the shade of Oedipus and the Erinys. This juxta-position stresses the daemonic forces behind this twisted allotment process and its outcome.[59]

CLEROMANCY

One other aspect of the lot ought to be mentioned. That is the possible allusion, in line 414, to cleromancy or divination by means of lots. There Eteocles, after giving reasons for his confidence in

Melanippus as Tydeus's opponent, says that "Ares will decide the result with dice." There is evidence that cleromancy was practiced in several places and that Apollo was its patron. It was apparently a very ancient practice; at Delphi in particular it seems to have preceded the Pythian oracle. The regular word for the response of that oracle, ἀναιρεῖν, probably owes its origin to the "picking up" of lots in divination. Even at Delphi cleromancy was not entirely supplanted by the Pythian oracle but persisted well into historical times.[60]

In this trilogy, the family's problems are in part connected with the Delphic oracle and with Apollo. Thus mention of another type of prophecy associated with Delphi is not out of place in the *Seven*. Furthermore, dice were often used as lots in cleromancy.[61] In this case, however, Ares, not Apollo, throws the dice—the same god who, as arbiter, is to deal out the lots which apportion their moira to the brothers. This line, then, may anticipate the later lot imagery.

CONCLUSIONS ON THE LOT

In the *Seven*, Aeschylus uses the process of allotment as an image for the duel between Eteocles and Polynices, in accordance with the terms of their father's curse. He thus distorts the procedure whereby an inheritance would customarily be shared in peace into an expression of the brothers' enmity and doom. Several other themes are connected with the casting of lots; all are related to one another in a complex but coherent way. The lot suggests an arbiter—in this case the iron or Ares. One of the technical terms for this mediator implies division, but the division which results is not one of property, as would be expected, but of the brothers' bodies. These are pierced by the sword; the iron in the capacity of arbiter performs its particular kind of division. The idea of division, finally, evokes moira, the term for "share" which also means "fate" or "death." The allotment of shares is thus absolutely equal, but it brings only sorrow.

The discussion in this chapter has concentrated on the lot as it applies to the brothers themselves. It is, in fact, a theme of the whole play. Its transfer to the brothers, in anticipation of the start of the second stasimon, is made in the course of the shield scene and in the second epirrhematic scene; and in the latter the themes of iron and division are also introduced.

The importance of this image to the play may be measured by the fact that language of allotment occurs more frequently in the *Seven* than in any other extant drama by Aeschylus.[62] The other play with a heavy concentration of such words is the *Eumenides*. Anne Lebeck shows how, in the first stasimon of that play, Aeschylus sets up a correspondence between the respective λάχη of Orestes and the Furies. "Both are woven by Moira," she says. "It is the portion of the Erinyes to bind his apportioned lot upon the wrongdoer. . . ." Also, "the Erinyes who destroy their victim's honor, themselves now face dishonor. The allotted portion they pursue . . . as they pursue transgressors . . . is about to be snatched from them."[63] In the *Seven*, by contrast, the Erinys does her work all too well and is secure in her function. The justice of her task is never questioned. This marks the difference between the conclusions reached by the two trilogies. Miss Lebeck also notes that the voting pebbles of the judges in the *Eumenides* are twice referred to as if they were lots (πάλος, lines 742, 753). The significance, she thinks, is that Aeschylus thereby plays on Athena's name Pallas. I would say, rather, that this transfer of the word emphasizes that the portions woven by Moira have been replaced by, or at least mixed with, those determined by human reason. In the Theban trilogy, on the other hand, it is possible to discern, by conjectures based on the second stasimon of the *Seven*, a certain grim logic in the oracle given to Laius and in the operation of the Erinys. This logic is unerring, but it lacks humaneness.

A man perpetuates himself, in a sense, by having children; and he passes his prosperity on to them in the form of their inheritance. These are basic aspects of the rhythm of one man's life and of the generations. The family of Laius is cursed in both. Relations between parents and children are abnormal. And in the third generation, by the terms of Oedipus's curse, their patrimony becomes the focus of Eteocles' and Polynices' quarrel. They cannot divide it in the usual, peaceful way; in their case the process is twisted, like everything else which life needs if it is to flourish—family, city, gods, and earth.

CONCLUDING REMARKS ON IMAGERY

In the preceding chapters, two important elements in the creation of the *Seven* have been considered: Aeschylus's treatment of his mythic material in constructing a dramatic plot, and the recurrent themes and images of the play. It was argued that the various parts of the play are grouped in ring composition around the central shield scene in such a way that each section following that scene represents in some sense the fulfillment of the corresponding earlier one. This arrangement accentuates the progress of the plot toward a more explicit understanding of the situation and of the factors which have produced it. The imagery develops in the same direction and is therefore closely related to the plot and structure. Many images are introduced early in the play in connection with the city. There they depict the city's normal way of life and the value of what is threatened by war. They also stress the brothers' alienation from those qualities. As the play proceeds, however, these same images become attached specifically to the brothers and to their family, and thus contrast the family's destruction with the city's survival. Other themes at first describe the Argive army and the violence of its assault on Thebes. These also narrow in their application to the conflict between Eteocles and Polynices and to the curse. One of the latter is the language of allotment, which is carried through in the course of the play, with the later introduction of related themes, to depict the brothers' duel and its results.

The following table is intended to provide a synopsis of the major themes and images which have been examined, and of their development.[64] It should be evident from this table that most of these images are transferred from the city to the family during the shield scene—often around the break in the play (lines 653 ff.)—or in the second epirrhematic scene.

Every time a theme or image occurs, it connects with other themes and events in the play. There is a limit to what exegetical prose can do in explaining these themes. Each has to be experienced in its specific context. And at every moment of the play's performance, the effect of the imagery was reinforced and complemented by what the spectator saw and heard.

Table 1

	General Application	*Transition*	*Applied to Brothers and Family*
Nautical	2–3; 59–64; 114–15; 208–10	602–608; 689–91; 758–71	795–98; 819; 854–60; 992
Walls; Inside/ outside	32–34; 58; 68; 193–94; 284	556–61	727–28; 895–96; 900; 954–60
Earth (mother and nurse)	16; 415–16	580–86; 668	736–37; 753–56; 854–60
Plants and Crops	12; 71–72; 412–13	533; 587–88; 593–94; 600–601; 618	718; 736–37; 753–56; 951–52
Ages of Man	10–13	532–37	664–69
Family	16	582–86	695; 720; 792; 804; 889–90; 926–36; 940
Blood	42–48; 348	679–82; 718	736–39; 755; 938–40
Gods	14–15; 76–77; 109–80; 217–18; 312–20	639–41	653–55; 689–708
Debt and Commerce	20; 396; 437	656–57	684; 697; 797–98
Sounds	83; 247; 320; 380–81; 468–69	657	854; 900–902; 917–18
Music	122–23; 151–53; 192; 203–207; 463–64		835–39; 953–55
Dionysiac Language	155; 213–15; 497–98		835–39
Madness	355; 380; 392; 484	661; 686–88; 692–94	725; 730; 781; 935
Divination	8–9; 24–29; 414	536; 576–79; 670–71; 710–11	722; 808; 829–31; 838–39
Alternatives	4–9; 46–48; 477–79	636–38	
The Lot	55–58; 124–26; 375–76; 423; 451; 457–60; 504–14	690	727–33; 788–90; 816–19; 907–14; 947–50

Table 1 (continued)

	General Application	Transition	Applied to Brothers and Family
Arbitration (Iron, Ares)		715	720–33; 844; 884–85; 908–10; 941–46
Division		711	727–33; 735; 895–99; 900; 915–22; 934
Moira	263; 281		733; 907–908; 947–50; 975–77 (986–88)

4

The First and Third Parts of the Play

The imagery of the *Seven Against Thebes* has thus far been treated
as something of a framework which helps to give the play its shape.
To understand the *Seven* as a living entity, as it must have been
experienced in actual performance, we must put the individual
occurrences of the images into context. This task will involve examining each section of the play in greater detail, with attention to
language, the place of the several scenes and choral odes in the overall design, and the internal structure of each. Though worthwhile in
itself, this scrutiny will have as its particular object, and will be the
basis for, conclusions on the dramatic presentation (as defined above
in the introduction). Just what such ephemeral aspects as music
contributed to the performance cannot now be known, and the conditions of production in the theater of Aeschylus's time are uncertain. Nevertheless, much can be deduced from the text of the *Seven*
about the immediate effect of the dramatic presentation in each
scene and about this element's relation to the plot and imagery.
Indeed, only through an inquiry of this kind can these scenes be
fully appreciated.

I shall discuss here the early and final parts of the *Seven* and
reserve the shield scene for the next chapter. With some sacrifice of
continuity, this arrangement will emphasize the great shift in the
play before consideration of the scene in which that change begins.
First, however, more must be said about the play's setting and its
significance.

OBSERVATIONS ON DRAMATIC PRESENTATION

Aeschylus always made striking use of the possibilities afforded by
theatrical production. The *Vita* in the Medicean manuscript makes
a valuable statement about his purpose: that "he used spectacles and
plots with a view towards an awe-inspiring impact ($\pi\rho\dot{o}\varsigma$ $\H{\epsilon}\kappa\pi\lambda\eta\xi\iota\nu$

τερατῶδη) rather than for the sake of illusion (μᾶλλον ἢ πρὸς ἀπάτην)." The word ἔκπληξις is a strong one. It denotes the amazement caused by the onrush of any strong feeling—love, surprise, delight, or terror.

Aristotle also suggests that ἔκπληξις can be produced by tragedy, but he connects it specifically with *anagnorisis*, which is an aspect of plot.[1] *Opsis* can arouse pity and fear, but in his view that is less the function of the tragedian's art than the task of the *choregus*.[2] Of the six elements of tragedy, he says in another passage, opsis is powerful in its emotional impact (ψυχαγωγικόν), yet the least proper to the poetic art; it is, rather, the province of the σκευοποιός.[3] In the same passage, he calls music a ἥδυσμα; and clearly he would regard as essential to tragedy none of the effects I shall discuss in the category of dramatic presentation. For he holds that tragedy does not depend on production to accomplish its characteristic effect; as is true also of epic, merely to read it is sufficient.[4]

These statements accurately reflect conditions of the drama in Aristotle's period—the result of a trend, which began in the fifth century B.C., toward increasing specialization in the various tasks of dramatic production.[5] In Aeschylus's time, by contrast, the dramatist not only wrote his plays but also produced and even acted in them. He was responsible for every aspect of production from beginning to end. The tragic art was thus not simply verbal but visual and aural as well. A play was an integrated product of all the activities connected with composing, acting, and staging; and the dramatist himself planned and executed it in every detail. In later antiquity, Aeschylus was credited with innovations in costumes, masks, scene painting, and the figures of the choral dance.[6] Accurate or not,[7] these attributions at least suggest that he was active in all departments of production. Therefore the dramatic presentation in any of his plays is extremely important.

Along with later specialization in the theater came an increasing emphasis on spectacle for its own sake and a demand for illusion, or, as we should say, "realism." But watching a performance in Aeschylus's day had not yet become passive entertainment; it still involved active exercise of the imagination. The spectator shared in the creation of a drama. That is the point of the statement in the Medicean *Vita*, that Aeschylus did not use spectacle for illusion. He could rely on the simple resources of the theater of his time to create a setting in the spectator's mind. The details were imaginary, and the very sparseness of the scenic furnishings must have made what actually was there stand out as especially significant. Nor was Aeschylus bound by the normal conventions of time. For him it was not a problem, as it was for Euripides, that by the end of the parados of the *Seven* the enemy is assaulting the city walls, whereas in the shield scene there is time for lengthy descriptions. The point is not that the audience assented to a deception for the sake of illusion. Rather, dramatic time differs from actual time, because it is the medium in which events are abstracted from life as it is normally experienced, for the purpose of revealing their significance.

One of the most striking characteristics of the *Seven* is that so many events occur "offstage." The lot in the Argive camp, the enemy attack on the city, the battle, and above all the decisive duel at the seventh gate—all these "facts" of the plot take place out of sight of the audience. Many of them are carefully described, and we would do well to remember the principle enunciated by Miss Dale, that the most detailed descriptions in the texts of plays concern what the spectators could not see.[8] Now it is true that such occurrences as battles were normally recounted in tragedy by messengers and not directly portrayed. In part we may be dealing with convention and with the limitations of the Attic theater—but only in part. In considering spectacle in the *Seven*, we must assume that Aeschylus represented what he chose to, what he considered vital to the play. The audience could be invited to imagine the rest. The "facts" of the plot form the background or setting to what the spectators actually saw and heard; and Aeschylus abstracted from these "facts" the aspects of the action which were ultimately significant for his play. These were principally the mental and emotional effects of the events themselves.

In the *Seven*, Aeschylus presents the inexorable operation of an inherited curse. We see first its effect on the city of Thebes as a whole, with all the delicate qualities of rootedness and of civic and personal life threatened, and the balance they imply upset. Then, at the climax of the play, comes the spectacle of the curse taking hold of an individual member of the tainted family, as its influence overthrows his mental equilibrium. Finally, at the close, the spectators see the results of the curse's work, which is now complete in the destruction of the family's last male survivors accompanied by the city's release from danger. Like the play's structure and imagery, the dramatic presentation gradually concentrates attention on the two brothers and isolates them from the rest of the city. All the elements of the *Seven* thus work together.

In particular, the relationship between imagery and dramatic presentation is of fundamental importance. It was remarked earlier that one outstanding characteristic of Aeschylean images, besides their repetition and development, is their concreteness[9] —because they express abstract concepts in physical terms, but also in a literal sense, for Aeschylus physically represents some of them to the spectators. In Aeschylus's hands, image and dramatic presentation are ultimately one and the same.

It is remarkable that he could create this effect with such simple theatrical resources. The *Seven* requires no elaborate setting or machinery. The location of the play was imagined to be the acropolis of Thebes. As in the *Suppliants,* the action apparently took place on two levels. One was the orchestra, and the other was a raised area representing a common altar to the city's gods, on which stood their statues.[10] It is important to bear in mind the presence of these images, in a dominating position, throughout the play.

Possibly, as Arnott argues, a raised stage in front of a wooden scene-building already existed by this time, and an altar with statues was a regular part of its decoration.[11] Or, if even temporary backgrounds became part of the furnishings of the Athenian theater only a little later, to be replaced long afterward by a permanent scene-building and (later still) a raised stage,[12] the altar would have been a mound of some kind, placed somewhere on the circumference of the orchestra opposite the audience. Impressive arguments have been made for each alternative; for our purposes, it is not necessary to decide between them. What is important is that there was a raised area with access from the orchestra and large enough to accommodate the chorus, who take refuge at the altar during the parodos.

THE EARLY PART OF THE *SEVEN*

It is well known that in the prologue of each of his plays Aeschylus introduces the themes and images which will become important in the course of the drama. The *Seven* is no exception. Of some fifteen themes and images which have been discussed in the pre-ceeding two chapters, all ten of those which at first are associated with the city and its situation occur in Eteocles' opening speech (lines 1-38).[13] In addition, the spy mentions blood in connection with the Argives' sacrifice and oath (lines 42-48) and describes their drawing of lots in the same speech (lines 55-56). Thus Aeschylus deftly weaves all these themes together right at the start of his play.

Eteocles' first speech is constructed in carefully marked stages. The first nine lines, which concern his own duties as ruler, begin and end with references to Cadmus.[14] When he addresses the citizens, the phrase ὑμᾶς δὲ χρὴ νῦν in line 10 answers χρή in the first line, and the second part of the speech is in turn rounded off by the mention of the debt (χρέος) due the earth in line 20. Thus what is required for the city's defense is defined and distinguished: from Eteocles, vigilance and control; and from the citizens, loyalty to home and native land, with their wealth of associations. Eteocles speaks perceptively about the latter but does not directly associate himself with it. In this sense, von Fritz seems right to speak of Eteocles' solitude and isolation from the rest of the city.[15]

The last part of the speech (lines 21-35) is framed by mention of the gods. So far, says Eteocles, the gods have inclined towards Thebes in the war (εὖ ῥέπει θεός, line 21; καλῶς ... ἐκ θεῶν κυρεῖ, line 23). But now events are approaching the crisis; νῦν δέ in line 24 balances καὶ νῦν μέν three lines before.[16] After he urges the Thebans into action, he ends by encouraging them: εὖ τελεῖ θεός (line 35). Thus we find here, on the one hand, human preparations to meet the danger; on the other, recognition that the issue will finally be determined by the gods, and with it confidence that the decision will be favorable to Thebes. The rest of the prologue follows the same pattern. The spy describes the preparations in the Argive camp, including the lot, and then advises Eteocles to act in response, with a return of the nautical imagery (lines 62-65). Eteocles' prayer follows this speech directly. Divine action and human action are interwoven but kept distinct. Eteocles' closing lines (76-77), in which he sums up the relation between the gods and the city, are in keeping with this tendency.

Even this early in the play, it may already be significant that the images of the gods stand in sight of the audience. They have not yet been mentioned, but Eteocles might draw attention to them with a gesture when he invokes the city's gods (line 69). The gods, whose statues remain visible throughout the play, will decide the outcome in a way favorable to Thebes but unexpectedly fatal to Eteocles. Though the result will be made plain enough, their actions themselves will remain hidden. Their images are fixed, inscrutable.

In the prologue, what is invisible to the audience is also suggested to the imagination. Apart from their thematic importance,[17] mention of the walls, towers, and gates as the boundaries between the city and its enemies (lines 30–35) influences the spectators' conception of what they see. The participle πυργηρούμενος (line 22; cf. 184) helps to set the visible scene of the play *within* a ring of towers. Similarly, the gates, referred to by the periphrasis πυλῶν ἐξόδοι (lines 33, 58; cf. 284), are "exits" from the point of view of those inside. The spy is another device for making what happens out of the spectators' sight and hearing as vivid as possible. He is twice called a κατοπτής (lines 36, 41). The audience will see the Argives' activities through his eyes. In the same way, his final words before his exit, with another reference to his eye, prepare the audience for his description of the Argive chiefs in the shield scene. Though the spectators witness none of the enemy's preparations, Aeschylus is careful to make them present to the imagination.

Immediately after Eteocles ends his prayer with an expression of the balance of the city's life, the chorus enter in utter disarray. Their song strikingly exemplifies the chaos and panic within the city. The predominant meter of the parodos is dochmiac, which as *the* measure in tragedy for expressing violent emotion, is a fitting medium for the Theban maidens to give voice to their terror.[18] Often in tragedy (though by no means always) the chorus entered with anapaests delivered in recitative. The dochmiacs here indicate that, as Pickard-Cambridge points out, "the introduction is . . . sung, not recitative, but stands in the same relation to the following lyrics as the marching lyrics of *Persae* and other plays."[19] The movements of the chorus as they rushed into the orchestra must have been correspondingly agitated, in contrast to the orderly procession which anapaests would have accompanied.[20]

The astrophic introduction, which should probably extend no farther than line 107,[21] may not have been delivered by the chorus in unison. Since the text falls into clearly defined sections, different parts of the chorus, or individual members, might exchange excla-

mations on the Argives' progress towards the city, mingled with cries
to the gods.[22] This arrangement would contribute to the general
atmosphere of confusion.

Probably during the introduction, the chorus flee to the altar.
From this position they deliver the main body of the song (lines
109 ff.) in strophic responsion. But they do not remain stationary,
for they evidently carry out their intention, announced earlier (lines
95–99), of falling before the gods' images and clasping them in sup-
plication. The repetitions of σύ (lines 127, 135, 145, 149) suggest
that they actually gesture or move toward each of the statues in turn.
The order in which the gods are named provides a further clue to the
staging here. Those addressed in lines 109–50 are again invoked in
lines 151 ff. in reverse order, but with only one from each of the two
middle pairs specified. The single exception is that where Zeus is
named first and alone, Hera, his mate, is addressed first in the second
list. Figure 2 diagrams the structure of this section.

Lines 109 ff.:

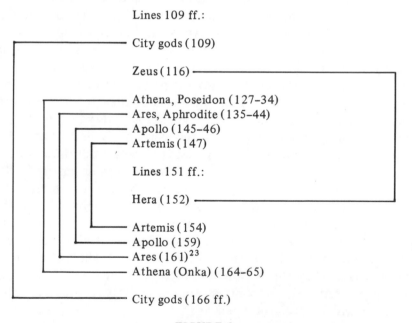

City gods (109)

Zeus (116)

Athena, Poseidon (127–34)
Ares, Aphrodite (135–44)
Apollo (145–46)
Artemis (147)

Lines 151 ff.:

Hera (152)

Artemis (154)
Apollo (159)
Ares (161)[23]
Athena (Onka) (164–65)

City gods (166 ff.)

FIGURE 2

This order may have been determined by the actual placing of the
statues. We might imagine them in a row, with images of Zeus and

Hera at either end. The chorus would then appeal to the gods in the order in which their images stand, beginning with Zeus and ending with Hera, and then moving back up the line in reverse order. At the beginning and end of this series of individual prayers, they would address the city's gods as a group.

For all its agitation, then, the parodos does not lack a definite form. We can observe this in another respect as well. The chorus's prayers are interwoven with, and prompted by, their comments on the assault on the city. Evidently they can look out over the plains and watch, as the audience cannot, the advance of the hostile army.[24] They simultaneously describe and react to what they see. The closer the Argives draw to the city, the more frantic the maidens become. The stages in the attack are clearly delineated. The army leaves its camp (line 79). At first only the cavalry is visible, with the dust it raises; there is no sound yet (lines 80–83). Then the clash of weapons grazes the chorus's ears (lines 83–84).[25] They hear more sounds, hovering in the air and still from rather far off, like the rush of a swollen mountain stream (lines 85–86).[26] Then, "out beyond the walls,"[27] the white shields of the foot soldiers can be seen. Now the banging of shields (line 100) and of spears (line 103) is audible. The wave of the enemy washes around the walls (line 113–15). The harnesses of the Argive horses rattle and the seven chiefs can be distinguished (lines 120–26). The Argives have surrounded the city. The noise of their chariots and the whistle of the axle boxes are heard (lines 151, 153). The air rages, shaken with spears (line 155), and a shower of stones hits the ramparts (line 158).[28] Finally, shields rattle in the very gates (line 160).

It is not necessary to suppose that these sounds were actually imitated. The chorus simply mention them in a regular progression, and the audience's imagination would do the rest. Here, as in the prologue, Aeschylus has taken care to make vivid what the spectators could not see or hear. And he has done it artfully. Mesk has drawn attention to the regular alternation of the visual and aural components of this description.[29] The two converge in the phrase κτύπον δέδορκα (line 103), which Stanford cites as an example of "synaesthetic imagery."[30] The visible counterpart of the assault is the chorus's response; their panic corresponds to the Argives' ferocity.

The invading army, invisible but a definite and swelling presence; the chorus with their agitated song and gestures; and the unmoving

statues of the gods—all are important elements in Aeschylus's presentation here. The parodos shows the effect of the war, and thus
of the curse, on the city. In the midst of the turmoil both within and
without, only the gods are stable (εὔεδροι, line 97), the one fixed
point in this reeling city. Their statues represent this steadiness and
evoke, more generally, the city's whole relation to them, on which
its safety and prosperity are founded. The gods, as we have seen,
form an important theme in the play, and in their statues this theme
becomes concrete. On the one hand, the images epitomize the
balance in the city's life, which is now threatened; on the other
hand, it is before these statues that the problems in Eteocles' own
relation to the gods are later made explicit.

The first hints of this—and they are little more than hints—occur
in the scene which follows between Eteocles and the chorus. It is
surely significant that the issue which divides them is how reverence
must be paid to the gods if the city is to survive. The other important dimension of the argument is Eteocles' diatribe against women,
which for the first time sets him apart from the idea of the family
and all that that implies.

The organization of the scene is important. It begins and ends
with speeches by Eteocles. Between them is a symmetrical epirrhematic section, followed by a short passage of stichomythia. In
the former, the chorus sing three strophic pairs, each of which consists mainly of dochmiacs but closes in other meters. Each pair
decreases by one line from the previous pair—five lines, four, and
then three. Eteocles is arguing the chorus into a calmer manner of
speaking (though the stichomythia too is rapid and excited), and
finally to silence (σιγῶ, line 263).[31] Between the choral utterances,
Eteocles himself delivers three lines of trimeters. These may have
been (but this is quite uncertain) what was known as παρακαταλογή—
iambics delivered in recitative to musical accompaniment.[32] In that
case they would have been more agitated than spoken lines, though
in the same meter. Eteocles too might thus appear upset—less so,
however, than the chorus, who sing in dochmiacs.

The matter of Eteocles' supposed impiety has already been discussed. The attitude towards the gods which his words in this scene
convey differs from that of the chorus but is not in itself arrogant.
Whereas the chorus trust entirely in the gods, Eteocles insists on the
need for both human action and divine aid. This attitude was apparent

also in the structure of the prologue. The chorus implore the gods to rescue the city; ῥύεσθαι and related words occur very frequently in both the parodos and the first stasimon. But Eteocles recommends that they ask the gods to be the Thebans' allies (ξύμμαχοι, line 266). The stage spectacle may reinforce this contrast. Throughout the scene, the chorus have remained at the altar, for Eteocles tells them to leave it only near the end (line 265). He himself stands apart from it, perhaps in the orchestra. The spatial distance would emphasize his self-reliance relative to the dependence of the chorus.

Yet, in keeping with the total effect of this scene, Eteocles' physical position also sets him apart from the close ties between the city and its gods. His vow to the gods at the end of the scene (lines 271 ff.) is entirely in keeping with the statement in his earlier prayer that the city which prospers honors its gods (lines 76–77), and so harmonizes with the reciprocal relationship with them which marks the city's piety. It is a perfectly proper attitude for a commander to take. And his confidence is not misplaced; the war goes in Thebes' favor. Eteocles' problem is rather his own situation.

The chorus leave the altar, in obedience to Eteocles' command, and deliver the first stasimon in the orchestra. In this ode the maidens do not run to the statues, though they continue to address the gods. The difference from the parodos in location and physical movement underscores the change in tone: the stasimon is more reflective.[33] Although the maidens are still terrified, they express their feelings no longer outwardly but by imagining the disaster they fear. The meter of this song is principally iambic, iambo-trochaic, and Aeolic. Dochmiacs occur only at the beginning of the third pair of stanzas (lines 345–47, 357–59), when the picture of the sack of the city reaches its climax. The chorus's fear is no longer explosive; it is lodged near the heart (lines 288–89), a settled dread (τάρβος; cf. προταρβῶ, line 332).

The statues of the gods are, however, still significant. In the prologue (lines 14–15), Eteocles has said that the altars of the gods need protection, and he has later told the chorus that the gods abandon a captured city (lines 217–18). In the stasimon, the chorus revert to this idea when they ask what better land the gods could dwell in than Thebes, and beg them to "stand well-fixed" (line 319). The repetition of εὔεδροι here from line 97 has concrete reference to the statues. Even their stability is threatened by the common danger.

The first strophic pair is constructed so that the stanzas correspond very closely. They fall into three distinct periods: first, iambic and iambo-trochaic (lines 287–94, 304–11), then a run of pherecrateans (lines 295–300, 312–17), and a close which combines iambic and Aeolic (lines 301-303, 318-20). In each, the first period expresses the danger and depicts what is at stake: in the strophe the young birds in the nest, in the antistrophe the city's fertility and harmony with its gods. The subject of the second period is the attack of the Argives. In the antistrophe this is put in the context of a prayer to the gods to repulse them; to the threat Thebes opposes her piety. Both stanzas end with prayers for protection, and ῥύτορες (line 318) echoes ῥύεσθε (line 303).

With the second pair of stanzas, the imaginative description of the plunder of a city begins. The initial word of the strophe, οἰκτρόν, is answered by κλαυτὸν δέ in the antistrophe. In the strophe, general descriptions of destruction and desolation frame what the chorus particularly dread—the violent seizure, by the hair, of women both young and old (lines 326-29). At the start of the antistrophe, this picture is made more specific in a description of the capture of young girls before their marriage.[34] Then the scope widens once more to pillage throughout the whole city (lines 338 ff.). The maidens of the chorus, who represent the city in general, embody some of the qualities most precious to it, such as the piety which attracts to Thebes the beneficence of the gods. They also possess the capacity for continuing the cycle of life through marriage and procreation, and thus they carry within themselves the potential for the city's future. In them, Aeschylus represents what is threatened in the war. Their presence thus complements that of the images of the gods.

The final stanzas continue the picture of the sack. Details of the destruction are juxtaposed with the ferocity and greed of the pillagers. The slaughter of babies (lines 348–50) and the waste of the earth's gifts (lines 357–62) add further dimensions to the depiction of what is endangered. The song closes with a recurrence of what is necessarily the chorus's own preoccupation: the lot of a captive girl.

Throughout the early part of the play the emphasis is on the war. The curse is mentioned only once (line 70), and there are merely hints of what is to come. It is apparently the city in general that is threatened. In addition, as Benardete notes, the first stasimon could describe the plunder of any city, not just of Thebes.[35] Thus the concerns of the play have become most comprehensive just before they begin to narrow in the central scene.

The overall picture given by this first section of the play is one of imbalance. The excess of the Argives' ferocity is answered by that of the chorus's panic. Though Eteocles seems, by contrast, self-controlled, there are indications in the first episode of a basic lack of equilibrium in him also. Even the relations between the gods and the city, which in peace take the form of a measured interchange, are now called into question. All of this is conveyed by the dramatic presentation, working in conjunction with the imagery. Perhaps the foregoing discussion will justify my interpreting "dramatic presentation" in the very widest sense. It is primarily what the audience actually sees and hears. But (at least when applied to the *Seven*) the term should also include what is out of sight and hearing but is so described as to be extremely vivid. The rush of the Argives across the plains to attack the city is virtually put before the spectators by the language and structure of the parodos, and especially by the actual portrayal of the chorus's terror. The audience shares in the creation of this effect as its imagination works on what Aeschylus gives it. He actually presents, however, not the occurrences outside the city but those within it. And that is where the significant problems of the play—even the war itself—begin and end.

The imbalance depicted here, however, because it results from an unusual situation, implies a norm: a way of life which is as fragile as it is bountiful and which is now under stress. The destruction of Thebes' ruling family removes that stress. This result, prepared for in the shield scene (which will be examined in the next chapter), is carried out in the third section of the play.

THE FINAL SECTION OF THE *SEVEN*

The end of the shield scene leads directly into the scene in which Eteocles prepares to meet his brother at the seventh gate. This is the climax of the play. The war's significance has suddenly been defined with a new and awesome explicitness, and in this second epirrhematic scene (lines 677–719) Aeschylus presents visibly the seizure of a man by a curse. The change is emphasized formally. In the shield scene, at the end of each of the first six pairs of speeches, the chorus have expressed their reaction in a short lyric passage. But now, after

the seventh pair, when Eteocles has declared himself Polynices'
opponent, the chorus begin to plead with him in a short speech of
iambic trimeters (lines 677–82). This is their only spoken, nonlyric
utterance in the entire play, except for single lines in stichomythia.
It comes in abruptly and perhaps indicates the chorus's altered position with regard to Eteocles, before their emotion leads them once
more to sing in agitated rhythm.

This scene is the counterpart to the earlier epirrhematic exchange
between Eteocles and the chorus. For the second and final time in
the play it brings together, in confrontation before the spectators,
the representatives of the city and of the ruling house. In the previous scene, however, the chorus's address to Eteocles as "child of
Oedipus" (line 203) held only intimations of potential disaster;
when that form of address recurs here (line 677), what was latent
has come to the surface. This is the scene in which it is guaranteed,
through the agency of the curse, that the disaster will occur. Here it
is Eteocles who is driven by something irrational, and the chorus are
now the ones who urge prudence.

Like the earlier one, this scene begins with dialogue in the form of
two short speeches and ends with stichomythia. In the center is
another epirrhematic section. The chorus again sing in dochmiacs,
with Aristophanean *clausulae*, while Eteocles replies once more in
three lines of trimeters (perhaps again in recitative) after each stanza.
But here too there is a difference. If Eteocles' lines are recitative,
they suggest determination and excitement; if spoken, a hard decid-
edness, which would be equally effective. The mental imbalance
hinted at in the previous scene becomes explicit here. The chorus,
for their part, are again frightened, as their dochmiacs show. Earlier,
however, they were afraid of the enemy attack and of what might
befall them. Now they fear for Eteocles. Whereas before they were
gradually calmed and their stanzas successively decreased in length,
here they become more agitated. Trimeters switch to lyrics, and their
stanzas grow in length from three lines to four.

The trimeter sections which frame the epirrhematic segment are
concerned, in both scenes, with human activities. The earlier scene
begins with Eteocles' invective against women and his command for
silence. It ends with a prayer, by which he shows the chorus how to
enlist the gods' aid in an enterprise in which he too will be active. In
both parts he is dealing with the immediate situation of the war. In

the later scene, as Regenbogen points out, the main subject of the framing sections is a warrior's honor.[36] Again Eteocles is responding as a soldier, but to a situation now perceived as involving him personally. The central part of each scene is concerned with the relation between men and gods. But Eteocles earlier observed that the gods desert a captured city and promised them proper sacrifice in the event of victory; he now rejects the chorus's confidence in the efficacy of sacrifice and asserts that his own family has been abandoned by the gods. As in the earlier scene, the chorus put forward the beliefs of conventional religion—not to be scorned on that account, since upon them the city's well-being rests in such large part. But a new factor, which has been active all along, though not obviously, has now been recognized. That is the curse. Against it, Eteocles sees no defense.

The role of the curse in contriving Eteocles' situation is stressed by the spectacle in this scene. Schadewaldt has plausibly suggested that when Eteocles calls for his greaves (lines 675–76), his full armor is brought, and that during each speech in his exchange with the chorus he puts on one article of it. By the end of the scene he stands before the audience fully armed.[37] This physical action (if it occurs) probably prompts Eteocles' language in line 715, where he says that he is "whetted" and will not be "blunted" by argument: τεθηγμένον τοί μ' οὐκ ἀπαμβλυνεῖς λόγῳ. Helen Bacon proposes that he takes up his last implement, the spear, as he delivers this line, not at line 719 (as Schadewaldt thinks).[38] This gesture, along with his words, would suggest that, equipped with his armor, Eteocles embodies the iron of a sword or a spear (cf. line 944: θηκτὸς σίδαρος).

The visual and verbal equation of Eteocles with the iron has manifold implications, which can best be explored by comparison with a passage in the *Prometheus Bound* (lines 860–69). There Prometheus prophesies to Io the Danaids' murder of their husbands, and then goes on to tell of the single exception, Hypermestra (lines 865–69):

> μίαν δὲ παίδων ἵμερος θέλξει τὸ μὴ
> κτεῖναι σύνευνον, ἀλλ' ἀπαμβλυνθήσεται
> γνώμην· δυοῖν δὲ θάτερον βουλήσεται,
> κλύειν ἄναλκις μᾶλλον ἢ μιαιφόνος·
> αὕτη κατ' Ἄργος βασιλικὸν τέξει γένος.

The word ἀπαμβλυνθήσεται here is striking. It apparently is suggested

by the mention, in line 863, of the "two-edged sword" (that is,
"whetted on both sides," δίθηκτον . . . ξίφος), which will be the
instrument of the Danaids' hatred. This passes into the metaphor of
Hypermestra's being "blunted in her intention," so as to prefer a
reputation for weakness to one for murder. There seems, then, a
deliberate contrast between the sharpness of her sisters' swords and
the dulling of Hypermestra's purpose. The reason for the latter is
given as ἵμερος, sexual desire, which will "charm" (θέλξει) her not to
kill her "bed-mate" (σύνευνον). The implication is that in relenting
she will accept her role as a woman. Thus only she, of all the Danaids,
will beget a royal race in Argos. Conversely, to use the weapon would
be to refuse that role—to end life rather than perpetuate it.[39]

Eteocles' use of similar language in line 715 of the Seven also
originates in an actual weapon—the spear which he may take at that
point. But unlike Hypermestra, he will not be blunted. He clearly
would rather commit murder—and murder in a particularly abhorrent form—than be known as a coward (cf. line 717). His purpose is
fixed, and he will not be swayed by the chorus's arguments (λόγῳ).
While they talk, he acts, by equipping himself and then by leaving for
the fight. If Schadewaldt's view of this scene is correct, the audience
watches Eteocles become less and less human with every piece of
armor he puts on. When he is fully armed and speaks of himself as
if he were a weapon, he is no longer a man. His humanity is concealed
behind the trappings of his role as a member of a cursed house. The
result is destruction, not only for himself but for his entire family as
well. This is the final and most important contrast with the story of
Hypermestra. It is the same contrast as the one suggested by the
imagery of earth and family between Thebes and her ruling house.[40]

Eteocles finally is, in fact, just what the chorus, at the start of the
scene, beg him not to become (lines 677–78).[41]

μὴ, φίλτατ' ἀνδρῶν, Οἰδίπου τέκος, γένη
ὀργὴν ὁμοῖος τῷ κάκιστ' αὐδωμένῳ.

"Do not become like your brother in temper."[42] But Eteocles' determination to fight matches that of Polynices. When he has armed
himself, Eteocles is the visible counterpart of his brother. The spy
has described Polynices' imprecations on the city, his challenge to
Eteocles, and his shield device. We learn nothing more about him;

Amphiaraus's rebuke of him enables us to evaluate Polynices' action rather than the man himself or his motives. That is as it should be. For his part, Eteocles loses any individuality he may have possessed when he covers himself with his armor.[43] He would be indistinguishable from Polynices, except for the latter's shield token.[44] Both are equally warriors acting under the compulsion of a curse.

The effects just described amount to a portrayal of the working of the curse. Later in the play, in the lament just after they learn of the fratricide, the chorus say that "the oracles have not been blunted" (line 844: θέσφατ' οὐκ ἀμβλύνεται).[45] On any interpretation of the evidence, the oracle Laius received and the curse were related.[46] Eteocles, "whetted" for battle, demonstrates visibly that the oracle is still "sharp" (that is, effective). It will be fulfilled, and so the curse will be accomplished.

But the iron and the Erinys are connected in another way as well. They are identified with each other in the opening stanzas of the second stasimon, where lot imagery is first used specifically of the brothers' duel.[47] Here, just before that ode, the lot, the iron, and the theme of division all converge in the figure of Eteocles. With the iron of the spear he holds, he will carry out the division of the inheritance, so that he and his brother will meet the fate they have been allotted. Thus, since the curse is manifested through the iron, and since Eteocles has come to personify the latter, he represents physically the operation of the daemonic force which is moving events to their result. Not only his words, but his very person makes it plain that he has become literally possessed by the curse. The sight of him thus overtaken stands out before the motionless images of the gods, under whose supervision Eteocles goes to meet the consequences of his inherited guilt.[48]

The Erinys has begun to accomplish her task, and at line 719 Eteocles exits for the last time. Appropriately, the stasimon which follows explores the origins of the curse. The chorus view the present moment as a stage in a pattern of events which started with a misdeed of Laius, and foresee all too accurately what the outcome must be. This ode, like the first stasimon with which it corresponds, has a few dochmiacs in the last strophic pair. Like the earlier song, this one too is contemplative. But dread of imminent defeat by the Argives has been replaced by consideration of the past as well as the near future, and by the more specific fear of the curse's fulfillment.

The second stasimon begins, however, with a new and striking element. When the chorus describe the curse through lot imagery (lines 720–33), they sing in Ionics, the meter of Asiatic and Dionysiac cults. This rhythm appears nowhere else in the *Seven*, with one probable exception.[49] The emotion which has built up through the preceding scene breaks out here in a vision that can only be called prophetic; and what the maidens foresee terrifies them. Their shuddering (πέφρικα, line 720) contrasts sharply with the dread (τάρβος) of the second stasimon. Only then do they settle down to tracing out the causes of their fear, which lie in the past.

Jacqueline de Romilly has observed that around the middle of each play Aeschylus customarily places a flashback to the distant past and considers its implications—usually ominous—for the future.[50] The *Seven* certainly illustrates this habit. In this ode, past, present, and future are telescoped into an all-encompassing vision of disaster. At least four stages of time can be distinguished: Laius, Oedipus, the present, and the near future, the latter two being the period of the third generation. The present is a transition between past and future, for the brothers' fate is a result of something Laius did.

The three generations are woven together in a complex structure.[51] The first two stanzas express the chorus's anxiety over the future—the outcome of the duel between the brothers. This subject is continued into the second strophe. But at the end of it, the mention of "the house's new toils mingled with ancient ills" (lines 739–41) associates present and past. In the second antistrophe and third strophe, the stories of Laius and of Oedipus's marriage to his mother follow.[52] With the third antistrophe the chorus revert to the present. Lines 758–61 repeat the idea of new misfortunes added to old, but in nautical language which, as was earlier remarked, expresses the fear that the city may yet be implicated in the curse. There is a distinct break after this stanza. Thus fearful anticipation of the future (second strophe), connected with the view of the present as a new stage in a pattern of misfortune (third antistrophe), frames allusion to past events (second antistrophe and third strophe). In the middle section, the second antistrophe tells of the oracle Laius received. The third strophe recounts the respective errors of Laius and Oedipus. Both errors are sexual and involve begetting children who should not have been born. Their juxtaposition emphasizes the disruption within the family and, more generally, the pattern of the curse's effect.

Within the strophe, allusions to the birth of Oedipus frame the
account of his incestuous marriage if, as seems likely, lines 756–57
refer to Laius and his wife.[53]

The second section of the ode takes its subject, Oedipus, from the
central part of the third strophe. It tells not of his marriage to his
mother (for that has been mentioned) but of the consequences of
that union: his rise to prosperity, his ruin, and his curse on his sons.
References to curses and dread of their accomplishment (τέλειαι,
line 766; τελέσῃ, line 791) frame the whole section. In addition, the
last lines of the song round off the whole with a clear echo of the
first strophe (cf. especially τελέσαι, line 724). Thus the idea of the
fulfillment of curses marks the beginning, middle, and end of the
stasimon.[54]

But are the same curses alluded to at all three points? Oedipus's
curses are certainly mentioned in the first and last stanzas, but since
the reference in line 766 is less specific, there is another possibility.
I suggested earlier that the rape of Chrysippus and Pelops's curse on
Laius were the origin of the family's troubles.[55] Though there is no
clear reference to the episode in this song or the entire play, the rape
may be Laius's "transgression" of line 743, and the curses of line
766 those not of Oedipus but of Pelops.[56] That would mark the ode's
structure even more clearly; for allusion to the story of Chrysippus,
as first cause of the misfortunes, would begin the narrative of Laius
(lines 742 ff.) and make the transition to the story of Oedipus (lines
766 ff.). The epithet παλαιφάτων might thus recall παλαιγενῆ in
line 742. The ideas which articulate the shape of the song could be
listed as shown in figure 3. If the curses of line 766 are those of
Pelops, Oedipus's fall from prosperity, which is recounted next, is
explained as a consequence of Laius's crime. Pelops's curses are thus
effective in Laius's death and in Oedipus's own ruin and curse on his
sons. If, however, the allusion in line 766 is to Oedipus' curses, the
story of Oedipus's sufferings has the effect of a digression, with the
main thread resumed only in the final stanza. Consequently, the
form of the song is less well defined.

Whether it contains references to Chrysippus or not, the song as
a whole progresses from the first generation to the second in the
earlier section, and in the next from the second to the third. Oedipus
binds the two parts together; he appears in the first as a son, and in
the second as a father, both times in an abnormal relation to other

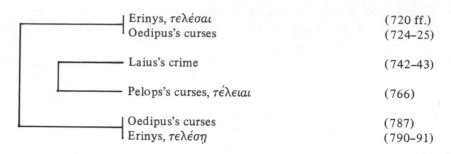

Erinys, τελέσαι	(720 ff.)
Oedipus's curses	(724–25)
Laius's crime	(742–43)
Pelops's curses, τέλειαι	(766)
Oedipus's curses	(787)
Erinys, τελέση	(790–91)

FIGURE 3

members of his family. Thus the plan of the stasimon stresses the
continuity of the curse through three generations.

The messenger's scene which follows, though brief for structural
reasons, is important. It announces the fulfillment, in an unforeseen
way, of Eteocles' prayer at the end of his first exchange with the
chorus.[57] And since, in a more general way, the scene signifies the
completion of everything in the play up to this point, Aeschylus
draws together in it many of the major themes and images and
applies them specifically to the battle's result. The scene reveals the
direction in which the play has been moving all along.[58] At the same
time, it leads into the lament which follows. The messenger's remark
(line 814) that there is cause for both weeping and rejoicing is immediately picked up by the chorus (lines 822 ff.), and the lot imagery,
which he employs (lines 816–19), becomes the basis of their song.

If the anapaests which introduce the third stasimon (lines 822 ff.)
are genuine, they are at least badly corrupted.[59] If that is so, certain
words, at any rate, can be picked out which have structural and
thematic significance. This ode, together with its introductory section, corresponds to the parodos. There the city gods (line 109)
and Zeus (line 116) were invoked and asked to save the city (cf.
ῥύσεται, line 92). In this passage, the same deities are addressed
(line 822), and some form of the verb ῥύεσθαι is apparently employed
(line 824). It is worth pointing out once again that this song too is
delivered within sight of the statues of the gods, who have now
heeded the maidens' prayers.

But it is most likely delivered in the orchestra and preceded (probably) by the orderly recited anapaests that might have been expected

to introduce the parodos. These contrast sharply with the excited dochmiacs which actually appear there. Terror has given way to grief as the outcome of the battle is both welcomed and mourned.

The final lament (lines 875–1004) balances the prologue and, though under unforeseen circumstances, is the "hymn" of woe which Eteocles has mentioned as a possibility (lines 5–9). The tone of this lament is one of sorrow, and yet also of reconciliation as the curse ceases, having overcome the two brothers (lines 959–60), and as the chorus meditate upon the ultimate decision of the lot.

We have observed how, in this part of the play, Aeschylus distorts the allotment procedure into an image of the brothers' mutual hostility. The ideas suggested by this image, particularly the ambiguous notions of moira and division, are now represented physically. Near the end of the antistrophe in the third stasimon the brothers' bodies are brought onto the scene on biers. The chorus signal their arrival with the words (lines 846–47):

> . . . ἦλθε δ' αἰ-
> ακιὰ πήματ' οὐ λόγῳ.

The natural antithesis to λόγῳ is, as Tucker points out, ἔργῳ, and these lines indicate that the audience will actually see what the words describe. Then, as the corpses are placed in the orchestra, the chorus continue (lines 848–53):[60]

> τάδ' αὐτόδηλα · προῦπτος ἀγγέλου λόγος ·
> διπλᾶ μερίμναιν διδύμαιν ὁρᾶν κακά,
> αὐτοφόνα δίμορα τέλεα τάδε πάθη. τί φῶ;
> τί δ' ἄλλο γ' ἢ πόνοι πόνων ἐφέστιοι;

The last line recalls language used in the second stasimon, where the imminent duel of the brothers was viewed as the third stage in the hideous pattern of the curse (lines 739–41). Here we actually see the third and final achievement of the Erinys (cf. τέλεα, line 850). The wounds in the brothers' bodies are the literal correlate of the idea of division. But there is also an emphasis on doubleness (διπλᾶ, διδύμαιν, δίμορα): the brothers are spoken of together as a pair. They have been allotted an equal fate, and the presence of their bodies, together, stresses this ghastly impartiality.

The effect of words and spectacle, working together, must have been powerful, especially in passages like lines 938–40:

πέπαυται δ᾽ ἔχθος, ἐν δὲ γαίᾳ
ζόα φονορύτῳ
μέμεικται· κάρτα δ᾽ εἰσ᾽ ὅμαιμοι.

Here the mingling of the brothers' blood on the ground adds a new dimension to the idea of the identity of their fate. Death has brought them together in peace at last, and the spectacle emphasizes this. Immediately after these lines, the lot imagery recurs; the spectators *see* the outcome of the lot.

In the closing part of the *kommos* (lines 961–1004), if not before, the chorus probably divide into two groups, each taking a position near the bier of one of the brothers.[61] The semichoruses sing short phrases in turn, each answering the other. Their theme is the paradox of the brothers' death at one another's hand and the final similarity of their fates. Here too words and spectacle contribute equally to the effect. The play probably does not end with a procession, but the final lines of the lament make it clear that Eteocles and Polynices will be buried together, returned to the darkness of the maternal earth.

Above and behind the orchestra, the statues of the gods still stand immobile, the benefactors of the city through the destruction of its ruling house. In front of these images the spectators have seen the panic of the women yield to grief in the end; they have seen Eteocles become possessed by the curse until he literally *is* the iron for a moment; and finally they see, in the brothers' corpses, the result of the lot.

THE ROLE OF THE CHORUS IN THE DRAMATIC PRESENTATION

The chorus are not just a group of panic-stricken virgins. As previously remarked, they represent Thebes as a whole, and they embody much that is fragile and precious in the city's life. Their reactions to the events of the play not only are those of young girls but also stand for the effects of those events on the entire city. They thus provide an effective foil to Eteocles.

Of Aeschylean choruses, de Romilly says that their dance and song are the tangible equivalent of a situation or emotion.[62] The Greeks considered the dance in general mimetic. Aristotle says that it imitates καὶ ἤϑη καὶ πάϑη καὶ πράξεις.[63] There is a fair amount of ancient testimony that Aeschylus, like the other early dramatists, himself devised the dance figures for his plays and taught them to his chorus members.[64] The chorus's movements, then, were an important aspect of the staging. What these were in the original performance of the *Seven* we cannot know, but we should bear in mind that the odes involved more than a bare text. Certainly it is not hard to imagine how the chorus's physical motions at the beginning of the parodos, for instance, or of the second stasimon, vividly expressed their fear.

Dance was mimetic not only through bodily movement but through gestures with the hands as well.[65] The text of the *Seven* gives two indications of these. In the parodos, the chorus implore the gods to hear their χειροτόνους λίτας (line 172). They probably stretch out their hands to the statues or to heaven,[66] using the γυναικομίμοις ὑπτιάσμασιν χερῶν which the defiant Prometheus scornfully rejects as characteristic of female helplessness.[67] In the same way Eteocles, shortly after the parodos, attacks the chorus's femininity. The other motion suggested by the text is one of lamentation for the brothers, when the chorus rhythmically beat their heads and compare the sweep of their hands to that of oars (lines 854–60). This contrast in physical gesture marks the change in the chorus's emotions from general fear to mourning specifically directed.

Music also was a form of imitation.[68] It must have been as important in the production of the *Seven* as the choral movements it accompanied. It also furnishes another example of imagery made concrete, for music, as we have seen, is a recurrent theme of the play.[69]

Although the music is lost, the lyric rhythms can give us some idea of its effect. These progress from panic through dread and mantic excitement to sorrow. The dochmiacs of the parodos are continued in the chorus's first scene with Eteocles. The meter of the first stasimon is, with a few exceptions, more settled, as the maidens, calmer now but not silent, imagine the consequences of defeat upon a city. Their lyric comments in the shield scene, however, are again mainly in dochmiacs, and they employ the same rhythm as their agitation mounts in the second epirrhematic scene. Then, with the vision born of sudden understanding, they burst out in wild Ionics in the first strophic pair of the second stasimon. This passage might be called the high point of the chorus's fear. In the rest of the ode they return to quieter rhythms for contemplation, as in the corresponding first stasimon. Finally, as the maidens grieve over the brothers' death, they sing in iambic, iambo-trochaic, and Aeolic rhythms, with only a few scattered dochmiacs. One would have expected a far heavier incidence of the latter here. Aeschylus seems to have used them sparingly to emphasize the contrast, in situation and in tone, between the beginning and the end of the play.

The dramatic presentation, like the structure and imagery, stresses the shift in the play between the first section and the third. The shield scene paves the way for this change. It is itself carefully constructed and contains very important themes. And though it consists principally of description, its full effect can have been achieved only in performance. These aspects of the scene will be examined in the next chapter.

5

The Shield Scene

In the lengthy and—in all senses—central scene of the play, the spy, returning once again from the enemy camp, describes the appearance, boasts, and shield devices of the seven Argive chiefs and tells which gate each of them is to attack. Their respective positions have been determined by lot, as the spy reported in the prologue. In this scene, the Theban countermeasures are announced and made final. The process itself is somewhat uncertain. Against each of the Argives Eteocles sets a Theban defender; or else, having selected at least some of his champions and assigned them to the gates during the first stasimon, in accordance with his words at lines 282–86, he now comments on the fitness of each Theban to face his particular Argive opponent. In either case, the arrangements, by an uncanny coincidence, can be so interpreted as to appear advantageous to Thebes, and Eteocles does so in his responses to the spy's descriptions. The reason, then, for the length and special position of this scene is that in it the battle is virtually fought out in words and symbols before the event itself.

The seventh pair of speeches presents, however, a special case. The shield scene not only assures Thebes' victory; it also culminates in matching Eteocles and Polynices in battle at the seventh gate. Thus the war, which has earlier been treated as a conflict between two cities, concentrates here on the fighting between seven pairs of champions. And by the end of the scene, the issue lies between the two brothers, where it turns out actually to have been all along. The central scene is thus the turning point in the war, but the war, once decided, loses importance. As it does so, the curse, previously unobtrusive but never inactive, becomes prominent.

THE PLAN OF THE SCENE

The structure of the shield scene can be viewed in two ways. One is to regard the first six pairs of speeches as a unit, with the seventh and culminating pair set off from the rest. Short lyric comments by the chorus, arranged in strophic responsion, follow each of the first six pairs and bind them together. After the seventh, this symmetry is broken, for, as I noted in the preceding chapter, this pair is followed not by lyric but by the chorus's short passage of spoken trimeters (lines 677–82), which is actually the beginning of the next scene. Moreover, the first six Argive attackers are grouped, on the basis of their shield devices and by recurrent themes in the spy's reports, into three successive pairs; the seventh, Polynices, stands alone. Tydeus's taunts at Amphiaraus in the first pair of speeches are answered by the seer's reproach of both him and Polynices in the sixth. Thus the first six exchanges are rounded off, and the seventh is more or less appended to them. Finally, Eteocles responds to the news of his brother's presence at the seventh gate (lines 653 ff.) entirely differently from the way he dealt with the descriptions of the previous six attackers. By isolating the matching of Eteocles and Polynices in these ways, Aeschylus emphasizes that it is the result to which the entire scene has been leading. Against the background of the verbal battle which engages all the Argive chiefs and Theban defenders, the brothers stand out, for on them the weight of the war finally rests.

Even so, the fourth exchange falls at the middle of the scene and so receives special emphasis.[1] It opposes not only two men who are, for some reason, personal enemies, but also, on their shields, Zeus and his monstrous rival Typhon (lines 509–11).[2] As Eteocles asserts, since Zeus overcame Typhon there is good reason to expect that Hyperbius, the Theban, will prevail over Hippomedon. After this pair of speeches, the city's victory with the aid of Zeus cannot be in serious doubt.[3] The first three pairs lead up to it, for they all concern mainly the outcome of the war in general and its effect upon the city. But the central pair not only is decisive in regard to the war; it also anticipates in important ways the situation of Eteocles and Polynices that will emerge at the end of the scene. The speeches which follow it, the fifth and sixth pairs, also carry significant implications for the brothers' position. Thus the latter part of this scene, starting with the central pair of speeches, begins the process of concentration on the brothers, and so prepares for Eteocles' outburst at the end. The epirrhematic scene which follows continues this narrowing of focus, but the shift occurs in the shield scene.

Considered either way, the plan of the scene facilitates and stresses this shift. Probably we ought to think of both views of the structure as valid simultaneously. That is, Aeschylus seems to be emphasizing both the final pair of speeches as isolated and different—the culmination of the scene—and the central fourth pair as decisive for the war in general and the point at which attention begins to center on the brothers.

THE SHIELDS AND THE MAJOR THEMES

As he describes the shield of each Argive chief, the spy presents Eteocles with a riddle, the correct solution of which will make a Theban victory probable, if not absolutely assure it. The shields are a form of omen, and Eteocles' task is to interpret and accept the omen.[4] At the same time, the Argives play into his hands. Their boasts are so excessive that they seem without substance. Κομπάζειν and its derivatives are used again and again in connection with them.[5] When Eteocles names the Theban champions, by contrast, he stresses their disposition for action rather than for speech.[6] The Argives affront even the gods, while Thebes seeks to enlist their aid, both in the early part of the play and, through Eteocles, in this scene. It is as if each Argive, in the spy's account, challenges Eteocles directly in his capacity of commander. By his piety, however, Amphiaraus poses a special problem to the city; and the anomaly of his position among the Argives throws light on Eteocles' own situation. Polynices, finally, in his appeal to justice, confronts Eteocles with a problem that is less military than personal, and the latter's confidence in the gods' favor and in his own ability to meet the challenge suddenly evaporates.

The first four pairs of speeches can conveniently be considered together. On the one hand, those concerned with Tydeus and Capaneus, the first two Argives, have particular affinities with one another, and the same is true of the third and fourth pairs. At the same time, certain themes run through all the pairs and converge in the description of Hippomedon at the center of the scene.[7]

Tydeus is a picture of unbridled ferocity. Aside from his appearance, the noises he makes render him formidable. They are summed up in the word βρέμει at the start of the spy's description (line 378). He is impatient of Amphiaraus's religious scruples. His violence and eagerness for battle are depicted in two similes: he cries out like a snake in the midday heat (lines 380-81), and resembles a horse champing at the bit, waiting for the signal to begin the race (lines 391-94). These similes, one near the beginning, the other at the end of the spy's speech, are tied together verbally: βοᾷ in line 392 is repeated from line 381, while μάχης ἐρῶν recalls the earlier μάχης λελιμμένος (line 380). Between them, the spy tells of Tydeus's abuse of the seer, the bells on his shield, and the shield device itself, which is the one visual element of the description. It represents stars shining in the night sky, with a full moon, the "eye of night," prominent in the center. Its intended meaning is probably, as Fraenkel says, "I, Tydeus, am the full moon, the others only stars."[8] Eteocles, however, twists it into an omen of Tydeus's death by producing, from the association of "eye" and "night," the phrase "night upon the eyes." Amphiaraus's hestitation thus appears well founded, and the fact that the sacrifices are unfavorable (line 379) bodes ill for the Argives.

Except for his scorn of Amphiaraus, however, Tydeus is not impious. It is in his self-assertion that he is excessive, his claim that he outshines all his fellow warriors.[9] The picture on his shield is called "arrogant" no fewer than three times.[10] Thus Melanippus is a fit opponent for him, for he "honors the throne of Αἰσχύνη" (lines 409-10). In addition, Tydeus is an intruder; his noisy violence is the absolute antithesis of the city's normal calm and balance. Melanippus, on the other hand, descended as he is from the *Spartoi,* has an especially close relationship with the Theban soil; and in confronting Tydeus he will be defending both his mother, the earth, and his blood kin, his fellow citizens (lines 412-16).

Capaneus's boast, by contrast, exceeds what is appropriate to mortals (line 425) and defies Zeus himself. Not even the thunderbolt, he says, will keep him from sacking the city.[11] Far from fearing the lightning, he carries his own kind of fire. On his shield is a naked man with a torch in his hands and the motto, in gold letters, "I shall burn the city." It is unnecessary for Eteocles to interpret this. So obviously dangerous is Capaneus's presumption that Eteocles need only predict that Zeus's thunderbolt will indeed fall upon him, and that Capaneus will find it more terrible than he expected. Moreover, to the fire on Capaneus's shield Eteocles opposes Polyphontes, who is "blazing in spirit" (line 448) and so more formidable than any

picture or words. And where Capaneus proudly scorns Zeus, Polyphontes is under the special protection of Artemis and the other gods
(lines 449–50).

Thus the speeches concerning the first two attackers are connected,
in that Capaneus surpasses Tydeus in self-assertion. At the start of his
description of Capaneus, in fact, the spy explicitly compares him
with Tydeus (lines 424–25):

> γίγας ὅδ᾿ ἄλλος, τοῦ πάρος λελεγμένου
> μείζων, ὁ κόμπος δ᾿ οὐ κατ᾿ ἄνθρωπον φρονεῖ . . .

Aeschylus here is probably alluding to the Homeric description of
Tydeus as "small in stature, but a warrior."[12] But Capaneus is
μείζων in another sense as well—his boast. That seems to be implied
by the progress of the sentence, which introduces his defiance of
Zeus. The first phrase has the same effect, if we take it, as Fraenkel
paraphrases, "gigas hic redivivus."[13] Capaneus resembles a giant in
challenging Zeus. Tydeus's boast has not gone so far.

Diverse noises were associated with Tydeus, while the description
of Capaneus emphasizes the visual. The only sound Capaneus makes
is his defiance of the thunderbolt. The counterpart of that boast is
the motto on his shield, for the man there depicted speaks (φωνεῖ,
line 434). Thus shield and boast are related; both, in addition, involve fire. Taken together, they imply that although Capaneus need
not fear Zeus's lightning, the fire which he himself brings threatens
to consume the city.

The progression from the first Argive to the second is reflected
also by their shield devices. The natural elements on Tydeus's shield
express his claim to personal distinction as a warrior. Capaneus's
shield has a contrasting element—fire—and a human figure, and he
not only asserts his own strength but also threatens the city directly.
A curious play on the idea of fire and heat, which runs through
both pairs of speeches, should probably be connected with these
shield tokens. Tydeus's emblem, the moon, is the sun's antithesis.
Heat is not his element. Accordingly, in his lust for battle he is
furiously agitated, like a snake reacting to the heat at noon, the
period of the sun's greatest intensity (lines 380–81):[14]

> Τυδεὺς δὲ μαργῶν καὶ μάχης λελιμμένος

μεσημβριναῖς κλαγγαῖσιν ὡς δράκων βοᾷ.

But Capaneus apparently is not affected by that kind of heat; Zeus's thunderbolt is no more forbidding, and he seems to feel that he can disregard both (lines 430–31):

τὰς δ᾿ ἀστραπάς τε καὶ κεραυνίους βολὰς
μεσημβρινοῖσι θάλπεσιν προσήκασεν.

He has a torch on his shield, and the thunderbolt will not prevent him from setting it to the city. Finally, Eteocles matches Capaneus's fire with the person of Polyphontes (αἴθων λῆμα, line 448) and says that when Zeus's thunderbolt falls upon Capaneus, it will defy comparison (line 445). He echoes Capaneus's words but denies his boast: the thunderbolt *is* hotter than the sun.[15]

The arrogance of both Tydeus and Capaneus, though it takes different forms, is self-defeating. Eteocles seeks to ensure this result in a way that he specifies in answering the description of Tydeus (lines 402–406):

τάχ᾿ ἂν γένοιτο μάντις ἡ ἄνοια τινί.
εἰ γὰρ θανόντι νὺξ ἐπ᾿ ὀφθαλμοῖς πέσοι,
τῷ τοι φέροντι σῆμ᾿ ὑπέρκομπον τόδε
γένοιτ᾿ ἂν ὀρθῶς ἐνδίκως τ᾿ ἐπώνυμον,
καὐτὸς καθ᾿ αὑτοῦ τήνδ᾿ ὕβριν μαντεύσεται.

Note μάντις and μαντεύσεται at the beginning and end of his interpretation of the shield device. Divination, an important theme in the whole play,[16] has particular significance in this scene. Here Eteocles is interpreting and accepting the omen which Tydeus carries on his shield, to the latter's disadvantage. There seems to be a certain order in things which gives words and names a special power in predicting—and even in shaping—the outcome of events. Hence the phrase ὀρθῶς ἐνδίκως τ᾿ ἐπώνυμον (line 405)—an idea which recurs more than once in this scene. Eteocles' language in speaking of Capaneus is similar (lines 438–39):

τῶν τοι ματαίων ἀνδράσιν φρονημάτων

ἡ γλῶσσ᾽ ἀληϑὴς γίγνεται κατήγορος.

This is a clear case of cledonomancy.

The actual fulfillment of these omens, however, is by no means mechanical. Eteocles always recognizes that the gods will decide the issue. Ares, he says, will judge the battle at the first gate with his dice (line 414). And even in the case of the fourth pair of champions, where a Theban victory seems most assured, it is probability (εἰκός, line 519) that he invokes.

The description of the third Argive, Eteoclus, like that of Tydeus, includes both sights and sounds. In his impatience for battle, Tydeus was likened to a horse. This simile now becomes concrete in Eteoclus's mares, which are eager to assault the gates (lines 461-62). They too are noisy; their cheek pieces whistle in a perversion of music (συρίζουσι, line 463). Like the bells on Tydeus's shield, the sounds here are intrusive, disruptive of the city's normal peace (cf. lines 122-23, 205-207). Thus once again in contrast, Eteocles asserts that Megareus, the Theban defender, will repay his debt to the earth if he is killed (line 477). Eteoclus's shield, like that of Capaneus, combines the aural with the visual. It too has a motto, which is shouted (βοᾷ, line 468).

With Eteoclus and Hippomedon, the fourth aggressor, there is a growing tendency toward abstraction. Eteoclus's shield shows a hoplite scaling a ladder against an enemy tower and shouting that not even Ares would throw him back. Benardete speaks of "the absorption of Eteocles into his image."[17] Eteocles plays on it in his response (lines 478-79). In the next pair of speeches, as Benardete also notes, the emblems become more important than their bearers. The personal enmity of Hyperbius and Hippomedon is reflected, it is true, by the rivalry between Zeus and Typhon; but the real issue lies between the latter pair. The battle at the fourth gate will be fought and decided in the sphere of images.

There is thus a steady progression in the shield tokens of all four Argives. Tydeus's device, bare of human figures, simply exemplifies his claim to surpassing physical prowess. Capaneus's shield presents a man carrying fire, which is opposed to the moon that Tydeus bears because it is akin to the sun and the day, and which poses a direct challenge to the thunderbolt of Zeus. But the man depicted there is

naked, and only the motto threatens the city. Eteoclus's device
shows a warrior fully armed in a direct attack on a city's towers. And
where Capaneus defied Zeus through his own words, Eteoclus's
challenge to divinity (in this case Ares) is on the shield itself. Thus it
is no longer the motto, but the picture itself, which menaces the city;
the words on the shield go still further and taunt a god. Finally, in
the fourth pair, the whole battle is assimilated to the archetypal
struggle between Typhon and Zeus. On Hippomedon's shield, the
god is challenged by an image alone, which sums up the Argives'
monstrous arrogance. This defiance of Zeus has been anticipated by
the description of Capaneus as a giant and by his scorn of the thunderbolt, but it is now represented solely by the emblem. Thus the
shields themselves gradually assume an independent life and over-
shadow their bearers. Hyperbius, for his part, carries on his shield an
anthropomorphic Zeus actually wielding the thunderbolt (line 513).
It is remarkable that only here in the whole scene is the shield of a
Theban described. This shield token has, of course, a special purpose:
to oppose the city's piety to the Argives' excess; but it also seems far
from accidental that this confrontation takes place at the very heart
of the scene.

Several themes also converge in this central pair of speeches.
Tydeus was earlier (line 381) compared to a serpent. In the early
part of the play too the Argives are spoken of in animal terms. But
just as the horse to which Tydeus was also likened anticipates the
mares of Eteoclus, so here the snake assumes tangible form on the
rim of Hippomedon's shield (lines 495–96). The comparison culminates in Eteocles' first words in answer to the description of
Hippomedon (lines 501–503):

$$\pi\rho\tilde{\omega}\tau o\nu \ \mu\grave{e}\nu \ \text{'}\text{O}\gamma\kappa a \ \Pi a\lambda\lambda\acute{a}\varsigma, \ \mathring{\eta}\tau\text{'} \ \mathring{a}\gamma\chi\acute{\iota}\pi\tau o\lambda\iota\varsigma$$
$$\pi\acute{u}\lambda a\iota\sigma\iota \ \gamma\epsilon\acute{\iota}\tau\omega\nu, \ \mathring{a}\nu\delta\rho\grave{o}\varsigma \ \mathring{e}\chi\vartheta a\acute{\iota}\varphi o\upsilon\sigma\text{'} \ \ddot{u}\beta\rho\iota\nu,$$
$$\epsilon\mathring{\iota}\rho\xi\epsilon\iota \ \nu\epsilon o\sigma\sigma\tilde{\omega}\nu \ \dot{\omega}\varsigma \ \delta\rho\acute{a}\kappa o\nu\tau a \ \delta\acute{u}\sigma\chi\iota\mu o\nu.$$

This recalls a simile used earlier by the chorus of their fear (lines
291–94):

$$\delta\rho\acute{a}\kappa o\nu\tau a\varsigma \ \ddot{\omega}\varsigma \ \tau\iota\varsigma \ \tau\acute{e}\kappa\nu\omega\nu$$
$$\mathring{u}\pi\epsilon\rho\delta\acute{e}\delta o\iota\kappa\epsilon\nu \ \lambda\epsilon\chi a\acute{\iota}-$$

ων δυσευνήτορας
πάντρομος πελειάς.

Eteocles' tone is, however, confident. Like Artemis "who stands before" (προστατηρία, line 449), Athena, whose shrine is in front of the fourth gate, will defend what is vulnerable in the city. She will "ward off" the serpent (εἰρξει), as Melanippus will "ward off" (εἴργειν, line 416) the enemy spear from the maternal soil. The things within the city's walls may be delicate, like nestlings, but they can summon powerful allies. At this point in the play, the signs at least indicate victory.

Fire also becomes prominent once again in this fourth pair of speeches. The spy describes Typhon on Hippomedon's shield as breathing fire (lines 493-94):

Τυφῶν᾽ ἱέντα πύρπνοον διὰ στόμα
λιγνὺν μέλαιναν, αἰόλην πυρὸς κάσιν.

In his answer, Eteocles repeats the epithet πύρπνοον, as if to contrast Typhon's murky flame with the clear blaze of the thunderbolt which Zeus wields (lines 511-13):

. . . ὁ μὲν γὰρ πύρπνοον Τυφῶν᾽ ἔχει,
Ὑπερβίῳ δὲ Ζεὺς πατὴρ ἐπ᾽ ἀσπίδος
σταδαῖος ἧσται, διὰ χερὸς βέλος φλέγων.

Typhon is merely monstrous; Zeus's power is overwhelming. Capaneus defied Zeus by belittling the thunderbolt, setting over it the fire on his shield. There φλέγει (line 433) is like φλέγων in the description of Zeus (line 513). Eteocles answered Capaneus's boast by sending against him the blaze of Polyphontes' spirit. With Hippomedon the contest is between clear flame and fire obscured by smoke. If, however, Stanford is right in saying that Capaneus's name suggests καπνός, to which Polyphontes is opposed, then the same contrast runs through the second pair of speeches as well.[18] In any case, the ideas of both fire and snake start from the comparison of Tydeus to the serpent stimulated by the noon heat (line 381) and culminate in the speeches about Hippomedon.

Thus the noise, violence, and arrogance of the Argives reach their height in Hippomedon and seem, by the middle of the scene, to ensure the city's victory and deliverance. The responses of the chorus to these descriptions show a parallel progression up to the fourth set of speeches.[19] Their first two corresponding stanzas, which follow the descriptions of Tydeus and Capaneus respectively, express the same mixture of emotions: a prayer for the defeat of the aggressor (lines 417-19, 452-53) accompanied by fear of the consequences if the Theban champion should fail (lines 419-21, 454-56). The second strophe (lines 481-85), which comes after the speeches about Eteoclus, reflects more trust that Zeus will punish the Argives for their boasts, but this is still couched in the form of a prayer. The antistrophe (lines 521-25), which comments on the fourth pair of speeches, expresses real confidence for the first time; and πέποιθα there (line 521) answers ἐπεύχομαι in the strophe (line 481).

If the shield scene lies at the heart of the play, its central pair of speeches is the play's midpoint. And it is precisely here that the outcome of the wider struggle between Argos and Thebes is decided. For the omens contained in these shields will be fulfilled in the event. In these first four exchanges, however, there are also two elements which anticipate the matching of Eteocles with Polynices. First, Hippomedon and Hyperbius—the middle pair, ominously—are personal enemies (line 509): ἐχϑρὸς γὰρ ἀνὴρ ἀνδρὶ τῷ ξυστήσεται. . . . So are the brothers, and Eteocles later echoes his own words (line 675: ἐχϑρὸς σὺν ἐχϑρῷ στήσομαι). Secondly, the ἔρως and ἵμερος (lines 688, 692) which drive Eteocles into battle are like Tydeus's fierce impatience for the attack (lines 380, 392). Thus Eteocles will associate himself with all the Argives' martial ferocity— but in a battle which by then will have shrunk to his individual struggle with his brother. The next three exchanges do pose special difficulties to the city, but these can be met. At least as important is that in these speeches the operation of the curse is gradually uncovered. The fifth and sixth pairs point ahead to Eteocles' true position, and the last fully reveals it.

From the city's point of view, Parthenopaeus is forbidding because he is a riddling figure. His relation to the earth is ambivalent.[20] His fierce personality belies his name and is not ἐπώνυμον (line 536; contrast line 405); in him, then, the word has lost its power to enlighten. And he carries on his shield a picture of the Sphinx. None of the other shields has displayed a threat aimed specifically at

Thebes. Even the tower under assault on Eteoclus's shield could belong to any city, and the other picture of a monster in this scene (Typhon) was meant to challenge Zeus. Parthenopaeus's avowed purpose is to force the defenders to aim their weapons at the Theban whom the Sphinx holds in her claws and so to hit one of their own men.[21] He thus threatens the city not only with violence but with internal strife, Theban against Theban. Eteocles' answer, a general wish that such arrogant men receive their deserts from the gods (lines 550–52), displays rather less assurance than his response to the description of Hippomedon. The chorus, for their part, are once again terrified. The account of Parthenopaeus pierces the maidens' breasts, and their hair stands on end; they too pray that the gods punish impiety (lines 563–67). Their tone here contrasts sharply with the confidence they express in the second antistrophe (lines 521–25). There is good reason; because of his shield device and the paradoxes he embodies, Parthenopaeus is the most formidable of the aggressors yet described.

Like the other Argives up to now, however, Parthenopaeus is vulnerable because he is presumptuous: he reveres his spear more than a god and takes an oath by it to sack the city in spite of Zeus (lines 529–32).[22] He dooms himself. Yet though Eteocles can avert from Thebes the danger presented by the shield token, he fails to catch this emblem's implication for himself. His language in lines 556–61 raises the question of the Sphinx's identity. Parthenopaeus's threat to carry her into the city has no substance, but she is probably a reminder of the curse on the house of Laius.[23] As Eteocles suggests, moreover, the Thebans would naturally aim at the Sphinx rather than her victim, so that the danger of bloodshed among the citizens is likewise a phantom. But one instance of Theban fighting Theban will occur when Eteocles and Polynices both do what the other Thebans will avoid: strike at one of their own—not in civil war, however, but in fratricide. Parthenopaeus's shield, then, menaces the city only superficially, but it does foreshadow the brothers' duel. The most significant paradox he presents concerns the uncertain distinction between internal and external. An invader so foreign to Thebes that his relation to Argos and Arcadia is stressed (lines 547–48), he nevertheless carries an image which recalls the true location of the conflict, within the city's royal family. The ambiguity of Parthenopaeus is that of the war itself.

Amphiaraus and Parthenopaeus form a unit because each presents a special challenge. But they do so in contrasting ways, and they are opposites in behavior and outlook. Parthenopaeus, himself like a plant, poses a threat which is intended to make troubles sprout for Thebes (ἀλδαίνειν, line 557). Amphiaraus will enrich the Theban soil (line 587). Whereas Parthenopaeus is arrogant, the seer's mind is like a deep furrow, from which grow wise counsels (lines 593–94). Parthenopaeus is an alien determined to destroy the city; Amphiaraus, though an Argive, will be incorporated into the land of Thebes.

Amphiaraus differs from all the other Argives in being temperate and pious. His shield is blank and he holds it still, in contrast to the way Hippomedon whirls his (line 490). The Theban champions' prowess in action has been opposed to the empty and hybristic boasts of the other Argives. In like manner, Amphiaraus's virtues are juxtaposed with the failings of his comrades (lines 610–12):

σώφρων δίκαιος ἀγαθὸς εὐσεβὴς ἀνήρ,
μέγας προφήτης, ἀνοσίοισι συμμιγεὶς
θρασυστόμοισιν ἀνδράσιν βίᾳ φρενῶν.

Where the others are excessive, Amphiaraus is restrained. There is a sharp contrast between μέγας προφήτης and θρασυστόμοισιν: they speak arrogantly, whereas the truth of his words is guaranteed by his knowledge of divine will. Amphiaraus represents substance over appearance (line 592).[24] His qualities, summed up in the spy's opening words (lines 568–69) make him—at least potentially—the most dangerous enemy among the Argives. As the spy concludes, δεινὸς ὃς θεοὺς σέβει (line 596). With no shield device to interpret and no boast to turn against Amphiaraus, Eteocles can reply only by recognizing the seer's moral worth and by predicting that he will not fight because he knows that it will mean his own doom. Eteocles rather diffidently sends to the sixth gate a Theban who is a strong and intelligent warrior, and the chorus round off this pair of speeches with a general prayer for the Argives' defeat.

As in the case of Parthenopaeus, however, the threat to the city is not serious; either Amphiaraus will not attack or, if he does, he will be swallowed into the earth. But his character and his position in the invading army shed light by implication on the situation of Eteocles and Polynices. Amphiaraus's rebuke of Tydeus contains two ambiguous phrases: τὸν πόλεως ταράκτορα (line 572) and Ἐρινύος κλητῆρα (line 574). These could be simply general terms of abuse. But by urging Adrastus to undertake the war, Tydeus, as Polynices' accomplice, has disturbed not only Argos but Thebes as well. He has also been the instrument of the Erinys by furthering the quarrel within the Theban ruling house.[25] The earth and crop imagery prominent in this set of speeches, taken with the same language used later to describe the fratricide, associates Amphiaraus with fertility and the brothers with the ruin of crops.[26] That the seer, a foreigner, will benefit the land continues the confusion between the internal and the external, which began with Parthenopaeus.

The speeches devoted to Amphiaraus occur just before Eteocles recognizes the truth of his own position. A clear sign that they represent a step toward this knowledge is that they mention Polynices explicitly for the first time in the play and make him conspicuous. With regard to Eteocles, Amphiaraus is a pivotal figure. He brings discord into an otherwise united army. Cameron says that he is "the counterpart in the Argive camp of the women in Thebes, each speaking words of ill-omen although Amphiaraus does so in full knowledge."[27] This statement describes the seer's function in relation to the early part of the play. And there Eteocles is analogous to the other Argive chiefs: as they are bent on attacking the city, he is determined to defend it militarily. Like them, he will tolerate no opposition (cf. Tydeus's mockery of Amphiaraus, lines 382–83). But in his reply to the spy's account of Amphiaraus, Eteocles seems to feel a bond between himself and the seer. They do have this in common: each stands alone against a majority of his fellow citizens. This correspondence, however, does not cover vital details; in fact, it seems designed to call attention to the contrast between the two figures.

This contrast is hinted at when Eteocles compares Amphiaraus's predicament to that of a reverent man on a ship manned by an impious crew, or of a just man among unrighteous citizens (lines 602–608).[28] But this is not Eteocles' own position; the moral strength of the Thebans has been emphasized throughout the play. At the same time, the use of city and ship as vehicles of these comparisons invites us to consider the situation in Thebes. We are thus led to think of the converse of Eteocles' statement. What of the passengers on a ship whose captain is cursed?[29] Or the inhabitants of

a city ruled by a man who carries guilt in his blood? They too are
infected and threatened with ruin. This is the position of Thebes in
relation to Eteocles. The result is an inversion. Amphiaraus resembles
the Thebans, but on the basis (it now appears) of moral qualities
rather than ill-omened words. Eteocles, when he arms himself in the
second epirrhematic scene, becomes once again like the Argives, and
like Polynices in particular, but no longer with the laudable purpose
of defending the city. He lusts fiercely for blood. Thus our perceptions of the significance of Amphiaraus change as the meaning of the
curse is unravelled. The speeches which describe him ultimately show
that there is disunity on both sides and that both the Thebans and
the Argives are endangered by moral fault. But whereas the Argives
as a group are guilty, in Thebes the taint is within, and limited to, the
ruling family. Accordingly, the Thebans, except Eteocles and Polynices, survive, and the Argive champions, except Amphiaraus, perish
utterly.

There is irony in Eteocles' tribute to Amphiaraus: he perceives the
seer's predicament clearly but is blind to his own. This irony is
especially marked when he says that Amphiaraus probably will not
attack the gate (lines 616–19):

> οὐχ ὡς ἄθυμον οὐδὲ λήματος κάκη,
> ἀλλ᾽ οἶδεν ὡς σφε χρὴ τελευτῆσαι μάχη,
> εἰ καρπὸς ἔσται θεσφάτοισι Λοξίου·
> φιλεῖ δὲ σιγᾶν ἢ λέγειν τὰ καίρια.

Even while he speaks, a prophecy by Apollo about his own family is
being fulfilled. Though some have doubted the authenticity of the
last line, I should like to understand it, with Apollo as the subject of
the verb, as a parenthetical statement eliminating any doubt which
the preceding line (618) might have admitted as to the truth of
Apollo's utterances.[30] Eteocles attributes to the god the quality of a
good commander (cf. line 1). His own words in this scene have been
carefully chosen to produce a Theban victory. These lines too seem
intended to ensure Amphiaraus's defeat if he should attack, but they
are ill-omened for Eteocles himself. Apollo's oracle to Laius will bear
the bitter fruit of his grandsons' fratricide. It is ultimately the god
who λέγει τὰ καίρια.

Amphiaraus will fight and meet his doom; his words to Polynices (lines 587–89) leave no doubt of that. After the next pair of speeches, Eteocles will find himself in the same situation: he knows that if he enters the battle he will die, in accordance with an oracle from Apollo. Here, from an objective point of view, he concedes to Amphiaraus the option of holding back without disgrace, though the seer himself apparently never considers it. Later he will refuse to entertain the same possibility for himself, dismissing it as shameful.[31] For Amphiaraus, as for Eteocles soon after, the demands of the situation are clear. But once again, the differences which result from Eteocles' being under a curse are important. Amphiaraus's fate, though it may seem arbitrary, will be honorable (line 589). Eteocles will be mourned, but his death fits into a coherent if horrible pattern. The surface likenesses between Eteocles and Amphiaraus only make us reflect upon the more fundamental differences. Eteocles, the ruler, is cut off from the rest of the city, as his brother is. Amphiaraus, though out of sympathy with his fellow Argives, will find rest in Theban soil. By these dislocations we may gauge the effects of the curse; but Amphiaraus's death in an important way will be redeemed.[32]

With the last set of speeches, the action of the play focuses clearly on the brothers' dispute. Their personal enmity, which now overshadows the city's struggle, is emphasized. At the beginning of every other speech, the spy names the gate to be attacked, but here he stresses instead the number seven, which is peculiarly fateful for the brothers (line 631). It is true that Polynices calls down curses upon the city as a whole (lines 632–33); behind them, however, stands the curse he is under. Moreover, the picture on his shield pleads his private case against Eteocles. G. H. Chase has pointed out that though most of the emblems in this scene appear to have been conventional and have parallels on existing monuments, that of Polynices is different in that it refers to the personal fortunes of the bearer.[33] The issue has become individual, inside the family.

By the break in the play (lines 653 ff.), then, the war has gradually narrowed in scope from the middle of the scene, and concern has begun to shift from the city to the family. Eteocles' sudden outburst completes this shift. His words explicitly recognize the consequences of this final match for his house and for himself. Thus he makes no attempt in this case to turn the shield token into an omen unfavorable to his brother.[34] Instead, he confronts Polynices' claim directly and denies it.

In doing so, however, he does point to and accept an omen—the significance of his brother's name (line 658): ἐπωνύμῳ δὲ κάρτα, Πολυνείκη λέγω. . . . Polynices is all too truly named. Amphiaraus too dwelt on Polynices' name in condemning him (lines 577–78).[35] Here, however, the significance of the word is by no means necessarily to Eteocles' own advantage. This concern with names continues as he asserts that Dike has never stood on Polynices' side and does not do so now. He refers to her with an interesting phrase: ἡ Διὸς παῖς παρθένος Δίκη (line 662). The mention of father and daughter together seems intended to play on what would seem, to a Greek ear, a similarity in their names, which have the syllable Δι- in common.[36] The suggestion is that Dike shares in the nature of her father and is therefore just. But the collocation παῖς παρθένος recalls Parthenopaeus's name, which his nature belied (line 536). The question thus is whether Justice will be true to her name. Eteocles claims, in effect, that she will not if she favors Polynices against him (lines 670–71):

$$\text{ἡ δῆτ᾽ ἂν εἴη πανδίκως ψευδώνυμος}$$
$$\text{Δίκη, ξυνοῦσα φωτὶ παντόλμῳ φρένας.}$$

Here ψευδώνυμος contrasts with ἐπωνύμῳ in line 658. Eteocles is invoking a fundamental order by which a name reveals the character of its bearer. Polynices obeys it all too well; Parthenopaeus stood it on its head. And Dike, if she were to side with Polynices, would be falsely named "by all rights" (πανδίκως). Where, then, does justice lie? In this speech we are given only one side of the question; the other is depicted on Polynices' shield. The outcome of the play, with the utter impartiality of the brothers' fate, will show that Dike stands somewhere above their conflicting claims. We might say that she is finally revealed in the essential rightness of the Erinys' machinations. Like Polynices, Dike will prove all too ἐπώνυμος.

Thus the prophetic power of the word, so important to the scene as a whole, is used here to highlight the problems of Eteocles' situation. His sense of the order implicit in this power leads him finally to accept his brother's challenge (lines 672–73):

$$\text{τούτοις πεποιθὼς εἶμι καὶ ξυστήσομαι}$$
$$\text{αὐτός · τίς ἄλλος μᾶλλον ἐνδικώτερος;}$$

ἐνδικώτερος echoes not only πανδίκως a few lines before, but also ἐνδίκως in line 405. He is, as he goes on to say, the right opponent for his brother in every sense (lines 674–75):

> ἄρχοντι τ᾽ ἄρχων καὶ κασιγνήτῳ κάσις,
> ἐχϑρὸς σὺν ἐχϑρῷ στήσομαι.

As leaders and as brothers, they are enemies; both aspects are summed up in the word ἐχϑρός. They stand in the same relation to each other as do Hyperbius and Hippomedon. Lesky says that Eteocles' words bring out his "tragische Doppelrolle."[37] But they do more; they put the whole war in perspective. Its cause is the fraternal dispute, which has had wider repercussions because the issue is the control of Thebes. Thus even if the intent of the words is to insist that the war is at once civic and personal, their actual effect is to concentrate it in the duel between Eteocles and Polynices, where it properly belongs.

In summary, then, the city can no longer be in serious danger by the end of the set of speeches which occurs at the middle of both this scene and the whole play. After that point, the contest narrows gradually to the fight at the seventh gate, which is the result of all that takes place in the scene. In the last pair of speeches, the break in the play occurs, and the distinction between the fortunes of city and family, hinted at in the similes Eteocles uses to describe Amphiaraus, is made explicit. The structure of the scene stresses both the central speeches, which are decisive for the war, and the eventual matching of the brothers. The shield tokens are closely related to the important themes in the speeches. In a sense, they represent these themes concretely. Both themes and emblems harmonize with the structure in converging on the fourth exchange and in subsequently pointing ahead to the seventh. Thus the scene as a whole moves, by the elimination of all other possibilities, toward the confrontation between Eteocles and Polynices.

As one looks back from the end of the scene, this confrontation seems inevitable. Indeed, the formal similarity of all the pairs of speeches except the last creates the effect of relentless progress towards the fatal end. What is behind this development? It is not, I think, anything that Eteocles himself does or can do. I cannot accept, then, Kitto's view that in the shield scene Aeschylus "makes Eteocles not merely a prudent commander but also a man of acute moral perceptions, and ruins him this way,"[38] or Cameron's statement that "it is not really fate or the Erinys alone that brings about the duel, but Eteocles' *belief* that the curse must come true which causes him to choose as he does."[39] Instead, we probably should throw off our modern obsession with freedom of choice and admit that Eteocles has little or no leeway. The spy presents him with the omens; Eteocles accepts them and, somehow, matches with each Argive the one Theban who is in every way fit to oppose him. At work here is a very narrow logic, by which Eteocles himself is finally entrapped. As Benardete says, "It is the consistency of image and interpretation when put together and in order that constitutes the compulsion in Eteocles' choice."[40] It seems better, however, to discard the idea of "choice," or to view any apparent opportunities for choice in this scene as illusory, and to concentrate rather on the curse.

Throughout the scene, there is a consistent recognition that the gods will decide the outcome of the battle. Every speech in the fifth and sixth exchanges, for instance, ends with a reference to the gods.[41] But since the conflict is already joined here through words and images, and since what occurs in this scene determines the results of the actual fighting, one might expect a superhuman agency to be active also in the matching at the gates. There are, in fact, indications of this. In commenting upon the particularly appropriate pairing of Hyperbius with Hippomedon, Eteocles gives credit to Hermes (line 505). The chorus's final words in the first epirrhematic scene are (line 263), "I am silent; I shall suffer with others what is fated" (τὸ μόρσιμον). Eteocles echoes this soon after, when he tells them that their noisy panic is fruitless (line 281): οὐ γάρ τι μᾶλλον μὴ φύγῃς τό μόρσιμον. In the very next line (282), he announces his intention of selecting six champions and stresses that he will be the seventh. There σὺν ἑβδόμῳ occupies the same metrical position as τὸ μόρσιμον in line 281. What is in store for the chorus and "the others" is safety; Eteocles will meet his brother at the seventh gate. The number seven, as the shield scene demonstrates, is his fate. And the term τὸ μόρσιμον, which is related to μοῖρα, foreshadows the latter word's significance later as the fatal portion which results from the lot.[42]

Eteocles closes his answer to the description of Amphiaraus with a gnomic statement (line 625): ϑεοῦ δὲ δῶρόν ἐστιν εὐτυχεῖν βροτούς. In its context, this refers primarily to the doubtful result of the duel between Lasthenes and the seer, if that should take place. But it is applicable also to Amphiaraus's whole situation, to that ὄρνις (line 597) or chance (only apparently random) which has associated him with overbearing companions. Thus line 625, along with 281, anticipates Eteocles' last utterance in the play (line 719): θεῶν διδόντων οὐκ ἂν ἐκφύγοις κακά. Through a series of apparent coincidences in the central scene, the gods have aligned the Argives' arrangements and those of Eteocles with each other and with the requirements of the curse. In the same way, the spy's information about Polynices causes Eteocles to exclaim that the whole family is hated by the gods (lines 653-54). His language suggests that his confrontation with Polynices at the seventh gate has been contrived by something more than human volition or random chance.[43]

I shall return to this matter in due course. Just how the pairing is accomplished is a difficult problem. It is part of the larger question of how we are to view this scene. To answer that, we must consider the scene's effect in performance.

DRAMATIC PRESENTATION IN THE SHIELD SCENE

Like the parodos, the shield scene describes the assault of the Argives on Thebes; but there are important differences between these sections, which reflect the movement of the play. In the shield scene, attention is concentrated on the seven Argive chiefs. Their prominence here has been anticipated by lines 124-26 of the parodos, but there the enemy was viewed principally as an overwhelming mass. Moreover, speech largely replaces lyric now, as active preparations to repulse the attack succeed the panicked response of the chorus.

Here, as in the parodos, Aeschylus carefully balances the unseen and the visible. The presence of the seven chiefs is made almost palpable, and their ferocity is experienced immediately, through the spy's account of them. The descriptions in this scene, like those of the parodos, contain both sights and sounds; and the shields which carry not only pictures but also mottoes that are said to shout are a form of the "synaesthetic imagery" noted earlier (line 103). There is also the same tendency as elsewhere in the play toward concreteness, as in the case of Eteoclus's mares or, more significantly, of the shield tokens themselves, which—though invisible to the audience—embody themes used to depict their bearers.

Yet all of this is vividly described rather than shown. Not a single Argive ever appears. In particular, Aeschylus does not present a debate between Eteocles and Polynices, as Euripides did later in the *Phoenissae*.[44] Such a meeting would not only have been unnecessary here but would actually have weakened the scene. We learn from the spy all we need to know about Polynices. Of central importance to the play are his rival claim (summarized by his shield device) and, above all, Eteocles' own response—just as earlier, in the parodos, the actual attack by the enemy mattered less than the terror it provoked in the chorus.

How many Thebans appear? It has sometimes been suggested,[45] and more often denied,[46] that Eteocles is accompanied by the other six Theban soldiers and dispatches them to the proper gates one by one. Although this idea has no support in the text, the arguments against it are not conclusive either.[47] In itself, the presence of these mute figures would add little.[48] But their departure in succession would allow the audience actually to watch the elimination of other possible pairings, until Eteocles alone is left as Polynices' opponent. This abacus-like effect would express physically the development traceable in the sequence of speeches. It may fairly be objected, however, that this arrangement is too stiff and stylized; and a simpler presentation would have one great advantage. Eteocles is fighting the battle in words and symbols, and ultimately falls victim himself to these weapons. Their magical power could be felt most fully if Eteocles received and dealt with the spy's descriptions alone. The actual warriors, like their Argive counterparts, have only secondary importance. Their essential characteristics are described, and they do not have to appear in person—in fact, they should not if their presence and exits divert attention from the verbal battle. But each way of staging the scene has its own virtues.

Without a direct encounter between enemies, indeed without any physical action (except, possibly, each Theban soldier's departure), the shield scene might seem dull to the tastes of a later age. Yet it must have been intensely exciting to an Aeschylean audience, and it can still be so to us if we try to understand more exactly what occurs in it. Words here assume an independent life, and a sense that superhuman powers are at work pervades the scene. Thus during performance there would be considerable excitement in viewing the process by which all the other Thebans and Argives are paired off appropriately, until only the two brothers remain. The scene's effect, of course, can never have depended upon suspense in the audience about the identity of Eteocles' adversary. Even the spectators at the first performance must have known that the brothers would kill each other. But Eteocles himself, as a stage personage, does not know it, and the audience watches him taking in ignorance just those steps which ensure disaster for himself. Eteocles thus becomes a paradigm of the ultimate truth of curses and prophecies. As the scene develops and the spectators are drawn into its logic, they perceive the process of elimination by which the fatal duel is being arranged, together with Eteocles' peculiar position as both instrument and victim. At the end, it is clear that all has been contrived by the curse according to a consistent and inescapable method. Even in reading the scene today, we sense that something is being worked out with the precision and symmetry of a mathematical problem.

It is, however, difficult to account for this impression. Clearly more is occurring than simple description and the execution of military tactics—but what? This question can be approached only by asking how the Thebans and Argives are matched. We know that the Argives have determined the order of their attack by lot, as the spy reported in the prologue. On the Theban side, however, the situation appears vague. Just before the first stasimon, Eteocles announces that he is leaving to place six champions at the gates, with himself as the seventh, before any further news arrives (lines 282–86). After the ode, he re-enters in haste that matches the spy's (lines 369 ff.), but no reason is given for his appearance. Has he, in the intervening time, made his gate assignments? If so, in this scene he merely reveals and comments on them. Or has the arrival of the spy interrupted his preparations? In that case, he would be making some if not all of the dispositions on the spot, as he is informed of the Argive order. The apparent inconsistency in Aeschylus's language has complicated attempts to decide this matter. The verbs used by the messenger to report the placing of the champions are all future or have future force (lines 395, 435–36, 470, 499, 595–96, 650–52). But the tenses of the verbs with which Eteocles announces the assignments vary: one present (line 553); two futures of the same verb (lines 408, 621); two aorists (lines 505, 508); and two perfects (lines 448, 473).[49]

The timing of Eteocles' gate assignments, and so the implication of the verb tenses, have been much debated in various attempts to define the roles of Eteocles' own decision and of necessity (the gods or the curse) in bringing about his duel with his brother. If Eteocles has already completed his arrangements by the time he re-enters (so the argument runs), then his position opposite Polynices is involuntary. Those who take this view (without necessarily denying Eteocles all freedom in choosing to fight his brother) have sought to explain away the two future verbs.[50] If, on the other hand, Eteocles has not made his assignments, it has been maintained, then what he does in this scene is undetermined, and he decides freely to oppose Polynices. This position involves giving the future verbs their literal force but accounting for the aorists and perfects in such a way that they do not imply completed action.[51] There is also a third possibility: to accept the full literal force of *all* the verbs. This is the view of Wilamowitz and of Lesky, who both conclude that Eteocles has made some gate assignments but not others, for he has been interrupted by the spy's return.[52] This explanation is the most natural way of interpreting the verb tenses and has some support in lines 285–86. As a way of determining when Eteocles makes his dispositions, it seems preferable to the other two.

If we accept this suggestion as to the timing of the gate-assignments, we have to ask why Aeschylus makes the situation so complex. According to Lesky, he does so to portray the fulfillment of the curse, and at the same time to give the spectators the impression that something develops before their eyes (that is, that the matches are made only during the shield scene).[53] Dawe, who quotes Lesky with approval, similarly concludes that Aeschylus was making "a conscious attempt to give the play, besides its sense of predestined doom, an element of free will."[54] But these terms cannot appropriately be applied to an Aeschylean drama, and it is hardly credible that Aeschylus worried about balancing "free will" against necessity.[55] In fact, the opposite conclusion is more plausible. As was argued earlier, the outcome of this scene is the work of the gods, or, more immediately, of the curse. If, at the same time, Aeschylus conveys an impression of spontaneity, that only emphasizes the inevitability of the curse's effect: whatever Eteocles does, he cannot escape it. More than that, what he does is reasonable in view of his own and his city's evident situation, but it plays right into the hands of the Erinys. Although the assignments he has made before the scene begins do not reflect decisions based on knowledge of the enemy order, they are actions he has taken on his own in his capacity as commander. But, through no design of his, they match precisely the Argive positions. When he places Melanippus against Tydeus, on the other hand, the future verb in line 408 seems to imply that he is making a decision on the basis of the spy's description. But what real choice has he? Melanippus is the one Theban with the qualities needed to defeat Tydeus. Eteocles only seems to decide.[56] The same is true of the other occurrence of the future tense (line 621). Lasthenes, with his intelligence, strength, and fighting skill, is fit–if anyone is–to oppose Amphiaraus (cf. lines 620-24). That this second future tense comes just before the crucial seventh pair of speeches is surely no accident. If Eteocles' announcement that he will be the seventh Theban (line 282) means that he has already decided to defend the seventh gate himself, then the sixth gate is the only place left for Lasthenes. The future tense thus indicates that Eteocles thinks he is making a decision, just when that is out of the question. Or, if Eteocles has not yet chosen a gate for himself (and it is not necessary to infer from line 282 that he has), presumably he thinks that Lasthenes is a more appropriate adversary for Amphiaraus. The "selection" of Lasthenes for the sixth gate is therefore dictated by the position and character of Amphiaraus, and it leaves Eteocles to fight his own brother. Thus on either alternative, through the future tense in line 621, Aeschylus is showing how illusory is Eteocles' power to decide. The "choice" of Lasthenes is the right one; it is also the only one practicable. And it is the last step in a relentless process which makes Eteocles' ruin complete. In fact, this moment—when Eteocles seems to make a decision, but is actually least able to—directly follows the spy's mention of Polynices' presence among the Argives (lines 576 ff.). The audience thus would foresee who the opponents at the seventh gate must be. Eteocles' apparent choices simply make his understanding of the curse, when it comes, all the more sudden and dreadful. His manner changes abruptly at line 653 because he realizes that he has never been in control of events, despite appearances to the contrary in the early part of the play and through most of the central scene.

The spy has concluded most of his other speeches with questions (line 395: "Whom will you station against this man?") or with admonitions to Eteocles (sometimes expressed with the imperative of πέμπειν—for example, lines 435, 470) to send an appropriate champion against the Argive he has just described. But he ends his account of Polynices with different language, though he again uses an imperative: "You yourself decide whom it seems best to send" (line 650). If the spy stopped speaking here, we might infer that he at least thinks that Eteocles' choice is still open. But he uses the imperative γνῶϑι twice, if the text is sound. His language falters in a way that may indicate his realization that no one but Eteocles is left to face Polynices. His second command, in line 652 (the authenticity of which is not doubted), urges Eteocles in nautical language to "determine how to direct the city's course." But the only reason this form of expression is appropriate is that Eteocles' continued guidance of the city is precisely the question raised by Polynices' position at the seventh gate. Eteocles does act in the city's interest, in that he is the right opponent for Polynices; but that is not his concern. He begins his reply by recognizing the curse's meaning for himself (lines 653–57). When he says that he will fight his brother he uses the future tense in lines 672 and 675. The future verb in line 675 occurs in a sentence which indicates that the issue between himself and Polynices is personal.[57] Moreover, these are not verbs of placing. There can be no question at this point of Eteocles' station. Thus the future tenses here do not indicate that Eteocles decides among alternatives. He simply accepts the situation in which the curse has placed him.

If Eteocles' decisions are not at issue here—if everything that occurs in the scene, even what Eteocles seems to do on his own, is really guided by the curse—then the process by which the champions are paired should be considered more closely. The Theban preparations, both those made before the scene and those made during it, tally exactly with the Argive order of attack, which has been decided by allotment. Both early and late in the play, the lot is a recurring theme. As previously observed, Aeschylus typically presents themes and images concretely. I suggest, then, that the shield scene represents allotment, and that therefore what the spectators witness is the literal fulfillment of Oedipus's curse on his sons as stated in lines 788–90. For the brothers' actual duel is later described as the sharing of their inheritance under the arbitration of the iron. And if the symbolic struggle which anticipates it and which brings Eteocles and Polynices together in combat is associated with the same process, then in an important sense Aeschylus shows here the division of their patrimony by lot.

The language of several passages in the play suggests that the lot is connected with the events of this scene. In the prologue, the spy's report contains what seems a significant juxtaposition (lines 55–58):

κληρουμένους δ᾽ ἔλειπον, ὡς πάλῳ λαχὼν
ἕκαστος αὐτῶν πρὸς πύλας ἄγοι λόχον.
πρὸς ταῦτ᾽ ἀρίστους ἄνδρας ἐκκρίτους πόλεως
πυλῶν ἐπ᾽ ἐξόδοισι τάγευσαι τάχος.

Immediately after this first reference to the lot in the play, the spy goes on to urge Eteocles to station selected defenders at the gates. Thus even at the outset Aeschylus suggests that Eteocles' arrangements will be a response to the lot. The spy leaves at the end of this speech to observe the enemy further. Eteocles exits at line 286 to select and station his champions. When they reappear in the shield scene, the spy announces the results of the Argive lot, Eteocles the Theban order. The association of ideas in the above passage thus anticipates the way the Argive and the Theban preparations will converge in the central scene, and in particular it suggests that Eteocles' measures will somehow complement the Argive lot. This inference seems all the more likely in view of how carefully Aeschylus introduces ideas and themes in the prologue which will become important later in the play.

In the parodos, the chorus emphasize the method by which the Argive chiefs have determined their order (line 126). This procedure is also alluded to regularly in the first three exchanges in the shield scene (lines 375–76, 423, 451, 457–60). Aeschylus takes great pains to keep the lot in the spectators' minds.

Eteocles refers to the lot, explicitly and unmistakably, right after the shield scene (lines 689–90), if λαχόν there is given its full literal force:[58]

ἐπεὶ τὸ πρᾶγμα κάρτ᾽ ἐπισπέρχει θεός,
ἴτω κατ᾽ οὖρον, κῦμα Κωκυτοῦ λαχόν,
Φοίβῳ στυγηθὲν πᾶν τὸ Λαΐου γένος.

The phrase κῦμα Κωκυτοῦ λαχόν, which reflects the knowledge Eteocles has gained in the shield scene, gains force if it is taken to imply that the brothers have been brought face to face by the lot, and thus

that the family has, quite literally, been "allotted Cocytus's wave."
Like the nautical language, the theme of allotment narrows in these
lines to the family. It is reasonable to suggest that the shield scene
prepares for this change.

In the shield scene itself, Eteocles' language in commenting on the
fourth pair of opponents strongly suggests the importance of the lot
(lines 504–508):

> Ὑπέρβιος δέ, κεδνὸς Οἴνοπος τόκος,
> ἀνὴρ κατ' ἄνδρα τοῦτον ᾑρέθη, θέλων
> ἐξιστορῆσαι μοῖραν ἐν χρείᾳ τύχης,
> οὔτ' εἶδος οὔτε θυμὸν οὐδ' ὅπλων σχέσιν
> μωμητός· Ἑρμῆς δ' εὐλόγως ξυνήγαγεν.

Hyperbius has been chosen (ᾑρέθη) to face Hippomedon—by whom
we do not yet know, for the passive verb leaves the agent vague. But
then Eteocles rounds off this part of his speech by saying that Hermes
has brought the two together. This is surprising, since everything up
to this point suggests that Eteocles himself has stationed Hyperbius
at this gate. But Hermes, in accordance with his role as god of lucky
finds and draws (cf. the word ἕρμαιον), is particularly associated
with the lot.[59] Thus Eteocles' selection of Hyperbius, made to all
appearance independently of the enemy order, has set precisely the
right opponent against Hippomedon; and the agent in aligning these
warriors has been, not random coincidence, but Hermes. And if he
has guided this match, presumably he has been active at the other
gates also.

This passage occurs in the pair of speeches at the center of the
scene. In view of the way other themes come together here, this
seems hardly accidental; Aeschylus appears to be stressing the lot as
the basis for what is happening. Moreover, the passage immediately
precedes mention of Hyperbius's personal hostility to Hippomedon
(line 509), which, as we have seen, foreshadows Eteocles' own position with regard to Polynices. As with this pair, therefore, the lot is
perhaps behind the matching of the brothers in combat. In that case,
on Eteocles' lips the lines quoted achieve an additional and ironic
effect. He acknowledges the lot and divine will as the basis for the
assignment of battle stations; but he fails to recognize that under

his father's curse allotment in the form of warfare is the way he is to divide his inheritance with his brother.

In line 508, Hermes is said to have worked "fittingly" ($\epsilon\dot{\upsilon}\lambda\acute{o}\gamma\omega\varsigma$), both because these two champions are personal enemies and because they bring Zeus and Typhon into conflict on their shields. But the literal sense of this adverb relates the passage to the idea, so prevalent throughout this scene, of the appropriateness of words and names, and thus to the larger pattern of omens and their acceptance which underlies all the speeches. Like all omens, these have been sent by divinity; and the identity of the god in this case indicates that the mechanism by which the omens have been given in the shield scene is the lot. As was noted earlier, allotment and prophecy are closely related, and they are explicitly connected with one another in this scene if there is a reference to cleromancy in line 414.[60]

The Greeks employed allotment constantly, in both personal and political affairs, as a device for attaining complete impartiality. This practice was probably never considered mechanical, however, but was based instead on religious belief. Its purpose could be fulfilled because it was a way of placing decisions in the hands of the gods. By its nature, then, the lot involves the surrender of human choice to divine judgment. At the same time, like divination, it is an attempt to ascertain the will of the gods. Today we naturally think of allotment as a matter of chance. But in the Greek view chance or *tyche* (sometimes personified) was originally not a random or irrational force but divinely ordained, a manifestation of order imposed by the gods. Only later, in the course of the fifth century B.C., when such unpredictable events occurred that it seemed no longer possible to believe in a divine scheme, did chance become (in Knox's words) "the principle of chaos."[61] The older belief, by contrast, made it possible for Tyche to be linked with the goddess Moira.[62] In Aeschylus, chance, often in the form of good or bad fortune, is mentioned sometimes in contexts where the agency of the gods is not actually stated but is not ruled out and is, in fact, probably implied. Very often in his plays, however, tyche is directly attributed to the gods or divine powers.[63] This occurs frequently in the *Seven*.[64]

Thus when Eteocles ends his speech in the fourth exchange by saying that Zeus "happens to be" on Hyperbius's shield (line 520), the word evokes the tyche which is essential to the lot.[65] But that is coincidence directed by divinity.[66] A phrase with which Eteocles describes Hyperbius is also significant (lines 505–506):

$$\ldots \vartheta \acute{\epsilon} \lambda \omega \nu$$
$$\dot{\epsilon} \xi \iota \sigma \tau o \rho \tilde{\eta} \sigma \alpha \iota \; \mu o \tilde{\iota} \rho \alpha \nu \; \dot{\epsilon} \nu \; \chi \rho \epsilon \acute{\iota} \alpha \; \tau \acute{\upsilon} \chi \eta \varsigma$$

Here tyche and moira are considered closely related: what befalls one by chance reveals one's portion. Tyche is thus anything but random.[67] In these lines, "chance" is the fortune of the battle itself and "fate" is the battle's outcome. But since the pairing of opponents anticipates the fighting and determines its result, Eteocles' words describe what is happening in the shield scene as well. From a series of appropriate matches, which are only apparently coincidental, a consistent pattern emerges. This pattern becomes completely clear when Eteocles receives his own moira—his pairing with his brother.

With the possible exception of line 690, none of the passages discussed above shows conclusively by itself that allotment is the human procedure on which this pattern is based. Yet in their cumulative effect they associate the lot with the events of this scene. The nature of this connection depends on when Eteocles makes each gate assignment, and we return to the significance of the verb tenses. If they are taken literally, as seems best, Eteocles makes on the spot at least the two assignments for which he uses verbs in the future. These depend directly on the casting of lots in the Argive camp. When the spy describes Tydeus, Eteocles selects from the Thebans he has not yet stationed the one most likely to defeat him. Regardless of whether Lasthenes alone is then left unassigned, so that only the sixth gate remains for him, he is the right man for that position.[68] Eteocles has distributed at least the second, third, and fourth gates among the other Thebans before the spy's return. In these cases, of course, he does not match his warriors with the results of the enemy's lot during this scene. But his assignments, though made independently, precisely correspond to the Argive order, which *has* been fixed by lot. Tyche has been at work not only on the enemy side (through the lot) but also on the Theban. Eteocles' dispositions are related to the Argive lot in the sense that by a coincidence which is really the design of the gods, he has placed his men so that each will face the opponent for whom he is most suited.[69] In the shield scene, the Theban and Argive orders at these gates are compared and found to be in perfect alignment. These matches, combined with those Eteocles makes during the scene, ensure at once a Theban victory at six gates and the destruction of the two brothers at the seventh. The shield scene therefore shows the consummation of a process that has reference everywhere to the literal casting of lots by the Argives—a process which, as becomes clear in the seventh set of speeches, is controlled in every detail by the Erinys.[70]

As for Eteocles himself, if he has decided earlier to take the seventh gate, his chosen position corresponds to Polynices' allotted place by divinely guided chance. But if—and this would make the scene more effective—he has not previously selected his own gate, then the assignments he makes in this scene (which are direct responses to the enemy lot), together with those he has already made, eliminate all other possibilities for him. Either way, he and his brother meet their fate through allotment. Undoubtedly there would have been simpler and more straightforward ways to suggest the importance of the lot in this scene. It is hard to believe that Aeschylus rejected them because he wanted to make the audience believe that Eteocles could influence events by his own choices, when everything that happens points in the opposite direction. He meant instead, I suggest, to show that even when Eteocles appears to have acted independently or to make decisions in the course of this scene, he really has no control.[71]

The suggestions made above still hold if one of the alternative explanations of the verb tenses is adopted. If Eteocles makes all his dispositions during the scene, the Theban order is directly determined by the Argive lot. As the spy describes each enemy chief, Eteocles picks out the appropriate defender. Since in each case there is only one Theban whose attributes will give him the advantage over the Argive, Eteocles' assignments are not really choices at all. With this particular sequence of the Argives, the Theban distribution could not be other than it is. Thus everything, especially the pairing at the seventh gate, results from the lot. If, on the other hand, Eteocles has assigned all the gates before the shield scene, the crucial point is the exactness with which these dispositions tally with the outcome of the Argives' draw. In this case the lot plays the same role in the pairing at all the gates as was described above for the second, third, and fourth matches.[72]

It is important to keep in mind that this scene presents a battle waged in words and images, and that the literal conflict afterward is of less consequence. Since, then, in the last part of the play the brothers are said to have divided their inheritance by lot under the arbitration of the iron, the spectators see this process actually carried out in the shield scene. The pairing of Eteocles and Polynices leads to their duel. Like Hyperbius, they "inquire into moira in the stress of chance" and receive their portions through allotment. Aeschylus shows the spectators only a part of this procedure, but that is its culmination. Since the brothers share not land but death, the family of Laius can be said in actual fact to have been allotted the wave of Cocytus. Thus in the final pair of speeches, as the full meaning of the curse is revealed, the audience witnesses its literal accomplishment, apparently as Oedipus uttered it.

In this scene, as everywhere else in the play, it is of the utmost importance that the statues of the gods stand in full view of the audience. In front of them, as the spy gives the Argive order and Eteocles the Theban, matches—all of which are both appropriate and prophetic of the result of the battle—are made at the gates. As other possibilities are eliminated and the scene moves toward the vital seventh pair, the decision of the gods becomes more and more plain. For whether the agent behind the pairing of champions is called chance or Hermes, there is everywhere a sense, reinforced by the sight of the statues, that something more than human guides it. The logic behind what occurs is understood ultimately to be that of the Erinys. It might justly be said that the gods deliver Eteocles and Polynices to her; but it is also by their will that the city survives.

The proposals made here concerning the importance of allotment in the shield scene cannot be proved objectively. No interpretation of this puzzling scene can hope for that degree of certainty. Nevertheless, these suggestions seem plausible in the context of a total interpretation of the *Seven* and particularly because of these considerations:

(1) The lot is among the major images of the play and, like the others, narrows in its reference from the circumstances of the war in general to the situation of the two brothers.

(2) As with the other images, this development occurs around the end of the shield scene. Verbally, the new significance of the lot imagery is signalled in line 690. Shortly afterward, the related themes of division and the iron appear (lines 711 and 715). But

all of this is a result of what has happened in the central scene. The actual lot in the Argive camp is described in the prologue; upon the lot is based much of the imagery of the whole last part of the play. The shield scene mediates between the two.

(3) Since the shield scene, which is emphasized by its position at the center of the play, shows the battle fought through words, and since the brothers' duel in the actual battle is later described in terms of allotment, it is fitting that the manner in which they are matched should also be associated with allotment. The literal casting of lots would then pass into the sustained image of the last part of the play through what the audience witnesses in the shield scene.

(4) Aeschylus habitually makes imagery concrete through the dramatic presentation, and we have seen instances of this practice elsewhere in the *Seven*.

If these proposals are accepted, the dramatic presentation stresses all the more clearly the development of the plot, just as the structure and the imagery do. At first, there is the panic in the city while the Argives rush to the assult. Then, in the central scene, the spectators see the completion of the lot, which, as it removes the cause of that general terror, concentrates the burden of the fighting upon Eteocles and Polynices. Directly afterward, Eteocles arms himself for battle and finally stands before the audience as the embodiment of the iron which will mediate the quarrel between himself and his brother. Thus just as the lot in the shield scene is the contrivance of the curse, Eteocles manifests in his own person the curse's operation. At the end of the play, the two biers which carry the corpses tangibly display the outcome of the lot. The brothers' equal portions are their deaths. Division, not of land but of their bodies, is visible in their wounds and audible in the cries of grief which pierce the city. The fixed and significant presence throughout is that of the statues of the gods, by whose assent and under whose guidance the Erinys brings to completion her awesomely consistent design.

Appendix 1
The Ending of the *Seven*

In my interpretation of the *Seven Against Thebes*, I have supposed that with the death of Eteocles and Polynices Thebes is released from danger, that no further troubles are in store for her, and therefore that the ending of the play given in the manuscripts was not written by Aeschylus. Since, however, the matter is anything but settled, it must now be considered briefly.

In the text of the play as it has come down to us, Antigone and Ismene, the sisters of Eteocles and Polynices, are introduced by the chorus in an anapaestic passage (lines 861–74) as if they enter to be present during the lament over their brothers' bodies. The manuscripts assign parts of the "lyric stichomythia" of lines 961–1004 to them. In the final scene (lines 1005 ff.), a herald enters to announce the decision of the city's *probouloi* to forbid burial to Polynices. Antigone defies the prohibition, and the scene ends with anapaests chanted by the chorus, apparently as they accompany the biers off the scene.

The authenticity of this ending has been the subject of a long and complicated debate.[1] Is the ending of the play, as it now stands, the work of Aeschylus himself? Or were the passages in question added by an actor for a new production of the *Seven* toward the end of the fifth century B.C., perhaps under the influence of Sophocles' *Antigone* and possibly also of Euripides' *Phoenissae*? These appear to be the possible alternatives, and I would accept the latter. The balance of the arguments seems to favor the conclusion that the final scene is a later addition, that the sisters did not appear in the original version of the play, and that, consequently, at least lines 861–74 and 1005–78 should be rejected as interpolations. The play may thus have ended at line 960, as Bergk suggested long ago.[2] The passage from line 938 to that point has the feeling of a coda, with its emphasis on the end of the hostility and of the curse. It is probably much better, however, to consider the amoebaeic lament in lines 961–1004 the conclusion of the play as Aeschylus wrote it. Accordingly, in the discussion in chapter 4 it was treated as authentic, though with the parts taken by semichoruses rather than by the sisters. As a conclusion, this section has a good parallel in the ending of the *Persians*.[3] Within it, however, the line between the work of Aeschylus and that of the interpolator cannot be drawn exactly. Lines 996–97 probably should be rejected as more appropriate to Antigone and Ismene than to parts of the chorus, and so should lines 973–74 if their corrupt text has a reference to the sisters' presence.[4]

The arguments for and against authenticity have been made by others, and I have little to add. Discussing every point would serve no purpose, and I shall simply list those which seem to me persuasive.

The most obvious argument is also the least conclusive—that a trilogy ought to end with some kind of resolution and should not raise further problems. We have only one complete trilogy by Aeschylus, and though that has a very satisfying ending, it is dangerous to draw conclusions from it about the shape he usually gave his trilogies. Nevertheless, there are indications in the uncontested parts of the text of the *Seven* that the family dies out with the brothers' fratricide and that the curse, satisfied by it, ends also and does not remain to afflict the city further. Eteocles' words in the second epirrhematic scene envision the extinction of the whole family as a result of his duel with Polynices (lines 689–91, 702–704). I can see no other way of interpreting them. Accordingly, the chorus call the Erinys a "house-destroyer" in the second stasimon (line 720), and later, in their lament, they say that the brothers have ruined the house by their enmity (lines 877–78; cf. 881–85). And finally, they say that the family "has been turned in utter rout" by the curse (lines 954–55). The consequences of Laius's error, moreover, were to last to the third generation (lines 744–45); and the chorus later state very clearly that having overcome the two brothers (rather than the whole city?) the daimon has ceased (lines 959–60). In this connection, we should also consider the emphasis on the end of strife in lines 938 ff. As for the city, its fate is very different from that of the family (lines 814 ff., 825 ff.). It has been maintained that line 843 expresses anxiety over future troubles for the city. But μέριμνα does not have to refer to the future; one need only point to Aeschylus's use of the same word in line 849.[5]

Most important, however, is the clear implication of line 828 that the brothers die without offspring. Lloyd-Jones's attempt to give

ἀτέκνους there a meaning other than "childless" has not met with
agreement. If the word means what it should, it rules out any thought
of the Epigoni, and so of a fourth generation and further danger to
the city. Thus some other explanation should—and can—be found for
ἐπιγόνοις in line 903. I see no difficulty in understanding the word as
"those born later."[6] The property remains intact, not for the brothers'
direct descendants or even necessarily for their kin, but generally for
those who come after them, produced by and participating in the
normal cycle of life, from which they have been cut off. This sense of
the word would thus fit the pattern of disruption in Laius's family
which is stressed throughout the play.[7] What awaits the brothers is
"shares in their father's grave"—the contrast is emphasized by the
repetition of μένειν only a few lines later (line 912).

Many have wondered, however, whether Aeschylus could simply
have disregarded the story of the Epigoni. Thus Wilamowitz—and he
was not alone—attempted a compromise. The ending, he said, is
spurious, but the tradition of Thebes' eventual destruction was too
strong for Aeschylus, who therefore glanced at the story by referring
to the Epigoni here.[8] It is hard to accept this solution without also
acquiescing in Wilamowitz's view of the play as an unsuccessful
attempt to combine two traditions. If we are not prepared to do that,
we might approach the question differently. As Kirkwood points out
(against Lloyd-Jones), we cannot tell whether even the well-informed
members of Aeschylus's audience would have known the story; and
the earliest use of ἐπίγονοι as a proper noun referring to the sons of
the seven against Thebes may have been Aeschylus's play by that
name, of unknown date.[9] Thus it is by no means certain that the
spectators would have caught such an allusion, if there was one, in the
Seven. These arguments aside, Aeschylus no doubt *could* have ignored
that entire stage of the myth for the purpose of this trilogy, as
Sophocles apparently did in his *Antigone* (599–600). As was argued
in chapter 1, dramatists must have had considerable freedom in their
treatment of myth.[10]

Furthermore, much in the suspected passages themselves invites
criticism.[11] It is true that a fair amount of the Greek is above
reproach, and that several times some images from the rest of the play
are employed.[12] But on any view the passages were written in the
fifth century B.C., and no one has denied that the interpolator (if
there was one) knew his Aeschylus. Still, the passages contain some

language to which objections have properly been raised, and their dramatic value in general is questionable. This is especially true of the anapaests which introduce the sisters (lines 861–74).[13] They severely damage the effect of the beautiful image in lines 854–60, both by their poor phrasing and because they separate it from the lament into which Aeschylus must have intended it to lead.

The manuscripts assign the sisters parts in the lament of lines 875–960 haphazardly, in only three places (lines 933, 947, and 951), and even if they are present they probably do not participate. Their prolonged silence, after the flourish of their entrance, is strange. To infer from a similar situation in the *Iliad* (24.719–22) a customary form of ritual lament[14] goes far beyond the available evidence; and the chorus are hardly the professional mourners mentioned in the Homeric passage.

In the closing scene, the herald's surrender in his dispute with Antigone (line 1053) seems oddly abrupt. The *probouloi* of line 1006 do not necessarily smack of political conditions in Athens in the wake of the Sicilian disaster, as many have claimed.[15] Yet Nicolaus seems right in objecting that their introduction violates "dramatic economy": at the end of the drama Thebes is suddenly given a new regime whose only purpose is to issue an ineffectual order which has no consequences for the play.[16] If line 1039 means that Antigone proposes to bury Polynices by covering his body with dust, that could well be an indication of dependence on Sophocles. The absence of a specific object for φέρουσα is, in any case, strange.[17] A final remark on the style of this scene might be made. I would hesitate very long before attributing to Aeschylus the frigid antitheses of lines 1033–34:

> τοιγὰρ θέλουσ' ἄκοντι κοινώνει κακῶν,
> ψυχή, θανόντι ζῶσα συγγόνῳ φρενί.

Antithesis is by no means foreign to Aeschylus, but he usually employs it with great effect, as in the juxtaposition of φίλου and ἐχθρά in line 695. The device is pointless here.

Many other points can and have been raised, but I have noted the ones I consider important. Since, however, as Lloyd-Jones shows, there is no way of demonstrating objectively that the ending of the play is spurious, perhaps I may end with a more subjective argument. It is difficult to see what the presence of the sisters or the closing

scene adds to the *Seven*. With the transmitted text, the family survives in an attenuated form, and the play trails off indecisively.[18] Not
only is nothing gained by this; renewal of conflict at the close of the
Seven would run counter to the movement of the myth, the trilogy,
and the play itself as I have interpreted them.[19] The wording of lines
744–45 implies that the curse would end with the death of the
brothers in the third generation. In the course of the *Seven*, accordingly, the fates of city and family have become separated. I cannot
believe that the city would fall into further difficulties thereafter.
That would break the curve followed by the story. Moreover, a final
scene would disrupt the symmetry in the play's structure. And both
the imagery and the dramatic presentation converge on the brothers'
duel and on their fate; is the reference of these elements to widen
once again? That would make no sense. It may seem circular reason-
ing to study the play on the assumption that the ending is a late
addition and then to seek to justify that assumption on the basis of
the interpretation. But that problem is only apparent. For if it can be
shown that the play and the whole trilogy (so far as it can be reconstructed) make sense in themselves, and that their internal coherence
would be disturbed by further strife at the end, then we must either
reject the ending or admit that Aeschylus made a severe error of
artistic judgment. From what we know of Aeschylus, the latter
appears extremely unlikely.

Appendix 2
The Importance of Imagery

The study of imagery, though of relatively recent origin, is by no means a new approach to Greek tragedy.[1] Yet since it has been criticized by some as more suited to modern than to ancient literature,[2] its application to the *Seven* needs justification. A related objection must also be met. Greek abounds in traditional metaphors and figures of speech; how can we be sure that what, because of our experience of later poetry, we are inclined to call an "image" is not really one of these? The problem, then, is to defend this approach to the literary criticism of an ancient poetic text from the possible charge of mere subjectivity or fancifulness.

The decisive consideration is the sheer frequency with which what I have called "images" are repeated in the *Seven*. This in itself emphasizes them and warns the spectator to be attentive to them. Simply to notice these recurrences, however, is not enough, even though one may sense their importance by intuition. There is a reasonably objective method for testing whether the repetition of language associated with a given idea in a particular Aeschylean play is deliberate and systematic, and that is to examine the distribution of these words among the surviving plays of the corpus. This kind of control, necessary and obvious though it may seem, is all too rarely applied. Three of the apparently major themes and images of the *Seven* will therefore be investigated in this way.

(1) Nautical Language. There can be no disagreement that language of the sea is used frequently in the *Seven* to depict Thebes as a ship threatened by a storm. On the other hand, such language naturally formed common figures of speech for the Greeks, especially the Athenians of the fifth century B.C., for whom the sea had become a major concern. But although, predictably, words for water, wind, ship, and navigation occur often in Aeschylus, the *Seven* accounts for about 52 percent of the instances in his plays of the *figurative* use of this vocabulary. Next comes the *Agamemnon,* with 13 percent, and the whole of the *Oresteia* has some 23 percent.[3] But these numbers,

impressive though they are, do not tell the whole story. The usual word for "ship," ναῦς, occurs most often by far in the *Persians* (thirty-six times, apart from the very doubtful reading in line 342); but it is used there every time in a *literal* sense, and the majority of these instances are in the messenger's account of the battle of Salamis (lines 249 ff.).[4] In the *Seven*, by contrast, ναῦς appears only twice, but both times in a *figurative* context (lines 62 and 210). The situation in the *Persians* arises from an actual naval expedition and battle; in the *Seven*, an inland city is implicitly equated with a ship. The two cases are quite different. It seems, moreover, that in the latter play Aeschylus wanted more to suggest than to state the parallel between Thebes and a ship, and that he did so not principally with a single denotative noun, but by means of a whole complex of words connected with the sea. Some of these words, in fact, occur nowhere else in the complete extant dramas of Aeschylus.[5] Others, though they are employed elsewhere, have a nautical flavor only in the *Seven*.[6] In richness of vocabulary, and frequency and manner of use, language connected with the sea sets this play off from the other six.

(2) Earth, Plant, and Crop Imagery. As we have seen, the Thebans in this play are often spoken of as plants, and the earth as their mother. Of the figurative uses of terms for land, crops, sowing and reaping, and of related words, the *Seven* contains more than 56 percent, followed by the *Agamemnon* and *Choephori*, each with about 12 percent, while the whole *Oresteia* has 29 percent.[7] Once again, nouns for "earth"—γῆ, γαῖα, αἶα, and χθών—occur rather less often in the *Seven* than one would expect, relative to other plays (the *Seven* has about 10 percent of the instances of γῆ in Aeschylus, for instance, the same as the *Prometheus* and *Choephori*, as against the heaviest concentration, over 21 percent, in the *Suppliants*). But many other words connected with the earth are used figuratively in the *Seven* more frequently than elsewhere in Aeschylus, and some only there among the extant plays.[8] The word ἄλοξ, for instance, occurs three times in Aeschylus. At *Agamemnon* 1015 it refers to literal furrows; at *Choephori* 25 it describes the furrows scratched in their cheeks by the mourning chorus. The latter may rightly be called a figure of speech or an isolated metaphor. Far different is *Seven* 593, where Amphiaraus, in his wisdom, is said to "reap the deep furrow in his mind." This line and the next are closely related to all the other

language of earth and crops in the play, since the seer's feeling for, and future association with, the Theban soil has been emphasized (lines 580–88), in ironic contrast to Polynices' aggression. Most remarkable of all is that μήτηρ, while it has a figurative meaning in other plays (*Agamemnon* 265, *Persians* 614), is used four times in association with the earth in the *Seven* (lines 16, 416, 584, and 753), and elsewhere in Aeschylus only once (*Prometheus Bound* 90). [9]

It is true that in other plays Aeschylus describes the land as the begetter and nurse of men and of all life (for example, *Choephori* 127–28). In part, we may be dealing with a characteristic attitude toward the earth, of which no reader of Aeschylus can fail to be aware. But the facts stated above indicate that nowhere did he employ figurative language drawn from the earth and the raising of crops so frequently and so consistently as in the *Seven*.

(3) Terms of Debt and Commerce. These are also prominent in the *Seven*, which contains fully half of all the figurative uses of such language in the plays. [10] The *Agamemnon*, with 21 percent, is a very distant second.

The table below gives the percentages for each play of the total figurative uses in Aeschylus of the language discussed above. The numbers are rounded off to the nearest tenth of a percent. Similar

Table 2

	Seven	Pers.	Supp.	P.V.	Ag.	Cho.	Eum.	Oresteia
Nautical	52.1	9.6	6.4	8.5	12.8	7.4	3.2	23.4
Earth, Crops	56.5	10.1	2.9	1.4	11.6	11.6	5.8	29.0
Debt, Commerce	50.0	0	8.3	8.3	20.8	4.2	8.3	33.3

statistics could doubtless be obtained for the rest of the recurrent language of the *Seven*. [11] Those listed in the table, however, seem sufficient to support a claim that the repetition of such language forms a distinct pattern of meaning and deserves to be studied. But perhaps even more important than the statistics is the fact that, as was argued in chapters 2 and 3, all the themes and images of the *Seven* develop in a remarkably uniform manner, which also corresponds to the effect of the structure and the dramatic presentation. The consistent and sustained way in which they are employed clearly shows that they are far more than random figures of speech. In other plays, isolated instances of similar language may appropriately be called "traditional metaphors," "figures of speech," or the like, and must be carefully distinguished from what we have been discussing here. On the other hand, groups of words which reflect different concerns are evidently prominent as recurrent images in certain of Aeschylus's other dramas, while appearing seldom or never in the *Seven*. Obvious examples are repeated references in the *Oresteia* to hunting and to light shining from darkness.

In view of these arguments, the objection that this approach may be too "modern" for application to ancient poetry is less serious than it appears at first. Although the concept of "imagery" as a critical tool is of relatively recent origin, the phenomenon itself may be much older. There is no difficulty in believing that poetry of widely different ages might use similar devices.

It may still be wondered how a spectator at a single performance of the play could have grasped all the shifts in relation and meaning which have been claimed for the imagery in the course of this study. He could not, as we can, turn the pages of a written text to compare passages. One reply might be that even if we discern more than an actual audience could, we still may discover how Aeschylus himself, consciously or unconsciously, conceived of his material.[12] That would be a valid undertaking—always provided, of course, that the dangers of overinterpretation were recognized and avoided.

We should, however, be at least as concerned with the effect on the spectator of the play in production; and probably the importance of the imagery of the *Seven* would not have been lost on the original audience. Its members were closer than we are today to the customs and beliefs reflected in the imagery, which formed the environment of their daily life and had long since molded associations on which that imagery could play. The sea, the earth and crops, the family, and the handing on of property from one generation to the next, were of fundamental concern to Aeschylus's spectators; images drawn from these aspects of life would have been intelligible and vivid to them. Moreover, this immediate impact would have been reinforced by the numerous repetitions of the images. At first their significance is uncertain and their reference vague. But with each occurrence their meaning, their relations to one another, and the direction in which they tend become better defined. They work both within a given context and cumulatively; and even a spectator who could not understand their import in particular passages would at least have been aware of their general movement. And finally, the development of the imagery must have been all the clearer because it was experienced, not in isolation, but along with the other elements which were coordinate with it.

Appendix 3
The Character and Freedom of Eteocles

What view, it is often asked, should be taken of Eteocles, at first apparently the leader who demands calm within the city, and then the curse-maddened Labdacid? Is his character consistent? To what extent is his action in opposing his brother at the seventh gate voluntary, and how far (if at all) is it determined by external forces? A subsidiary problem is what the particle γε in line 71 implies. And the timing of Eteocles' gate assignments has been discussed mainly in this context. Various plausible answers have been offered.[1] These questions, however, may be less important than is commonly thought.

In the first place, it is highly debatable whether Greek tragedy was *primarily* concerned with characterization—that is, the consistent depiction, in psychological depth, of individuals and their personalities. Aristotle, at any rate, takes the position that character is secondary to plot, since tragedy imitates not men but actions. He even asserts that tragedy could exist without character, but not without action.[2] It seems methodologically questionable, therefore, to center attention on Eteocles himself.

Aristotle does not deny the importance of character, but indicates that it must be viewed in relation to the plot. The plot of the *Seven* does not require much characterization. Eteocles is presented selectively; Aeschylus shows us his exterior conduct—that is, certain words and actions chosen for the sake of the play as a whole. Any attempt to infer Eteocles' essential nature from these outward signs is futile and misdirected. True, the fratricide occurs because Eteocles responds as he does to the knowledge that his own brother will attack the seventh gate, and dismisses as shameful the alternative of avoiding battle. But that means simply that his character serves the plot. The structure of the second epirrhematic scene, as Regenbogen has described it, retains the proper perspective.[3] The central section is concerned with the consequences of the curse, which Eteocles maintains are inescapable. The situation is thus stressed as primary. In the framing trimeter passages, Eteocles bases his arguments on the concept of a soldier's honor. *Ethos* is presented, but not in the most prominent position.

Thus Eteocles is interesting mainly as the heir of a curse-laden house.[4] Similarly, what he does or does not know about the curse at any particular moment matters little.[5] What is properly of interest is the way Aeschylus leaves the curse in the background during the early part of the play, aside from a single mention of it in line 70. Then, when understanding of it comes, the dramatic effect is most important—not only the suddenness, but also the way the whole logic of the Erinys' work becomes clear in retrospect.

Worry about the unity of Eteocles' character also seems misplaced. For if, under new and shocking conditions, a personage begins to act differently from the way he has previously behaved, that is no cause for wonder. Such a change is credible either in life or in literature. Eteocles' behavior varies with the external circumstances; the situation is paramount, character incidental to it.

In itself, diminished emphasis on Eteocles' personality implies less need for concern with his freedom of action. Moreover, even raising the question of free will in connection with a play of Aeschylus seems inappropriate. The Greeks of his time thought of freedom and necessity (to the extent that they distinguished them at all) in far more concrete terms than we do; they did not even have a word for "free will." Nor did they conceive of individual freedom and necessity as polar opposites. If a man's life was fated to take a certain course, his voluntary actions, whether he intended it or not, would accord with that design. A tension is felt between the two, if anywhere in Attic drama, probably not before Sophocles' *Oedipus at Colonus.*[6] Even there the question is raised obliquely (for Oedipus's object is to deny all responsibility for his misdeeds) and in concrete terms (Oedipus's actions and the will of the gods). And Oedipus's emphasis, in rebutting Creon's charges, on the involuntary nature of his acts probably has more to do with Attic law than with theology.[7] Free will was not discussed as an abstract philosophical problem until much later. At the very least, the assumption, often accepted without question, that Aeschylus was exercised by the question of free will and conceived of it as a modern thinker might after centuries of Christianity, needs scrutiny and justification.

In fact, one of the results of this study (though not its principal aim) has been the conclusion that in the face of the inherited curse Eteocles has little or no freedom of choice. The whole logic of the shield scene seems to eliminate almost entirely any alternatives to the course he takes. Thus he never seems to make any decision, in the sense of weighing other possibilities; he simply announces his intention to fight his brother (lines 672–75) and resists the chorus's subsequent attempts to dissuade him. If this view makes the action of the *Seven* appear mechanical, perhaps that is because the modern audience makes different demands on drama from the Greeks.

Some writers do, in fact, argue that Eteocles has no control over events in the shield scene. But during the second epirrhematic scene, in their view, he becomes eager to fight his brother, so that what he wills fits the demands of the curse. Therefore, they say, Eteocles is guilty and deserves punishment, for he shares with Polynices responsibility for the fratricide.[8] It is true that the chorus call his attitude in that scene a savage desire, and as we have noticed, Eteocles' words and actions bear this out. But the attempt to determine how far necessity on one hand, and his own will on the other, influence what he does seems dictated by modern ways of thinking. Above all, it is unnecessary to try to sort out Eteocles' personal responsibility for the duel and the operation of the curse. Certainly the chorus term fratricide a deed which brings pollution and is unlawful (lines 682, 694; cf. 831). But there is little point in saying that the act which makes the brothers guilty (fratricide) is at the same time their punishment (death). In fact, the duel is the fulfillment of the curse. That is emphasized not only in the choral ode and lament later on (lines 822–1004) but also in lines 718–19, when in answer to the chorus's question, "Do you want to pluck your own brother's blood," Eteocles replies that evils given by the gods cannot be avoided. What he himself wishes does not matter. Though he longs for the battle, the decisive influence, here as everywhere else, is not his independent desire but the curse. Eteocles becomes possessed by the curse in the second epirrhematic scene, as I have tried to show. I doubt that Aeschylus attempted to unite two distinct factors in Eteocles' action —necessity and personal will—or that he thought of the scene in precisely those terms. Eteocles' appeal to shame (lines 683–84) and to a warrior's honor (line 717) is a response, admittedly courageous, to a situation from which he clearly sees no escape. And his mad desire to fight Polynices is really a consequence and a symptom of his possession by the curse.

Eteocles' character and its quality, his freedom of choice and personal responsibility as against the requirements of the curse—these are not, it seems to me, the questions we should be asking about the *Seven*. Even if these matters can legitimately be explored (that is, insofar as they do not represent the imposition of modern notions upon an ancient text), they should not be raised initially. Other, more fundamental aspects of the play can be ignored only at the risk of one-sided interpretation. Such topics as Eteocles' character and freedom should take their place in a total view of the play. Assessed in that context, their importance seems limited indeed.[9]

Notes

INTRODUCTION

1. Arist. *Poet.* 1449^{b}31–1450^{b}20.

2. Aristotle does seem to include "story" in the meaning of the term, since later in the *Poetics* (1452^{a}12–1452^{b}8) he discusses simple and complex plots, and *peripeteia* and *anagnorisis*.

3. Arist. *Poet.* 1450^{b}21–1451^{a}6.

4. *Poet* 1457^{b}6 ff.

5. See especially chapter 4, section "The Role of the Chorus in the Dramatic Presentation," below. The performance of the chorus, which involves both visual and aural effects, is a clear example of the impossibility of considering one without the other.

6. An outstanding example is the parodos, where the progress of the enemy attack is vividly described by the chorus even as they react in terror to it. See chapter 4, section "The Early Part of the Seven," below.

CHAPTER 1

1. Ar. *Frogs* 1021–22. Cf. Gorgias's similar judgment, cited in Plut. *Mor.* 715E (Gorgias B24 Diels-Kranz).

2. Ar. *Frogs* 1026–27.

3. Owen (1952), p. 40.

4. Murray (1940), p. 142.

5. This is true of Polynices from the start of the *Seven*. In the case of Eteocles it becomes apparent in the course of the play, as the full implications of the curse unfold.

6. Solmsen (1937), especially pp. 202–204.

7. Such a supposition underlies Wilamowitz's view of the *Seven* as an unsuccessful attempt to combine two incompatible epic tales (1914, pp. 82, 95–106). It has also colored the debate over the ending of the play, mainly in the question: could Aeschylus in the Theban trilogy simply have ignored the story of the Epigoni? See appendix 1.

8. These passages are collected by Baldry (1956), pp. 25–29.

9. Baldry, p. 29.

10. The fragments of the lost plays, which are of little help in this respect, will be discussed in section "The Form of the Trilogy," this chapter.

11. Given in hypotheses to Eur. *Phoen.* and Soph. *O.T.* That this is the older form of the oracle is argued by Robert (1915), pp. 62, 66.

12. Page's text is given here.

13. Cameron (1971), pp. 19–21. His words are cited only as a clear statement of the assumptions commonly made about the curse and the meaning of the oracle.

14. For example, Apollo's words have been taken as implying the eventual destruction of Thebes by the Epigoni (Wilamowitz, 1914, pp. 80, 82). The same conception of the oracle is the basis for the contrasting *Opfertod* theory, according to which Eteocles goes to fight his brother in the full knowledge that he will die, but knowing also that he will thereby save the city.

15. H. W. Smyth, *Greek Grammar* (rev. ed., Cambridge, Mass., 1956), 1865, 1870, 1998; E. Schwyzer, *Griechische Grammatik* (Munich, 1939–1950) 2, p. 296; R. Kühner, B. Gerth, *Ausführliche Grammatik der griech. Sprache* (Hannover 1898–1904) 2:1, pp. 195–97. Examples of aorist infinitive of single action in prophecies: *Il*. 13. 666–68: πολλάκι γάρ οἱ ἔειπε γέρων ἀγαθὸς Πολῦϊδος/νούσῳ ὑπ᾽ ἀργαλέῃ φθίσθαι οἷς ἐν μεγάροισιν/ἢ μετ᾽ Ἀχαιῶν νηυσὶν ὑπὸ Τρώεσσι δαμῆναι; Pl. *Rep*. 415C: ὡς χρησμοῦ ὄντος τότε τὴν πόλιν διαφθαρῆναι; Hdt. 4.178: ταύτην δὲ τὴν νῆσον Λακεδαιμονίοισί φασι λόγιον εἶναι κτίσαι. Present infinitive of continued action in prophecy: Thuc. 2.102.5: λέγεται δὲ καὶ Ἀλκμέωνι τῷ Ἀμφιάρεω . . . τὸν Ἀπόλλω ταύτην τὴν γῆν χρῆσαι οἰκεῖν. With this last, contrast the Herodotus passage cited above, where κτίσαι apparently means "colonize" or "found a city in." Here οἰκεῖν suggests rather "settle in and continue to dwell in."

16. Symptomatic of this is Tucker's explanation. In the introduction to his edition (p. xxv), he says that the oracle "thrice bade him die without children, if he would 'keep the country safe.'" Yet in his translation he renders the words in question, "thrice . . . did Apollo bid him save the realm. . . ." Manton, on the other hand (1961, p. 80), sees the implications of the oracle much as I do: "The sense of the oracle must have been that if Laius wished to preserve the city he must die without offspring. . . ." He goes on, however, to attribute the troubles which afflict family and city to Laius's "disobedience" of Apollo's command—a view of which I am doubtful.

17. Groeneboom (note ad loc., p. 212) says that σῴζειν reproduces a "prophetic present" in direct speech and cites *Ag*. 126. This would rule out the traditional interpretation of the oracle, since it would exclude a command by Apollo and thus the notion of Laius's disobedience. It would be impossible to tell the aspect of the action on Groeneboom's suggestion; but the sense "you will save" would still be liable to the objection that we know of no danger from which Thebes had to be delivered. A prophetic present meaning "you will keep the city safe" would be compatible with my view of the oracle's significance (see below).

18. E.g., Robert (1915), p. 253.

19. Winnington-Ingram (1966), p. 91.

20. Parke, *Oracles of Zeus* (1967), Appendix 1, nos. 2, 3, and 6 under "Public Enquiries."

21. Cf. Paus. 9.5.9.

22. Generally, εἰπεῖν means "command" when followed by an infinitive and takes ὅτι or ὡς when it introduces indirect discourse with the meaning "say." It does occur in the latter sense with the infinitive, however, rarely in Attic prose, but frequently in poetry (Smyth 2017c, with note; for additional instances, see L.S.J. s.v. εἶπον, 1.a). For this verb in the sense "foretell" with the infinitive, see *Il*. 13.666–68 (quoted above, note 15).

23. Hdt. 1.53.3.

24. Only Cameron (1971, p. 20) notes this difficulty, but he draws no conclusions. The story which comes closest of any I have found to illustrating punishment for disobedience of an oracle is Hdt. 5.45.1 (the story of Dorieus). But
it is not such an example because (1) the oracle in question was merely an
affirmative reply to Dorieus's inquiry as to whether he would obtain the land
(ch. 43), and thus quite different from the answer Laius received; and (2)
Dorieus's action was not disobedience: his alleged involvement in Croton's campaign against Sybaris was merely an incident on his journey to Sicily, something
he did in addition to the object of his trip. He did, after all, go to Sicily eventually (ch. 46). Admittedly the phrase παρὰ τὰ μεμαντευμένα seems at first to
imply disobedience, but since it is immediately explained by παρέπρηξε ("did
besides"), the preposition must mean "in addition to" rather than the more usual
"contrary to" (so Powell, Lexicon to Herodotus, s.v. παρά A.III.2) In any case,
the whole incident is doubtful, since Dorieus's participation, affirmed by the
Sybarites, was denied by Croton, and Herodotus leaves the question completely
open. As How and Wells observe (2, p. 18), ". . . the connexion of Dorieus with
the campaign is best regarded as an attempt on the part of the oracle to justify
the failure of its prediction that he would succeed."

25. Parke and Wormell (1956, 1, p. 299) content themselves with saying that
"his [Laius's] death at the hands of Oedipus becomes a penalty for his own disregard of the divine warning." They adduce no parallels.

26. Ἐξορθιάζων (line 271); ἐξαυδώμενος (272); ἔφασκε (276); εἶπε (279);
ἐφώνει (283).

27. See appendix 2 of Conington's edition of the Choephori (London, 1857)
and the notes ad loc. of Sidgwick (Oxford, 1884) and Tucker (Cambridge, 1901).

28. Hdt. 4.155-59.

29. See also Hdt. 8.20: the Euboeans suffered because they ignored a warning
from the oracle of Bacis. Here again there is no suggestion of personal vengeance
by the god; the story merely illustrates the consequences of disregarding an
explicit admonition.

30. Erinyes are mentioned in Apollo's warning to Orestes (Cho. 283-84), but
they would be "brought to maturity from the father's blood"—i.e., they would
not be sent by Apollo, but would embody the curses which would inevitably
fall on anyone who failed to avenge a kinsman. At Ag. 55 ff., gods are said to
send an Erinys, but upon transgressors of divinely protected limits on mortal
action. No such limits apply to the case of oracles. It may be imprudent to ignore
an oracle, but on the available evidence, it is not a religious crime. For a different
application of this passage to the story of Laius, see the following subsection,
"Laius's Crime."

31. What Laius's crime may have been will be discussed in the following subsection.

32. The infinitive μένειν (for the reading see note 33) requires that εἶναι be
supplied before ὠκύπουον.

33. For a temporal clause depending on an epithet rather than on the noun
which the epithet modifies, cf. Cho. 608-609: δαλὸν ἥλικ', ἐπεί . . . κελάδησε.

Most manuscripts read μένει in line 745 (μένοι, the reading of a few other mss., is impossible here). Since μένει would involve a hiatus not just within a period but in the middle of an iambic metron, I have assumed Wilamowitz's μένειν as correct. If μένει were retained, however, the εὖτε-clause would follow at least as naturally from ὠκύποινον as from παρβασίαν. The sense would be: "For I speak of an ancient-born transgression swiftly punished—but it remains until the third generation—when Laius. . . ." The sentence αἰῶνα . . . μένει in this case is a parenthesis; editors who retain the ms. reading (e.g., Paley, Groeneboom) set it off with colons or dashes (for δέ in a parenthesis, Wecklein, in his 1902 edition, compares *Cho.* 25-27). Thus even though παρβασίαν would be emphasized, ὠκύποινον is the closer word to the εὖτε-clause and is separated from it only by a parenthetical statement.

34. Since many years must have elapsed between Laius's crime and his death, ὠκύποινον may seem odd. Laius's suffering, however, is swift retribution in contrast to the extension of his crime's effect through the third generation. Besides, the epithet may draw attention to the fact that the original wrongdoer was punished at all. That did not always happen (e.g., Hdt. 1.13.2, 1.91.1: Gyges prospered as a result of his crime against Candaules; but four generations later, his descendant Croesus paid for that crime).

35. Cf. παράνοια . . . φρενώλης, lines 756-57 (if the reference is to Laius; on this question, see chapter 4, note 53).

36. For an Erinys causing atê, cf. *Il.* 19.86-89, and *Od.* 15.231-34. Pausanias (8.34.1) identifies goddesses called *Maniai* with the Eumenides. The end of the *Choephori*, though it is not an exact parallel, shows Erinyes confusing their victim's wits. In the *Seven* Eteocles ruinous desire to fight Polynices is called atê and atê is associated with curses as victors over the family (lines 687, 953-60).

37. Cf. *Seven* 531-32: βίᾳ Διός (for the reading, see note 22 to chapter 5 below); Soph. *Ant.* 79: βίᾳ πολιτῶν.

38. E.g., *Seven* 612: βίᾳ φρενῶν.

39. For Apollo's role in the fate of Oedipus's sons, see subsection "Family and City," this chapter.

40. See following subsection, "Laius's Crime."

41. Winnington-Ingram (1966). He also thinks that her role in the troubles would shed light on Eteocles' misogyny in lines 187 ff.

42. Fragment 171 (Mette).

43. Another argument against the notion that Laius's crime was to disobey Apollo is that he did not *entirely* ignore the oracle. It was, of course, a grave mistake to beget a child at all, but Laius did attempt to remedy his error by exposing the infant.

44. For passages bearing on the myth, see Bethe in *R.-E.* 3.2499-2500 (s.v. "Chrysippos").

45. Robert (1915), pp. 396-400. The corrupt passage in Aristophanes' hypothesis to the *Phoenissae*, while it need not imply that that play formed a connected trilogy with the *Chrysippus* and *Oenomaus*, still indicates, apparently, that all three dramas centered on the same group of myths. See Webster (1967), pp. 111-12.

46. Scholars are divided on this question. Against Aeschylean use of the myth, see Robert (1915), pp. 396–414. For a reply to his arguments, see Lamer in R.-E.12: 1, 476–81 (s.v. "Laios"). Dawe (1963, p. 40) also argues vigorously that Aeschylus knew and used the story. See also Smyth (1924), p. 128; Lloyd-Jones (1971), pp. 120–21. Cameron (1971, p. 20) sees "nothing to preclude" Aeschylus's use of the myth, though he observes that while Zeus should then punish Laius, "in the Seven it is Apollo that is offended." That is no difficulty if we discard the notion of Apollo's "offence," since in Aeschylus Apollo speaks and acts for Zeus (Eum. 616–21).

47. For this Peisander, see Huxley (1969), pp. 100–105, who, however, is silent on the subject of this scholion. He thinks it possible that Peisander flourished as early as ca. 648 B.C. See also Keydell in R.-E. 37.144–45. That ascriptions of other epics to Peisander were false does not concern us; we are interested here only in possible epic, and therefore pre-Aeschylean, treatment of the story, whoever the author may have been.

48. Robert (1915), pp. 149–68; Lamer in R.-E. 12:1, 478, 480, 507.

49. Farnell (1909) 5, pp. 437–40; Ernst Wüst in R.-E. Suppl. 8, 101–107 (s.v. "Erinys"). Cf. the linking of Oedipus's curse with his Erinys, Seven 70. See also Il. 9.565–72 (Althaea's curse on Meleager).

50. Schol. on Eur. Phoen. 60; cf. oracle in hypotheses to Phoen. and Soph. O.T If the form of the story given in the "Peisander scholion" is ancient, a curse by Pelops could be a variant at least as old as Aeschylus (and possibly invented by him).

51. In the Seven, an Erinys is mentioned only in connection with Oedipus's curse on his sons, but that is probably because the extant play treats only the last generation of the cursed family. An Erinys evoked by the initial crime probably hounded all three generations. Cf. Ag. 1190: συγγόνων 'Ερινύων, with Fraenkel's convincing explanation of the adjective as "inherent in the house" (1950, 3, pp. 544–45).

52. With παραβᾶσιν (Ag. 59) compare παρβασίαν in Seven 743.

53. Cf. Il. 9.447–57: Phoinix's offence against his father takes a sexual form. The father curses him and evokes Erinyes, and Phoinix is made sterile. For the power of Erinyes over the survival of a family, cf. Eum. 187–88 and (more pertinent to the Theban myth) Hdt. 4.149.2: the children of the male members of a Spartan tribe kept dying in infancy until, on the advice of an oracle, they founded a shrine to the Erinyes of Laius and Oedipus.

54. Fr. 182 (Mette): Σφίγγα δυσαμεριᾶν πρύτανιν κύνα πέμπει. The subject of the verb is not preserved.

55. Cf. Lamer in R.-E. 12:1, 478: "Es ist doch sehr wirkungsvoll, dass ein Frevel gegen die Gesetze der Ehe gerade in der Ehe des Frevlers bestraft wird." This statement needs some qualification. Laius's offence would not have been directly against marriage. Still, the aim of marriage is continuation of the family, and the rape (perhaps with Chrysippus's suicide) will have thwarted that purpose from Pelops's point of view—in part, at least, since he did have other sons.

56. For the connection of the Sphinx with an Erinys, cf. Eur. Phoen. 1029.

57. See below, pp. 99–100.

58. That is a plausible inference from *Od.* 11.274. If ἄφαρ there is taken in its usual sense of "right away," Oedipus would not have had time to raise children begotten with his mother-wife. So Baldry (1956), p. 25. Cf. Paus. 9.5.10–11, who adds that "the author of the epic they call *Oedipodeia*" used the same form of the story. In his edition of the *Odyssey* (2nd ed., London 1967, note on 11.271), Stanford understands ἄφαρ as "after that," and cites *Il.* 4.377, 386, where, he says, "Jocasta's sons by Oedipus are mentioned by Homer." But there, in fact, Eteocles and Polynices are simply mentioned by name; their mother is not even referred to, much less identified.

59. That Aeschylus used this form of the story we know from *Seven* 752–56, 926–32.

60. Baldry (1956), p. 31. That Aeschylus arranged the story this way is a reasonable deduction from *Seven* 772 ff. It cannot have been the Homeric version if the line of the *Odyssey* cited above (note 58) implies what it seems to.

61. The incurably corrupt line 784 of the *Seven* must refer to this.

62. Baldry (1956), p. 31.

63. Eur. *Phoen.* 63–66.

64. *Od.* 11.275–76.

65. Robert (1915), p. 171.

66. Howe (1962), pp. 130–33. "Had Oedipus merely conformed and mechanically fulfilled that oracle," she concludes (p. 133), "then there would have been no drama. When he expresses individual shame by his self-blinding, then his legend becomes transformed into drama."

67. Quoted by Ath. 11.465F–466A.

68. Schol. on Soph. *O.C.* 1375.

69. Apollod. 3.5.9.

70. Soph. *O.C.* 337 ff., 1375–79.

71. Cameron (1964).

72. Manton (1961), p. 82; cf. Baldry (1956), p. 31, note 1.

73. Manton, though rejecting Wilamowitz's emendation as "barely intelligible without its author's explanation," also considers Hermann's reading "not very probable." But the important point is that Wilamowitz's emendation is not inevitable and that there is at least one other possibility. A decision between ἐπικότους and ἐπίκοτος does not affect the interpretation (for an explanation of the former, see Baldry [1956], p. 31, note 1). It should also be pointed out that lines 785 ff. can be interpreted according to the Sophoclean scholiast with Hermann's emendation as well. See Wecklein ad loc. (his line 771) in his 1902 edition.

74. Cf. *Seven* 781: μαινομένᾳ κραδίᾳ.

75. The terms of the curse, given in lines 788–90, are that the sons will share their inheritance "with iron-wielding hand," and that is sufficiently ambiguous. Cf. Manton (1961), p. 78.

76. Eur. *Phoen.* 69–80.

77. Schol. on Eur. *Phoen.* 71.

78. See Paus. 9.5.12 for another account, which, however, is vague concerning the reason for the quarrel.

79. Cameron (1968), p. 252. See also idem (1971), p. 26.

80. E.g., *Seven* 906–907, 961.

81. That is the clear import of lines 580 ff. It is surprising that so many critics have missed this distinction. Patzer, on the other hand, takes it into account in a way I think questionable (1958, pp. 106–109). The issues of the quarrel, he says, are deliberately left vague; but they are unimportant by comparison with Polynices' overwhelming guilt in his assault on his native land. Now that is unquestionably a serious act, but it must itself be a response to something Eteocles did. Thus Eteocles himself shares in the responsibility for the danger to the city, even though he tries to defend it. Probably we are not meant to view one brother as innocent and the other as guilty. What matters is that both are equally under a curse and will suffer equally. This should not be ignored because of preoccupation with the character of Eteocles and an attendant anxiety to find him blameless.

82. The only significant variation among the mss., among τώς, τώσ', and τώς σ', is not pertinent here.

83. See Robert (1915), pp. 271–72. His attempt to explain the ms. reading along the same lines is unconvincing.

84. Winnington-Ingram (1977), p 20, note 42, observes that line 584 implies that Polynices himself claimed, and could argue for, justice on his side. The same point may be made about Polynices' shield device. Cf. *Cho.* 461, which could well be taken as a summary of the situation in the *Seven*.

85. Cf. Jones (1962), pp. 93–94: "No need asserts itself, or desire, to be precise about guilt when guilt is circumambient, atmospheric, blood-borne, often untethered to personal act or omission; where in the nature of things there can be no knowing how a man stands with his gods."

86. Robert (1915), p. 246; cf. Baldry (1956), p. 32.

87. Manton (1961), p. 80.

88. Fowler, for instance, sees in the city's survival Aeschylus's adherence to the mythical tradition as he had inherited it (1970, p. 37, note 12); Patzer considers it a mark of divine grace (1958, p. 116); and according to Solmsen (1937, pp. 207–208), Aeschylus felt in the end "that the curse when coming to a head should be confined to the family and not affect the city," which survives "because, like Athens in the Persian War, she is engaged in a defensive war in which she has justice and the Olympian gods on her side." Wilamowitz, on the other hand, thinks that Thebes *will* eventually be destroyed (see note 14 above); and the *Opfertod* theory offers yet another solution. It is unnecessary, however, to seek an answer either in the character of Eteocles or outside the trilogy in the mythological or epic tradition.

89. Cf. Manton (1961), p. 80: "The prediction of the oracle would be fulfilled if a son of Laius endangered the state, and it might be expected that the state would continue to be in danger as long as any of the descendants of Laius survived. But it might also be expected that if the descendants of Laius were wiped

out by mutual destruction the state would cease to be in danger, since the begetting of a son by Laius would be cancelled out. . . ."

90. Cf. line 813, where the daimon is said to "use up" or "consume" the family.

91. Cf. *Seven* 744–45. The difficulty with this scheme is that the myths actually encompassed not three but four generations, the last being that of the Epigoni. As the text of the *Seven* now stands, the closing scene seems to prepare for that final stage of the myth. I am as convinced as it is possible to be in the absence of conclusive evidence one way or the other that, for the purposes of this trilogy, Aeschylus simple ignored the story of the Epigoni, and that the final scene (lines 1005 ff.), the presence of Antigone and Ismene, and the anapaestic lines which introduce them (861–74) are the work not of Aeschylus but of a later interpolator. Reasons for this opinion are given in appendix 1. The main body of this study assumes it.

92. References are to Mette's edition of the fragments (Berlin, 1959).

93. Robert (1915), p. 278.

94. It seems better to consider, with Mette, fr. 172 as part of the *Laius* than as belonging to the *Oedipus* as Murray does. Cf. Robert (1915), pp. 273–78. The only reason for attributing it to the *Oedipus* is the highly questionable assumption that Sophocles, in his *Oedipus Tyrannus,* followed the same plan as that play.

95. I follow the restorations of Lobel (1952), pp. 29–31. Mette combines fragments 2, 4, and 1 in that order into a hypothesis to the *Laius* (his fr. 169). Of the heading of fr. 2, only a single letter (υ) remains. Mette restores:

ΛΑΙΟΣ]

ΑΙΣΧΥΛΟ]Υ

That is possible, though the letter could just as well be part of the name Οἰδίπο]υ[ς (so Lobel, and Page in his edition of Aeschylus). It seems, however, highly unlikely that frs. 4 and 1 physically can join (see Lobel, Plate V). Mette's arrangement is thus difficult to accept. There is no intrinsic improbability that the fragments belong to two different dramas, since they are in a group of hypotheses to various plays by Aeschylus.

96. It seems useless to try to reconstruct the lost plays scene by scene on the basis of such sparse evidence, as some have done: e.g., Robert (1915), pp. 273 ff.; Mette (1963), pp. 31–37; Stoessl (1937), pp. 171–225. See Podlecki (1975).

97. Cf. Stoessl (1937), pp. 13–82. His analysis of the *Oresteia* is enlightening. His method, however, in attempting to reconstruct the Theban trilogy according to the plan he sees in the *Oresteia*, seems questionable. From what we know of the story Aeschylus followed, it appears unlikely that the *Seven* can have stood as a contrast to the *Laius* and *Oedipus*.

98. Méautis (1936), p. 100.

99. Wilamowitz (1914), p. 69. My discussion of the play's structure starts from his remarks there and expands on them, with some alterations. Cf. also Lesky (1972), p. 94, who observes that the structure of the *Seven* is, in outline, like that of the *Persians*, with large choral parts framing a central section where

spoken verse predominates. Neither writer, however, points to the significance of this structure in the *Seven* in emphasizing the outcome of the action.

For a detailed discussion of ring composition in the *Persians,* established by verbal echoes and (more importantly) by varying conceptions of the causes of events, see Winnington-Ingram (1973), especially p. 218. His view of the effect of this kind of structure is similar to mine, particularly when he remarks (note 34) that ring composition ". . . can be used as a mode of emphasis and is perhaps most effective when what intervenes between the two occurrences casts a new light upon word or theme." In the *Seven*, the symmetry is effected by correspondences not just between large blocks of the play but also between individual scenes and odes.

100. Here I differ from Wilamowitz, who calls the prologue "ein Vorspiel."

101. Cf. Wilamowitz, (1914), p. 69, who says that the messenger scene, since it leads into the choral lament, corresponds to the "Eteocles-scene" (i.e., the first epirrhematic scene), which makes the transition from the parodos.

102. Another Aeschylean example of a symmetrical structure disturbed by the introduction of an additional element near the end is *Cho.* 479-509. There two- and three-line utterances of Orestes and Electra are arranged around eight lines of stichomythia in a symmetrical design, which is broken by Electra's three lines at 505-507, as follows: Or. (2), El. (2), Or. (3), El. (3); stichomythia (8); Or. (3), El. (3), Or. (2), *El. (3),* Or. (2). (I am grateful to Professor Herington for pointing out this parallel to me.)

103. Reinhardt (1949), pp. 123-25. Concerning Eteocles he says, "im Verteidiger verbarg sich der Verfluchte, im Beschützer der unselige Nachfahr, wie im Sieger Agamemnon der Besiegte, wie im Rächer durch seine Rache sich selbst Richtende Orest."

104. Eur. *Phoen.* 751-52.

105. *Phoen.* 1090-1199.

106. Von der Mühll (1964).

107. See chapter 5, section "Dramatic Presentation in the Shield Scene," below.

CHAPTER 2

1. E.g., Dumortier (1935)—basically a catalogue of images in Aeschylus (and valuable in that way). Hiltbrunner (1950) is in many respects a perceptive and helpful book. The chapter on the *Seven* (pp. 49-57) is, unfortunately, not the strongest part of it. Though he does, every now and then, seem to recognize a certain development in some themes, Hiltbrunner actually discusses very few of them.

2. E.g., Fowler (1970) treats *only* the nautical language. He does that thoroughly, however, and relates it in many ways to the play as a whole.

3. Van Nes (1963); Cameron (1971). See especially Cameron, p. 66 (on nautical imagery): "This complex of images undergoes in the last half of the play a remarkable development which reflects the shift in focus from the threat to the city to the danger to Eteocles and the race of Laius. The ship comes to

symbolize the royal house, and the waves and stream represent the misfortunes which the house has undergone." I had come to a similar conclusion about all the imagery of the play before I saw this book. My own discussion of nautical images parallels his in many ways, but is concerned more with placing those images in the context of all the imagery of the play and with tracing out their development in detail. There are also important points of disagreement. Cameron, for instance, makes much of Tucker's idea of irrigation imagery, of which I am skeptical, and discusses "horse imagery," which I consider relatively unimportant (see note 79 below).

4. See, for example, Fowler (1970).

5. These are the themes associated with the lot, which will be discussed in chapter 3.

6. Cf. Hiltbrunner (1950), p. 87: "Das erste Aufklingen des Motivs geschieht bei Aischylos in Ungewissheit, banger Ahnung und furchtbewegter Hoffnung. In welcher Richtung es führt, entzieht sich dem Blick. Die Fäden laufen im Verborgenen. Wo sie wieder emporsteigen, da geschieht es in einem Aufbruch von erschütternder Wucht."

7. For the discussion of individual themes and images which follows, the reader may find it helpful to refer to table 1, in chapter 3.

8. Cf. Tucker's note on line 60.

9. Cf. lines 206–207, where πηδαλιῶν gives a nautical flavor to the description of the Argive horses' shrieking harness-pieces.

10. Dumortier (1935), p. 38.

11. Tucker, note on lines 32 f.

12. Below, pp. 116–19.

13. For the details of this comparison, see Tucker's note on the passage (his lines 839 ff.); Dawson (1970), p. 106; and van Nes (1963), pp. 93–95.

14. The text given here is that of Page's edition.

15. This must be the import of lines 762–63, no matter how the textual problems are resolved.

16. Most clearly expressed in *Pers.* 598–602; but cf. also line 433 of the same play.

17. Textual problems again, but this much at least of the meaning is clear.

18. I cannot agree with Dumortier's statement (1935, p. 40) that these lines imply that "Thèbes pour être sauvé devra laisser périr son prince." The whole context is against it.

19. Similar, though with slightly different nautical terms, is *Eum.* 553–65.

20. See *L.S.J.* s.v. ῥόθιος.

21. Cf. Dawson (1970), p. 31.

22. Archil. 105 (West); Alc. 326 (L.-P.); Theog. 671–80.

23. Fowler (1970), p. 30.

24. Hdt. 7.141. Cf. Fowler (1970), pp. 31–32.

25. See below, p. 87.

26. The words are ἔξοδος, εἴσοδος, ἔξωθεν, ἔξω, θύραθεν, ἔνδοθεν, ἔνδον, εἴσω. They occur in the plays in these proportions (given in percentages): *Seven*, 38.2; *Pers.*, 2.9; *Supp.*, 0; *P.V.*, 8.8; *Ag.*, 11.8; *Cho.*, 29.4; *Eum.*, 8.8;

Oresteia, 50.0 Cf. also εἰσαμείβω at *Seven* 558, only there in Aeschylus, and in conjunction with the phrase ἔξωθεν εἴσω.

That words for walls, gates, and towers are more common in the *Seven* than elsewhere in Aeschylus is to be expected of a drama set in a city famous for its seven gates. But since these barriers divide what is inside the city from what is outside, the words for them, which concentrate attention on this contrast, are relevant here. They are: ἐπάλξις, θωρακεῖον, κλῆθρον, πύλαι, πυργηρέομαι, πυργοδάικτος, πύργος, πυργοφύλαξ, πύργωμα, and τεῖχος. If we add the occurrences of these words, and also of words for "outsider" (ἄποικος, μέτοικος, ξένος), to the figures given above, we obtain the following percentages: *Seven*, 60.2; *Pers.*, 4.2; *Supp.*, 4.2; *P.V.*, 2.5; *Ag.*, 11.0; *Cho.*, 12.7; *Eum.*, 5.1; *Oresteia*, 28.2.

27. Cf. Hdt. 1.78.2, where the word is contrasted with ἐπιχώριοι. Aeschylus is so intent on marking the Argives as alien that he not only stresses their white shields (line 91) but even implies that they do not speak Greek (lines 170, 72-73 —if 73 is genuine).

28. Cameron (1971), pp. 74-84; Bacon (see note 29).

29. Bacon (1964), p. 30. I am indebted in this section to her whole treatment of this subject (pp. 29-31).

30. The simplest and best solution to the problems in these lines is that adopted by Page, whose text is given here.

31. See above, pp. 16-17.

32. A fuller treatment of Parthenopaeus and Amphiaraus in relation to the internal/external theme is given below, pp. 115-17.

33. Cf. Bacon (1964), p. 30: "This ambiguity about who is really an enemy and an outsider, and about where he is, is the ambiguity of the house of Laius itself."

34. Cameron (1964), pp. 6-7. The story of the *Spartoi* may also be, as he says (p. 8), "a thematic anticipation of the birth of Eteocles and Polyneices, who sprang from the seed Oedipus sowed in the land of his mother and cut each other down in mutual fratricide." But there is no indication of this in the text of the extant play. The Spartoi are referred to only in connection with the Theban champions, to emphasize the city's close relations to its soil.

35. This seems the most plausible interpretation, despite the difficult textual problems in these lines. See the articles of Campbell (1931).

36. *Supp.* 625-709; *Eum.* 916 ff.

37. *Eum.* 976-83; cf. *Eum.* 861-65, *Cho.* 66-67.

38. Jones (1962), pp. 111-37.

39. For the imagery which marks the Argives as intruders, see below, this chapter, section "Themes Associated with the War"; for the similar effect of the dramatic presentation, see chapter 4, especially pp. 87-90.

40. The effect in the shield scene of the qualities of both Parthenopaeus and Amphiaraus will be discussed more fully in chapter 5, section "The Shields and the Major Themes."

41. Editors are divided on the authenticity of line 601. Even if the line does not belong here, however, the point made in the text is not materially affected,

since the undisputed line 600 contains a sufficiently clear occurrence of the type of imagery under discussion.

42. *Od.* 11.271.

43. Μητρός in line 584 is best considered a defining genitive (cf. Tucker, note on his line 571).

44. That Eteocles is at present defending Thebes does not make him any less a part of this pattern. He is simply in possession of the city for the time being. His earlier actions must have helped bring on the Argive attack, however. See p. 21 above. Amphiaraus's rebuke, of course, by the nature of the situation, can be directed only at Polynices, not at both brothers.

45. Cf. Dawson (1970), pp. 20–21; Caldwell (1973).

46. Cf. Bacon (1964), p. 31: "When the sons are laid beside their father-brother in Theban earth, they share their mother with him, as he shared her with his father, Laius."

47. Tucker thinks that the word in line 18 introduces the metaphor of an inn-keeper. That may well be, but the way it anticipates line 860 and aligns it with earth imagery seems more important.

48. This is the apparent meaning, in spite of the lacuna which follows.

49. The difficulty in this phrase concerns the genitive μητέρων. It is doubtful whether here and in the similar phrase at Soph. *Phil.* 3 the genitive can be taken as one of agent without a preposition. For that reason, Tucker and, more recently, Groeneboom, follow Verrall in understanding it as genitive of the source and implying "reared so that you are indeed mothers' children." Thus the messenger's tone is one, in Verrall's words, of "gentle contempt for their fears." That is, in fact, essentially how the Medicean scholiast understood the phrase. But we should remember that the phrase occurs immediately after the tale of distorted family relationships in the second stasimon. It would be appropriate for the city's life to be contrasted here with that history, just as the city's fate is contrasted with that of the brothers in lines 793–802. This could be the effect of the phrase whether it means "children reared by mothers" or "mothers' children." Cf. Dawson (1970), p. 100: "The messenger may feel a kindly superiority to these scared creatures, but at least, unlike Oedipus, they were brought up by their mothers." Whatever the messenger's attitude, it is less important than the thematic significance of the phrase.

50. See above p. 18.

51. For the possibilities, see above pp. 19–20. Nurture is at issue (though in different ways) whichever version Aeschylus used.

52. Cf. fr. 182 (Mette) and the descriptions of the Sphinx in the *Seven* as ὠμόσιτον (line 541) and τὰν ἁρπαξάνδραν κῆρα (lines 776–77).

53. See Chapter 1, section "The Form of the Trilogy."

54. *Il.* 4.30–49; cf. Eur. *Med.* 964, *Hipp.* 7–8.

55. Cf. Jones (1962), p. 131, who says that line 77, "in his [Eteocles'] mouth is no less reverent than the counter-proposition that those cities which honor their gods find prosperity."

56. Golden (1964), p. 83. Podlecki (1964, p. 291) asserts that "whether we

call Eteocles' attitude sceptical, or sarcastic and even atheistic, makes little difference." I would call it none of these.

57. It would take me far from my subject to argue this point at length, but cf. lines 4, 8–9, 21, 23, 35, 69 ff., 236, 264–81, 414 (hardly an expedient admission), and 625, among others.

58. E.g., *Supp.* 524–26.

59. These are probably the most discussed lines in the play. I take γε in its usual sense of "at least"; but I do not think that the particle will support elaborate theories of free will or its opposite.

60. Cf. Hiltbrunner (1950), p. 54.

61. Amphiaraus has already depicted Polynices' attack on Thebes as a religious transgression (lines 580–83). In line 653 the whole family is seen as implicated in the curse, including Eteocles.

62. Wilamowitz (1914), p. 66.

63. Cf. Hes. *Op.* 770–71; Parke, *Greek Oracles* (1967), pp. 80–81.

64. Benardete (1967), p. 24. Cf. Bacon (1964), p. 31.

65. I follow Page's text for this difficult line.

66. What the two forms of profit are is uncertain. For rather different explanations, cf. Tucker ad loc. (his line 424) and Fraenkel (1964), p. 289. The essential point for my purpose, however, is the use in this line of commercial language: profit (κέρδος) and the idea of interest in τίκτεται. Emendation of κέρδει to κόμπῳ (adopted by Murray), unnecessary anyway since the ms. reading can be satisfactorily explained, spoils the effect of the line.

67. See Tucker's note ad loc. (his line 644).

68. Winnington-Ingram (1977), pp. 25–28.

69. For ἐκπράσσειν as "exact payment of a debt," cf. Fraenkel (1950) 3, pp. 592–93 (on *Ag.* 1275); and for the idea of a curse calling in a debt, cf. *Ag.* 457, also with Fraenkel's note (2, p. 234).

70. The word μέριμνα in line 843 probably does not imply worry over further troubles for the city. See appendix 1 below.

71. Tydeus's shouts, for instance, are likened to a serpent's hisses at midday (lines 380–81).

72. Haldane (1965), p. 34. Cf. Haldane, pp. 36–37, for a detailed discussion of this imagery in the *Seven*.

73. Haldane (1965), p. 37.

74. This assumes that Schütz's emendation of the ms. τρόπον is right. Cf. Fraenkel (1964), p. 294.

75. Cf. Soph. *Aj.* 1202: γλυκὺν αὐλῶν ὄτοβον; Aesch. *P.V.* 574.

76. For the Ionics of lines 720–33, see below, p. 98. Their effect is like that of the Dionysiac language (cf. Euripides' use of this meter in the *Bacchae*).

77. See pp. 13–14, above.

78. Cf. line 831: ὤλοντ᾽ ἀσεβεῖ διανοίᾳ.

79. Related to the foregoing themes is the "horse imagery" discussed by Cameron (1971, pp. 74–84). Drawing attention to the many references to the Argives' horses, he observes that the maidens of the chorus are described as

animals, and as horses in particular. This parallelism indicates, he thinks, that like the Argives, the maidens, in their terror, pose a threat to the city. This is an important feature of the earlier part of the play. But since "horse imagery" is not carried through and developed like the other imagery we have been examining, it seems better to consider it part of a larger pattern of themes.

80. For the kinds of divination mentioned here, see Flacelière (1965), pp. 1-21.

81. Cameron (1970), p. 96. Detailed study here of this theme is made unnecessary by his article.

82. The suggestion by Hecht and Bacon (1973, introduction, pp. 14-15) that Eteocles' name means not only "man of true glory" but also "truly wept" does not seem linguistically possible, but a Greek ear might have detected such an overtone.

CHAPTER 3

1. I.e., by Cameron (see note 22 below).

2. *Il.* 15.185-95; cf. *Hymn. Hom. Cer.* 85-87. For later references to this story, cf. Pind. *Ol.* 7.54-58; *Ol.* 14.1-2; Pl. *Critias* 109b-d; Apollod. 1.2.1.

3. E.g., Ov. *Met.* 5.529.

4. Rose (1959), p. 49.

5. Hes. *Theog.* 73-74, 885.

6. Hes. *Theog.* 203-204, 421-27.

7. *Od.* 14.199-210.

8. Pind. *Ol.* 7.74-76.

9. Apollod. 2.8.4.

10. Paus. 4.3.5.

11. Strab. 8.5.6 (fr. 1083 N^2). Webster (1967, pp. 252-57) assigns this fragment to the *Temenos.*

12. See section "Arbitration," this chapter.

13. Plut. *De frat. amor.* 11 (483D).

14. There is an interesting occurrence of ἀπολαγχάνεω in Herodotus in connection with the division of patrimony (4.114.4; cf. 115.1). But it is not clear-cut, since the story is non-Athenian and the parents in this case are still alive. Still, the term itself in such a context could reflect common use of the lot for division in the fifth century B.C.

15. For a modern example which would indicate the stubborn persistence of this method, see Levy (1956).

16. Isae. 6.25.

17. Dem. 43.51.

18. Isae. 5.7 (cf. Wyse's note ad loc.).

19. Arist. *Ath. Pol.* 56.6. Cf. also the *Souda* s.v. Δατεῖσθαι καὶ Δατηταί.

20. E. Caillemer in Daremberg et Saglio 2: 1, 27-28. For a detailed description of this and other methods of sharing inheritance in the fourth century B.C., cf. Beauchet (1897) 3, pp. 638-56.

21. Both points are made by Beauchet (1897) 3, p. 643.

22. Cameron (1968).

23. For instance, Cameron's translation of lines 901 ff., which takes αἰνομόροις

as qualifying ἐπιγόνοις, seems forced. Hellanicus's account and a system of primogeniture fit the *Seven* only if, as Cameron asserts, the guilt for the quarrel rests solely with Polynices (see pp. 20–21, above, for arguments against this view). It is also more straightforward to understand the lot imagery as contrasting the brothers' enmity with the usual means of sharing patrimony than as an ironic comment on rival systems of inheritance. Finally, I see no difficulty in understanding ἐπιγόνοις as "those born after" (see below, appendix 1).

24. Fine (1951), pp. 177–208. Fine himself labels his opinion "unorthodox."

25. Guiraud (1893), pp. 90–110; Beauchet (1897) 3, pp. 423–32; Woodhouse (1938), p. 199; Lewis (1941). The decisive consideration seems to me that Solon abolished security on the person but did nothing to change the economic conditions which had forced so many into debt. Borrowing must still have been necessary, and it is difficult to imagine what form of security other than land would have been available for the long period between Solon and the Peloponnesian War. For different arguments which would still make land alienable before the fifth century B.C., see Finley (1975), pp. 153–60.

26. Woodhouse (1938), p. 79 (quoted in part by Cameron).

27. I have deliberately avoided the question of Solon's testamentary laws. Lewis suggests that they "assured the constant division of large estates" (1941, p. 156).

28. Beauchet (1897) 3, pp. 450–55. Primogeniture, as he remarks, is characteristic of feudal rather than patriarchal societies. Cameron objects that he, among others, does not "take into account the nature of land tenure," but that is precisely what Beauchet bases his argument upon.

29. Paus. 7.2.1 is irrelevant. In Paus. 3.1.4, Hippocoon claimed the rule in Laconia because he was older than Tyndareus, but he gained it only by driving Tyndareus out by force. Here, as in Pausanias's account of the Heraclids' allotment (discussed above), a claim based on priority of birth is not accepted. Strab. 8.7.1 tells of Hellen's eldest son succeeding to power in Phthia, but only at Hellen's direction. This would be unnecessary if the succession were automatic. Hellen's command to his other sons to emigrate can be attributed to the same motive as might have dictated Polynices' withdrawal from Thebes in Hellanicus's account: if one brother holds power it is inconvenient, and potentially dangerous, to have the others in the area.

30. Dem. 36.11; [Dem.] 48.13.

31. Burnett (1973). I regret that I saw this article too late to take it more fully into account.

32. Borecký (1968).

33. Murray's text is given here. Page obelizes lines 911–14.

34. There is no need to claim, as Borecký does, that the words ἴσον λαχεῖν in themselves would suggest death. The context makes this meaning clear enough.

35. Cf. line 1004 and pp. 46–47 above.

36. In his speech in the fourth pair, Eteocles also uses language which is important to an understanding of the lot in this play (lines 504–508), and which will be discussed later (chapter 5, section "Dramatic Presentation in the Shield Scene").

37. Similar is *Il.* 3.314–25, where, at the start of the duel between Paris

and Menelaus, the lot is used to determine which champion is to throw his spear first.

38. See chapter 5, section "Dramatic Presentation in the Shield Scene." There is the same mixture of the lot and nautical language at the end of the messenger scene (lines 815-19). The repetition stresses that Eteocles' words at the climax of the play come true in the event.

39. Fraenkel (1964), p. 401.

40. Engelmann (1967). He gives literary and inscriptional evidence for this practice and for its extension, in later periods, to smaller disputes.

41. Engelmann (1967), pp. 99-101.

42. Hdt. 4.62.2. This point is made by Benardete (1967), p. 26, note 4.

43. See above, chapter 2, section "The City's Walls."

44. Here πικρός is repeated from line 730, where the full image of the iron as arbiter is first introduced. The repetition shows once again that the chorus's fears for the brothers are fulfilled to the letter.

45. See section "The Lot and Greek Systems of Inheritance," this chapter.

46. This summary is based on E. Caillemer's explanation in Daremberg et Saglio 2: 1, 124-30 (s.v. "Diaitetai").

47. Arist. *Ath. Pol.* 53, 5.

48. Cf. Hesychius s.v. διαιτηταί.

49. Cf. Arist. *Rh.* 1374[b]: While the judge acts in accordance with the law, the diaitetes has equity (τὸ ἐπιεικές) in view: καὶ τούτου ἕνεκα διαιτητὴς εὑρέθη, ὅπως τὸ ἐπιεικὲς ἰσχύῃ. Cf. *Pol.* 1297[a].

50. For illustrations of the function of the diaitetai, cf. Dem. 21.83-84, 48.2, 59.71; Isae. 2.29-32, 5.31-32; Pl. *Leg.* 12.956B-C.

51. Bonner (1916).

52. Plut. *Arist.* 7.1.

53. Hdt. 5.95. That this is, once again, a case of political (rather than individual) dispute shows at once the pervasiveness of arbitration and the fluidity of its various forms. Note especially the word ἐπετράποντο, and compare the formal agreement (ἐπιτροπή) mentioned above. Cf. also Hdt. 4.161, 5.28-29, 6.108, 7.154.

54. Cf. lines 938-40.

55. Cameron (1970, pp. 111-15) argues persuasively that the prefix αυτο- in this word and the one which precedes it signifies primarily "self-" or "kindred-" and can bear the interpretation "each other" only in retrospect, after the issue of the duel has become known.

56. Lines 804, 812, 816, 921, 923, 959, 1000.

57. I give Page's text; but the main question in these lines—ἀχθέων for the ms. ἀχέων—does not affect my point. Note that this passage directly follows mention of the iron and Ares as arbiter and divider of the property (lines 941-46). For line 907, see section "Lot Imagery in the Play," this chapter.

58. See chapter 5, section "Dramatic Presentation in the Shield Scene."

59. For the close connection between Moira and Erinys in Aeschylus, cf. Fraenkel on *Ag.* 1535 f. (1950, 3, pp. 727-30).

60. The evidence is collected and discussed by Robbins (1916). Cf. also

Flacelière (1965), pp. 48–50, who discusses also an inscription from Delphi of the first half of the fourth century B.C., published in 1939; Parke and Wormell (1956) 1, pp. 18 f.; Parke, *Greek Oracles* (1967), pp. 85–88; and Ehrenberg in *R.-E.* 26.1452–54 (s.v. "Losung"). The latter's conclusions differ slightly from those given here.

61. For an example of the use of dice in a lot oracle, cf. Paus. 7.25.10 with Frazer's notes.

62. Cf. Borecký (1968), p. 264. These are the numbers of occurrences:

	Seven	Eum.	Other Plays
λαγχάνειν	10	3	5–8 (textual problems in three)
διαλαγχάνειν	2	0	0
λάχος	0	6	1
λαχή	1	0	0
διαπάλλειν	1	0	0
πάλος	4	3	2

Cf. Italie's *Index* (1964).

63. Lebeck (1971), pp. 150–59.

64. I have not attempted to list all the occurrences of these themes, but only a representative sample. In the first column are listed their occurrences in connection with the city, the war, or the Argives. The second shows passages in which they are first applied to the brothers and the family or begin to take on such significance. The third column shows passages in which the imagery is used directly of the brothers or (in some cases) is applied to the city in order to contrast its fate with that of the family.

CHAPTER 4

1. Arist. *Poet.* 1455^{a}17.
2. Arist. *Poet.* 1453^{b}1–8.
3. Arist. *Poet.* 1450^{b}15–20.
4. Arist. *Poet.* 1462^{a}11–13.
5. For this development and others, see Arnott (1962), chapter 7 (pp. 107–22). My argument in these pages owes much to his discussion there.
6. E.g., *Vita*, section 14; the *Souda* s.v. Αἰσχύλος; Philostr. *Vit. Apoll.* 6.11, *Vit. Soph.* 1.9; Hor. *A.P.* 275–80; Vitr. *de Archit.* 7, praef. 11. On the dance of the chorus, see note 64 below.
7. See Pickard-Cambridge (1968), pp. 190, 197–98.
8. Dale (1956).
9. See Introduction, above.
10. For the setting of the *Seven*, see Wilamowitz (1914), pp. 9–10, 72; Lesky (1972), p. 94; Hammond (1972), pp. 416–30.
11. Arnott (1962), pp. 1–41 (stage and *skene*), pp. 65–69 (statues).
12. Pickard-Cambridge (1946), chapters 1, 2, and 7. Lesky (1972, p. 94) agrees with him on this point. Hammond (1972) suggests a location for this raised area in the Athenian Theater of Dionysus.

13. See the first column of table 1 in chapter 3.

14. The structure of the speech is noticed also by Sheppard (1913), pp. 77 ff. The verbal repetitions in the speech, he concludes (p. 79), "have their effect on the dramatic value as a pious (therefore effectual, salutary) utterance, promising good on the whole, yet not without hints of evil." I agree, but think more can be said.

15. Von Fritz (1962), p. 213.

16. A similar transition from the general situation to the particular moment is marked by καὶ νῦν in the prologue of the *Agamemnon* (line 8).

17. See above, chapter 2, section "The City's Walls."

18. As the song progresses, there is some admixture of iambic and iambo-trochaic rhythm, with a very little Aeolic. But the introduction (lines 78–107), delivered as the chorus make their entrance, is entirely dochmiac except for three lines (100, 103, and 106). These are iambic and are probably recited (as opposed to spoken or sung) by the coryphaeus as he goads the rest of the chorus to ever more urgent appeals to the gods. Cf. Pickard-Cambridge (1962), p. 156.

19. Pickard-Cambridge (1962), pp. 242–43.

20. Similar, metrically, is the *epiparodos* of the *Eumenides* (lines 254 ff.), which is also astrophic and in iambic and dochmiac rhythm. There, however, the chorus deliver relatively calm trimeters at the moment of their actual entry, before they see Orestes.

21. Lines 109–50 can be made a strophic pair with emendations which, on the whole, improve the transmitted text (see the editions of Murray and Page). The contrary view is maintained by Wilamowitz (1914), p. 69, and Robert (1922), p. 161. Reasons for starting the main body of the ode at line 109 are (1) that the chorus must have reached the altar by line 127; and (2) that lines 109–50 form a unit on the basis of addresses to the gods (see figure 2 below).

22. For a possible distribution of parts, see Robert (1922), pp. 162–63.

23. With von den Bergh's emendation of line 161: παῖ Διός, ὅθεν.

24. It is worth asking whether the chorus can actually see out over the walls and view the attacking army. The Medicean scholiast comments on line 79, ταῦτα δὲ φανταζόμεναι λέγουσιν ὡς ἀληθῆ, and again on line 80, φαντάζονται δὲ ταῦτα πάντα. Nothing in the text proves that the maidens can see the Argives; even πρέποντες in line 124 could mean simply "outstanding among" and need not imply that these leaders are visible to the chorus, who might be merely imagining their appearance. Understanding the scene in this way has the advantage of making the chorus's terror more vivid: closed in and threatened, they cannot even see their danger, and their fantasy, we may suppose, outstrips the reality, grave as that is. On the other hand, the scholiast's remarks are confined to the opening lines of the song, where, even on the opposite interpretation, the chorus would not yet be able to see the Argive army and would only infer from a cloud of dust in the distance that the enemy has left the camp and is preceded (as would be normal) by the cavalry. The scholiast may have had the immediate context in mind rather than the whole ode. The care with which the attack is described step by step strongly suggests that the chorus can see it.

25. Though the text is corrupt, the meaning is clear from the Medicean scholion, and on that basis Page, following Paley, reconstructs the lines.

26. Stanford (1942, p. 22) points out that the simile in *Il.* 4.450-56 is "condensed" here. In the Homeric passage, it refers to sound heard from a distance and describes the clash of warriors in battle.

27. This is Dawson's translation of ὑπὲρ τειχέων (1970, p. 40).

28. Cf. Page's paraphrase in his *apparatus*, and Robert's explanation of this difficult line (1922, p. 168).

29. Mesk (1934), pp. 455-56.

30. Stanford (1942), pp. 106 ff. He compares *P.V.* 115. It is unnecessary to emend δέδορκα to δέδοικα, since Stanford's explanation of the ms. reading is more than satisfactory.

31. There may be a similar effect in the "persuasion scene" of the *Eumenides* (lines 778-880). There also the length of the chorus's dochmiac stanzas diminishes.

32. Pickard-Cambridge (1968, pp. 162-64) suggests that the word applies to recited iambics in symmetrical epirrhematic exchanges, which are found in all three tragedians. But he gives reasons for doubting that the trimeters in such scenes were *always* recited rather than spoken. Of the *Seven*, he says (p. 163), "it must be admitted that Eteocles' sentiments seem to demand violent speech rather than musical accompaniment." This may be correct. Still, if Eteocles' words are agreed to be vehement, why should he not deliver them in a more impassioned manner than speech—that is, recitative? That would still provide a contrast with the chorus, who *sing* in dochmiacs. This effect has been assumed in the discussion here, but it remains a suggestion, nothing more.

33. The differences between the parodos and first stasimon are treated in detail by Benardete (1967).

34. The intensity of the chorus's personal dread is underscored by the rhythm if (as is likely) lines 321-22 and 333-34 are in Ionics (see editions of Wilamowitz and Groeneboom ad loc.). If the lines are so considered, the endings of the metra and the word endings coincide consistently in lines 322 and 334 (though not in 321 and 333). For an Aeschylean example of Ionic rhythm mixed (as here) with Aeolic for particular effect (a play on Helen's name), see *Ag.* 686-98 (cf. Dale, 1968, p. 130). Ionics here would anticipate those at the beginning of the second stasimon, with which this ode corresponds structurally.

35. Benardete (1967), p. 25.

36. Regenbogen (1933), pp. 63 ff.

37. Schadewaldt (1961). It is unnecessary to postulate, as he does, a lacuna after line 676, in which Eteocles would call specifically for the rest of his arms. His action in equipping himself would be self-evident to the audience and would make description superfluous.

38. Bacon (1964), p. 36.

39. Cf. fr. 125 (Mette) of the *Danaids*, which suggests that the contrast between fruitful sexual love and destructive violence was a concern of the *Suppliants* trilogy also. The parallel would be especially striking if Aphrodite delivered those lines in defense of Hypermestra.

40. See above, chapter 2, section "Earth Imagery and Related Themes."

41. The precise meaning of the phrase τῷ κάκιστ' αὐδωμένῳ is uncertain, though it clearly refers to Polynices. The most likely possibilities are: "to him who has spoken most evilly" (Tucker); "to him who has that worst of names" (Paley); "to the one most ill reported of" (L.S.J., s.v. αὐδάω, II.3). Dawson, while granting that the phrase "probably refers immediately to Polynices," suggests that it "can clearly involve Oedipus." The juxtaposition with Οἰδίπου τέκος in the preceding line does seem significant. Polynices' imprecations, his name, and his attack on Thebes are, in fact, all symptoms of the curse. Perhaps Aeschylus intentionally made the phrase ambiguous to suggest all these meanings (and also, perhaps, a reference to Oedipus's curse). On any interpretation, the chorus are warning Eteocles not to act in accordance with the curse, like his brother and father.

42. The sense of ὀργή here also is uncertain. Though it may mean "disposition" (Medicean scholiast: τὸν τρόπον) or "zeal" (Italie), surely the main idea conveyed here is "anger." Eteocles clearly feels this emotion (lines 658–68), and it can be inferred from the spy's description of Polynices. The word in this sense shows how an irrational desire seizes men under a curse at the moment of crisis. It seems to have been common to Laius (for his ἀβουλίαι, see chapter 1, section "The Oracle Given to Laius"), Oedipus (line 781), and the latter's sons. Here, once again, we can see a regular pattern in the curse's effect. See also p. 59 above.

For an instance of ὀργή clearly in the sense "anger" and, interestingly, in association with τεθηγμένος, cf. Aesch. Supp. 186–87.

43. Cf. Astyanax's reaction to the sight of Hector in his helmet, Il. 6.466–75.

44. It may take us too far from the text to speculate whether there is a device on Eteocles' shield also, and if so what it is. Bacon (1964, p. 35) suggests a figure of the Erinys, and that would fit well with my view of the scene. Winnington-Ingram (1977, p. 19, note 40) rather diffidently proposes a picture of Dike to match the one on Polynices' shield. That would express well the complexity of the issues dividing the brothers. Yet none of the other Thebans is said to have an emblem on his shield except Hyperbius (lines 511–13), and his case is exceptional. There may thus be no point in wondering about Eteocles' shield. Even if there was a device, it must have been so obvious as to require no comment, and so we shall never know what it was.

45. This line, Seven 715, and P.V. 866 are the only instances in Aeschylus's extant plays of the forms of ἀμβλύνω. The adjective ἀμβλύς occurs once, in a sense similar to the verb in Seven 844, at Eum. 238 (Orestes' guilt worn away).

46. See above, chapter 1, section "The Oracle Given to Laius."

47. See above, chapter 3, section "Arbitration."

48. This scene has received considerable discussion in connection with the question of Eteocles' freedom of action. In particular, it is usually viewed as the moment in which he decides to face his brother. It seems more likely, however, that Eteocles has already made up his mind (if indeed there ever was any doubt of what he would do) by the end of the shield scene (lines 672–75). But I have ignored the question of freedom and necessity (see appendix 3) in order to approach the scene from a different direction.

49. For the anticipation of the Ionics here by apparently similar rhythms in lines 321-22 and 333-34, see note 34 above. There the chorus were afraid for the city in general and themselves in particular. Now the object of their fear is the brothers' fate.

50. De Romilly (1968), pp. 72-73.

51. Cf. Dawe (1963), p. 39. My remarks amplify his.

52. For discussion of this passage, see pp. 9-15, above.

53. See Tucker ad loc. "Derangement of wits" (παράνοια, line 756), like ἀβουλία in line 750, could describe the impulsive folly which resulted from the curse (see above, pp. 13-14). True, ἀρτίφρων in line 778 implies that Oedipus's error also was mental, but irrational error was evidently common, in one way or another, to all three generations of this cursed family. The word νύμφιοι, applied to Laius and his wife, is strange only if he consulted the oracle concerning childlessness, and that is unlikely. And lines 751 and 756 have the same rhythm ("paroemiac enoplion"—cf. Dale, 1968, p. 172). Reference to Laius at its beginning and end would give this strophe a clarity of shape which it would not otherwise have. For the opposite view, see Manton (1961), pp. 80-81.

54. For the thematic importance of τελεῖν, see above, pp. 52-53.

55. See above, chapter 1, subsection "Laius's Crime."

56. Of this idea, Dawe remarks, "it is not likely, but at the same time it is not impossible" (1963, p. 40). I am less skeptical, though certainty is impossible.

57. See chapter 1, section "The Symmetry of the Seven."

58. There have been innumerable attempts to mend the apparently confused ms. order of lines 803-20. It is not necessary and may not be desirable to rearrange the lines. The simplest solution is "to omit v. 804 and postulate, as Paley does, a lacuna between vv. 808 and 809" (Dawe, 1964, p. 119). Whatever solution one favors, however, one must bear in mind that every line has thematic importance, and none (except 804) should be excluded. Thus the idea of a double recension, which Murray adopts in his text, ought probably to be rejected.

59. Verrall (notes on his lines 809-16) considers these anapaests an interpolation. At the very least, however, lines 829-31 look genuine. Despite the lacuna in line 830, it can hardly be doubted that a play on the brothers' names is intended. The pun is introduced in a characteristically Aeschylean manner: for ὀρθῶς (line 829), cf. line 405; and for κατ' ἐπωνυμίαν compare not only line 405, but—more pertinent still—line 658. The significance of names, as we shall see in the next chapter, is highly important to the play.

60. In detail, the passage presents grave textual problems, but there can be no disagreement on its effect as a whole. Page's text is given here.

61. I am assuming that Antigone and Ismene do not appear. See appendix 1.

62. De Romilly (1958), p. 76: "De fait, il n'est pas rare que chant et danse prennent, dans la tragédie . . . une valeur de symbole. On dirait qu'ils expriment directement un sentiment ou une situation: en vertu d'une sorte de transposition immédiate et naturelle, ils en deviennent comme un équivalent plus concret ou plus stylisé."

63. Arist. Poet. 1447^{a}28. Cf. Pickard-Cambridge (1968), pp. 246-48.

64. A very early and vivid piece of evidence is a fragment of an unknown comedy by Aristophanes (fr. 677 Kock, Aeschylus fr. 246 Mette), where Aeschylus is made to say: τοῖσι χοροῖς αὐτὸς τὰ σχήματ᾽ ἐποίουν. Another character apparently answers in agreement, singling out the strenuous movements of the chorus in the *Phrygians* (last line of fr. 678 Kock): πολλὰ τοιαυτὶ καὶ τοιαυτὶ καὶ δεῦρο σχηματίσαντας. Athenaeus, who quotes both fragments (1.21D-F), also cites Chamaeleon's testimony that Aeschylus instructed his own choruses. Cf. also Ath. 1.22A, Plut. *Quaest. conv.* 8.9 (732F), and Pickard-Cambridge (1968), pp. 91, 250-51. The anecdote of Telestes preserved by Athenaeus (1.22A) may not be correct in assigning that dancer to Aeschylus's time. But whatever the date of Telestes or the nature of his dancing, the story may at least illustrate how memorable visual and choreographic effects could make a performance of the *Seven*.

65. Cf. Pickard-Cambridge (1968), pp. 248-49.

66. This is also the interpretation of the Medicean scholiast on lines 171-72: κλύετε πανδίκως· κλύετε ἡμῶν δικαίως εἰς οὐρανὸν ἀνεχουσῶν τὰς χεῖρας· τοῦτο δὲ τὴν ἐκ ψυχῆς ἱκετείαν δηλοῖ. Ὅμηρος· "χεῖρας ἀνασχόντες" (*Il.* 8.347). Stanford (1942, p. 61) calls χειρότονοι an Aeschylean coinage.

67. Aesch. *P.V.* 1005.

68. Cf. Pickard-Cambridge (1968), pp. 257-62; Lasserre (1967).

69. Cf. chapter 2, section "Themes Associated with the War."

CHAPTER 5

1. The central position of the fourth pair of speeches is noted also by Cameron (1970), pp. 103-104.

2. Cf. not only Hes. *Theog.* 820 ff. but also Aesch. *P.V.* 351-72.

3. Cf. especially line 516: πρὸς τῶν κρατούντων ἐσμέν, οἱ δ᾽ ἡσσωμένων.

4. Cameron (1970) stresses this aspect of the scene. As he says, "the important thing that he [Eteocles] is doing in these speeches is verbal" (p. 101). But, of course, Eteocles is also doing more. This is a contest not merely of words but of symbols and powers as well. All three, in this scene and by Aeschylean standards generally, are really identical.

5. Lines 391, 404, 425, 436, 480, 500, 538, 551. In addition, the messenger uses a related word in announcing the Argives' defeat (line 794). In this respect, as in so many others, his scene is a summation of what has gone before.

6. Aktor, for instance, in contrast to the κομπάσματα of Parthenopaeus (line 551), is ἀνὴρ ἄκομπος, χεὶρ δ᾽ ὁρᾷ τὸ δράσιμον (line 554).

7. My view of the shield devices of the first four Argives owes much to Benardete (1968), pp. 5-12, but I have filled in many details on my own. For a different and interesting interpretation of these shields, see Bacon (1964). My own approach differs from both of theirs in that it tries to connect the shield devices with the main themes of these speeches.

8. Fraenkel (1964), p. 278, note 3. He asserts that this meaning would have been self-evident to any Greek, and praises Tucker's explanation (see note 9 below).

9. Cf. Tucker's note on line 387 (his line 374): "The arrogance consists in representing himself as making the other warriors hide their diminished heads."

10. Line 387: ὑπέρφρον σῆμα; 391: ταῖς ὑπερκόμποις σαγαῖς; 404: σῆμ᾽ ὑπέρκομπον. Cf. line 410: ὑπέρφρονας λόγους.

11. For the identification of the *Eris* of Zeus (line 429) with the thunderbolt, see Fraenkel (1964), pp. 286–88.

12. *Il.* 5.801.

13. Fraenkel (1964), p. 285. Cf. also Wilamowitz (1914), p. 112. Dawson translates "a giant this one" (1970, p. 68). That makes the important point about Capaneus's *hybris* without associating Tydeus with it. Tucker's translation— "another giant this"—implies that Tydeus also might be so described, but he has not challenged Zeus. The word order too is against Tucker's version.

14. Cf. Tucker's note ad loc. (his line 368) and the Medicean scholion: τότε γὰρ μάλιστα μέμηνεν.

15. In line 445, οὐδὲν ἐξῃκασμένον ("not in image" or "incomparable") recalls προσῄκασεν of line 431. Thus if line 446 is spurious, the substance of Capaneus's boast is still evoked, and the idea of fire and heat is carried through in Eteocles' answer. Cf. Fraenkel (1964), pp. 290–92.

16. See above, chapter 2, section "Divination and Prophecy."

17. Benardete (1968), p. 8.

18. Stanford (1942), pp. 74 75

19. These lyric comments have been generally ignored, but the progress of the whole scene can really be read from them.

20. See above, chapter 2, section "Earth Imagery and Related Themes."

21. This, and not Parthenopaeus himself, is probably the reference in ἀνδρὶ τῷδε in line 544. Cf. Fraenkel (1964), p. 310.

22. For the reading βίᾳ Διός, see Dawe (1964), pp. 152–54.

23. See above, pp. 40–41.

24. Cf. Bacon (1964), p. 27: What distinguishes Amphiaraus from the first five Argives on the one hand and from Polynices on the other is that "he does not need either the mask of terror which would disguise his helplessness, or the mask of virtue which would disguise his desires."

25. This is the first mention of an Erinys since line 70—a sure sign that the scope of the play is narrowing and that the implications of the curse will soon be made explicit.

26. See above, chapter 2, section "Earth Imagery and Related Themes."

27. Cameron (1970), p. 106.

28. See above, pp. 34–35.

29. In line 604, the pious man is said to perish with the crew—ἀνδρῶν σὺν θεοπτύστῳ γένει. Later (lines 653–54, 691), Eteocles describes his own family, which has endangered Thebes, in similar terms. The thematic repetition reinforces the contrast between his position and that of Amphiaraus.

30. Most editors (but not Page) retain line 619. Fraenkel (1964, pp. 317–20) rejects it in spite of Aeschylean parallels. The only objection to the line is the apparent vagueness of the subject of the verb. It can hardly be Amphiaraus, but I

see no difficulty in understanding it as Apollo. The meaning in that case, asserts Fraenkel, is "geradezu absurd." But surely the line implies that when the god speaks he should be attended to. On Eteocles' lips these words have special point: to his own cost he fails to draw the lesson for himself.

For a defense of the line on different grounds, cf. Erbse (1964), pp. 15-17.

31. A verbal echo stresses both the similarity between Eteocles' and Amphiaraus's situations and the way Eteocles is finally driven to a more extreme attitude. Tydeus, accusing Amphiaraus of cowardice, has said that he "fawns upon fate" (σαίνειν μόρον, line 383). Eteocles himself defends the seer from this charge in predicting that he will not fight (lines 615-19), though Amphiaraus has expressed his readiness for battle (line 589). Later, when Eteocles rejects the chorus's advice to avoid combat, he uses Tydeus's expression (line 704): τί οὖν ἔτ᾽ ἂν σαίνοιμεν ὀλέθριον μόρον; His language reflects a martial frenzy like that of Tydeus. It is far more violent than the seer's resolve. Each forsees his own death. But Amphiaraus can hope for honor, while Eteocles is simply desperate.

32. Cf. Moreau (1976—this article appeared while the present work was under revision). Moreau also sees Amphiaraus as both mirror and foil to Eteocles. His view (which I cannot accept) that the seer serves also as a mouthpiece for the poet, assigning blame to Polynices and leaving Eteocles guiltless, is a separate point.

33. Chase (1902), pp. 69-70.

34. Cameron (1970, pp. 107-108) suggests that Eteocles might have played on the double meaning of κατάγειν as not only "lead back home" but also "lead down" to the underworld. In the final settlement of their quarrel, justice does in fact "lead down" both brothers. In this sense, the emblem *is* ominous.

35. In spite of the problems of text and interpretation in these lines, Amphiaraus clearly is manipulating Polynices' name. For an explanation, see Lesky (1955).

36. Cf. Hes. *Op.* 256, of which this line may be an echo: ἡ δέ τε παρθένος ἐστι Δίκη, Διὸς ἐκγεγαυῖα. The word play, unmistakable here, is characteristic of Hesiod's treatment of names.

37. Lesky (1972), p. 92.

38. Kitto (1950), p. 50.

39. Cameron (1970), p. 109.

40. Benardete (1968), p. 17.

41. The one possible exception is very doubtful. There is no need to transpose lines 547 ff. to follow line 537, or to delete line 549. Cf. Fraenkel (1964), pp. 306-308.

42. See above, chapter 3, section "*Moira* and Death."

43. Wolff (1958), Patzer (1958), and Lesky (1961) also maintain that Eteocles has no control over the process which pairs him with his brother. But they go on to assign him a share in the guilt for the fratricide. The extent of his personal responsibility for this act is not an important question of the play, in my view. See appendix 3 below.

44. Cf. Croiset (1965), p. 106. The absence of such a confrontation is probably attributable to something more basic to the play than (as Croiset suggests) the

lack, at the time of the *Seven*'s production, of a third actor. Or at least Aeschylus turned this deficiency in resources enormously to advantage.

45. E.g., Schadewaldt (1961, pp. 115-16) tentatively suggests that Megareus, who is described as "holding his boast in his hands" (line 473), actually appears carrying a huge spear.

46. E.g., by Wilamowitz (1914), pp. 75-76; Dawe (1963), p. 35.

47. The demonstrative τόνδε in lines 408 and 472 does not prove the warriors' presence. The first is easily emended, and the authenticity of line 472 is doubtful. In any case ὅδε can be used of someone who is absent but present to one's thoughts. It is applied to the Argives several times, and they cannot be visible (e.g., lines 395, 470, 553; cf. 404, of Tydeus's shield device). The frequent use of πέμπω could conceivably imply that the champions are present, but it is just as likely that Aeschylus used both it and ὅδε for vividness.

On the other hand, the arguments of Fraenkel (1964, pp. 276-77) against the champions' presence, though weighty, are not decisive: (1) that the chorus do not mention them in describing the manner of the spy's and Eteocles' entrance, lines 369-74 (why should they, when what strikes them as remarkable is that the two speaking characters arrive simultaneously and at such speed?); and (2) that Eteocles never addresses any of the warriors directly in the second person throughout the scene (but there is no need for him to do so; if these mute characters are present, it matters only that they should be visible).

48. It would probably have the effect described by Bacon (1964, pp. 37-38, note 7): "As the seven gates have seven attackers with seven shield devices we can expect to *see* on stage the seven defenders with their seven shields, each one claiming the protection of one of the seven gods whose statues stand on the stage." But this is tangential to the main effect of the scene.

49. The verbs in the future tense which Eteocles uses of himself in lines 672 and 675, since they do not signify sending, placing, or the like, are not pertinent to the question of when he makes the assignments and will be discussed a little later. The present ἔστιν in line 553 is usually left out of account, since it can signify either completed action or an immediate situation. Line 472, with its optative, raises such grave difficulties of text and interpretation that it is probably best rejected and will be ignored here.

50. Wolff (1958, p. 93) asserts that the futures imply "'ich werde ihm gegenüber stellen,' d.h. 'er wird ihm gegenüber stehen' (der gültige Akt der Auswahl ist aber schon getroffen)." Similarly, Erbse (1964, p. 6) thinks that they signify "ich will deine Mahnung mit folgender Disposition beantworten." See also Otis (1960), pp. 159-60.

51. Kirkwood (1969, p. 13) maintains that the past tenses "indicate the readiness with which Eteocles can match . . . defender for attacker," and so that Eteocles' determination to face Polynices "is a deliberate and rational choice . . . and . . . a reasonable *ad hominem* selection, just as all the other selections have been emphasized as being." See also von Fritz (1962), pp. 201-206.

52. Wilamowitz (1914), p. 76; Lesky (1961), pp. 6-9.

53. Lesky (1961), p. 9.

54. Dawe (1963), p. 37. The weakness of this position is evident when he says that Aeschylus "has contrived to make his audience believe two mutually exclusive things, because it improves the play when they do so." If Aeshcylus had tried this, I should think, he would have managed only to exasperate his audience.

55. See appendix 3 below.

56. That is why Aeschylus has Eteocles say (line 408), "I shall station" Melanippus at the first gate, and shortly thereafter, "Justice is sending him." This seems more plausible than saying that Aeschylus in this way is trying to offset necessity by injecting an element of "free will" (Dawe, 1963, p. 37, note 1).

57. See above, p. 121.

58. For Borecký's assertion that λαγχάνειν and related words always carried some of their literal meaning in the fifth century B.C., see above, chapter 3, section "Lot Imagery in the Play."

59. Cf. Hymn. Hom. Merc. 127–29, 550 ff. (though the latter passage is of doubtful interpretation); Ar. Peace 364–66, with scholiast; the Souda s.v. κλῆρος Ἑρμοῦ; Poll. 6.55. See also Ehrenberg in R.-E. 26.1452–53 (s.v. "Losung").

60. See above, chapter 3, section "Cleromancy."

61. For this development, see Knox (1957), pp. 164–68, 176–81. Cf. Gould (1970), pp. 26–27. Both show how, in Sophocles' Oedipus Tyrannus, Oedipus is induced to see chance as haphazard but later discovers to his sorrow that the gods have carefully shaped his own life. A similar pattern can be found in the shield scene of the Seven. At first the matches of the champions seem a series of wonderful coincidences which portend victory. Only with the final set of speeches does Eteocles discover that they are all aimed at himself and Polynices.

62. Archil. 16 (West); Pind. fr. 21 (Bowra; from Paus. 7.26.8). Both of these are cited by Knox.

63. E.g., Pers. 345–46, 601–602; Ag. 661–66, 1275–76, 1660; Cho. 138–39, 212–13, 783–88; P.V. 272, 375–76, 769 (cf. συμφορά, 758). In P.V., in fact, Prometheus often alludes to the sufferings with which Zeus has afflicted him as τύχαι, and does so even when he explicitly says that they are all fated and that he knows them in advance (line 106).

64. Seven 417, 422, 481–82, 625, 626–27. An indication of the identity of tyche with divine will is that whereas the messenger begs tyche not to accomplish Capaneus's threats in line 426, he later, in a nearly identical line (549), prays the gods not to fulfill those of Parthenopaeus. On the authenticity of line 549, see note 41 above.

65. The authenticity of line 520 cannot be in serious doubt. On the whole question of lines 515–20, see Fraenkel (1964), pp. 302–304.

66. Cf. κυρεῶ, line 401, and line 23, ἐκ θεῶν κυρεῖ. For a similar use of τυγχάνειν, see Hdt. 5.33.2: "Since it was not fated (καὶ οὐ γὰρ ἔδεε) for the Naxians to be destroyed by this expedition, the following incident befell (συνηνείχθη γενέσθαι). When Megabates was making the rounds of the sentries on the ships, it happened that no one was on guard aboard a Myndian vessel (ἔτυχε οὐδεὶς φυλάσσων). . . ."

67. Verrall (note on his line 493) proposes that χρεία, in conjunction with

ἐξιστορῆσαι, suggests the consultation of an oracle. If so, that would relate these words to the other kinds of prophecy and divination in this scene.

68. If the present tense in line 553 means that Eteocles makes his fifth gate assignment only at that moment, he there selects Aktor over Lasthenes. But since, as he makes clear, Aktor is the better choice for that position, and Lasthenes turns out to be the appropriate defender of the sixth gate, my point is not affected.

69. Eteocles' speech in the fourth exchange, which contains the language so strongly suggestive of the lot, also contains the two verbs in the aorist tense (lines 505, 508). Thus Aeschylus must have intended even the matches which involve Thebans assigned to gates before the scene to be connected with the lot.

70. Another indication that the lot in this scene is divinely guided is that lines 689-91, which, as was argued above, allude to allotment as the means by which the seventh match has been made, stress the role of divinity (689) and the hatefulness of the family to Apollo (691). Eteocles, who delivers these lines, evidently understands perfectly how his ruin has been concocted.

71. One minor way in which Aeschylus makes the matches seem more spontaneous (but for the reason I have suggested in the text) is that direct references to the lot cease after the fourth pair of speeches. Of Parthenopaeus and Amphiaraus, the spy says only that they have been "stationed" at the fifth and sixth gates (προσταχθέντα, line 527; τεταγμένος, line 570), and he uses no verb of placing at all in the case of Polynices. Yet surely all three have been assigned their positions by lot.

72. Cf. Wolff (1958), p. 93. He argues that Eteocles has made all his gate assignments before the start of the scene, and asserts that the human mechanism through which the gods contrive the matches is allotment. He refers to the lot almost in passing, however, and in the context of a discussion of Eteocles' freedom of choice in relation to necessity.

APPENDIX 1

1. See the bibliography given by Lloyd-Jones (1959). This comprehensive article covers most of the arguments made up to that date. The following discussions of the problem can now be added: Pötscher (1958); Fraenkel, "Zum Schluss der *Sieben gegen Theben*" (1964); Golden (1966), pp. 56-60; Dawe (1967), who, along with Fraenkel, answers Lloyd-Jones; Nicolaus (1967); Cameron (1968); Kirkwood (1969), pp. 23-25; Dawson (1970), introduction, pp. 22-26; Lesky (1972), p. 97; Brown (1976).

2. Bergk (1884), pp. 303-304.

3. For similarities in form and meter between the two passages, see Fraenkel (1961), pp. 133-35, and Lesky (1972), p. 94.

4. Cf. Wilamowitz's study of lines 961-1004 (1903, pp. 442-45).

5. For other parallels, see Klotz (1917-18), pp. 619-20.

6. This sense of the word is not attested until the fourth century. But ἐπιγίγνεται means "comes into being later" or "succeeds" at *Il.* 6.148, and in Herodotus the participle several times is used in the sense "those born later" (7.2.2, 7.3.3., 9.85.3).

7. This should answer Cameron's objection that this meaning is "not particularly apposite. We should like an interpretation more closely connected with the themes and plot of the *Seven*" (1968, p. 251).

8. Wilamowitz (1903), pp. 439-40.

9. Kirkwood (1969), p. 25.

10. See above, chapter 1, section "The Shaping of the Story."

11. See Nicolaus's detailed examination of these passages (1967, pp. 15-29, 59-84).

12. Dawson, for example, points to the "felicity of the final picture" in lines 1075-78 (1970, p. 25).

13. See Fraenkel's criticisms of the language in these lines ("Zum Schluss der *Sieben gegen Theben*, 1964, pp. 58-59); cf. Nicolaus (1967), pp. 15-29. Pötscher defends the lines (1958, pp. 143-47).

14. Cf. Wundt (1906), pp. 367-68.

15. Lloyd-Jones (1959, pp. 94-95) cites fifth-century uses of πρόβουλοι with the genitive in the nontechnical sense of "persons to take counsel on behalf of."

16. Nicolaus (1967), p. 49.

17. Lloyd-Jones's suggestion (1959, p. 98) that Antigone intends to carry the body away and bury it in the earth is sufficiently met by Dawe (1967), pp. 22 ff.

18. Brown (1976) has proposed that lines 861-74 are spurious and that the sisters do not appear; that Antigone's speech and the succeeding stichomythia (lines 1026-53) are an interpolation under the influence of Sophocles; but that the rest of the closing scene is genuine. The herald would thus exit "briskly" at the end of his speech (line 1025), and in his absence half the chorus would then defy the order he has relayed. Arranged this way, the scene would still be pointless and inept.

19. Hecht and Bacon (1973, pp. 7-8) assert that the closing scene "is integrated with the entire design of the play." They support this statement with only the most general indications of how they conceive that design. My own study has led me to just the opposite conclusion. Cf. Nicolaus (1967), pp. 85-92, who argues on the basis of the main themes (as he views them) that the ending is incompatible with the rest of the play.

APPENDIX 2

1. E.g., Hiltbrunner (1950); Goheen (1951); Blaiklock (1955); Knox (1957); Long (1958); Murray (1958); and Lebeck (1971).

2. E.g., D.W. Lucas, *CR* 72 (1958), pp. 229-32 (review of Knox); William M. Calder, III, *CW* 52 (1959), pp. 221-22 (review of Murray); H. Lloyd-Jones, *JHS* 92 (1972), pp. 193-95 (review of Lebeck). They are not all critical in general of the works reviewed, but they do raise questions about the method.

3. Cf. Italie's *Index* (1964). The percentages for all seven plays are given in table 2. I have been rather broad in my understanding of "figurative," but have tried to apply it consistently to all the plays. Thus although others might obtain different *numbers* of occurrences from mine, the *percentages* probably would not vary significantly.

The following words were investigated in connection with nautical imagery:

(a) ship and its parts: ἐρετμόν, θεωρίς, ναῦς, οἴαξ, πίτυλος, πλοῖον, πρύμνα, πρύμνηθεν, πρυμνήτης, πρῷρα, σέλμα, σκάφος.

(b) sailors and their activities: ἀντηρέτης, ἐρέσσω, ἐρέτης, ναυκληρέω, ναύκληρος, ναύστολος, ναύτης, ναυτικός, ναυτιλος, οἰακονόμος, οἰακοστρόφος.

(c) sea and water: ἀντλέω, ἄντλος, ἀπαντλέω, ἀποστέγω, ἀφρός, θάλασσα, κατακλύζω, καχλάζω, κλύδων, κλυδώνιον, κλύζω, κῦμα, πεδίον, πολύρροθος, πόντιος, πόντος, ῥεῦμα, ῥέω, ῥοθιάς, ῥόθιον, σταλαγμός, στέγω, τρικυμία.

(d) wind and weather: ἄνεμος, εὐδία, καταιγίζω, οὐριζω, οὔριος, οὐριοστάτης, οὖρος, πνεῦμα, πνέω, πνοή, τροπαία, φορέω.

(e) also: ἐκβολή.

4. Similarly, the word occurs nine times in the *Agamemnon* and eight or nine in the *Suppliants* (there is a textual problem in line 834). In the latter, every use refers to the ship of the sons of Aegyptus. Eight times in the *Agamemnon* it is used of the vessels in the expedition to Troy or of those wrecked on the way home. The ninth occurrence (line 897) is in a series of rapidly shifting figures of speech, where there is no question of sustained imagery. This is the only figurative use of the word in Aeschylus's complete extant plays outside the *Seven*.

5. E.g., καταιγίζω, line 63; καχλάζω, lines 115, 761; φορέω, lines 362, 819; ἀντηρέτης, lines 283, 595, 992; εὐδία, line 795.

6. E.g., ἀφρός, line 60 (used of blood at *Eum.* 183). In the same passage, σταλαγμος (line 61) could refer to a drop of any liquid, and πεδίον (line 60) to the actual plain before Thebes. But the context also suggests a picture of the wind causing the sea to foam, πεδία being the equivalent of *aequor* and σταλαγμοῖς the drops of foam on the surface of the water (see chapter 2, section "The Nautical Imagery," and Tucker's note ad loc.). Not only does ἀφρός color these words in this way, but the parallel is also explicitly drawn in lines 63–64 (especially the phrase κῦμα χερσαῖον στρατοῦ), following the comparison of Eteocles to a ship's helmsman. The words in question thus have both a literal and a figurative sense. By contrast, σταλαγμός is used of drops of blood at *Eum.* 247, and of poison at *Eum.* 783 and 813; and elsewhere in the complete plays πεδίον is used only of a literal plain. Cf., however, fr. 237 (Mette): δελφινοφόρον πεδίον πόντου/διαμειψαμέναι—from the *Nereids*, where this usage is appropriate. The passage cited from the *Seven* differs in implicitly likening an actual plain to the surface of the sea.

7. These are the words studied:

(a) earth and sowing: αἶα, ἄλοξ, ἄρουρα, βαθύχθων, γαῖα, γάιος, γῆ, παλαίχθων, πέδον, πιαίνω, σπείρω, χθών.

(b) plants, growth, and reaping: ἄδρεπτος, ἀμάω, βλαστάνω, βλαστέω, βλάστημα, βλαστημός, δρέπομαι, ἐκκαρπίζομαι, ἐξαμάω, θέρος, καρπός, καρπόω, πικρόκαρπος, ῥίζα, ῥίζωμα, σπαρτός.

(c) nurture: ἀλδαίνω, μήτηρ, μητρόθεν, παιδεία, τρέφω, τροφεῖα, τροφεύς, τροφή, τροφός.

8. E.g., πικρόκαρπος, line 693; παιδεία, line 18 (of the earth bringing up the Thebans); δρέπομαι, line 718 (but cf. ἄδρεπτος, *Supp.* 663, in a similar figurative use, and νεόδρεπτος, *Supp.* 334, and νεόδροπος, *Supp.* 354, both literal. Some

compound adjective from δρέπω may be used figuratively at *Seven* 333, but the reading is very doubtful).

9. Παμμῆτόρ τε γῆ. This occurs in Prometheus's invocation of the elements, and it is natural for him to call the earth the "universal mother." At *P.V.* 209–10, Gaia is Prometheus's own genealogical mother, and in the play no strong distinction is felt between her elemental and her anthropomorphic nature. There is a marked difference between this way of speaking and saying that the *Theban* earth is the mother and nurse of the *Thebans* and that the latter are plants sprung from her sowing. At *Prom.* 90 and in the *Seven*, figurative language is associated with the earth, but only in the *Seven* can one speak of it as imagery.

10. I.e., ἀποτίνω, ἐγγύη, ἐκπράσσω, ἐκτίνω, καπηλεύω, κέρδος, ὀφείλω, πιστός, τεκνόομαι, τίκτω, τίνω, φερέγγυος, χρέος.

11. Figures for words for "inside" and "outside" are given in note 26 to chapter 2, and for language of allotment in note 62 to chapter 3.

12. Cf. John Peradotto, *CW* 66 (1972), pp. 167–68 (review of Lebeck), who gives a general defense of this approach to ancient poetry.

APPENDIX 3

1. Concerning these questions there have been almost as many opinions as writers on the *Seven*, and to cite all the discussions would be to list very nearly the full bibliography for the play. The following might be considered a representative selection.

The Opfertod theory sought to affirm the unity of Eteocles' character by depicting him as the "ideal commander" throughout the play. This view is clearly outlined by Klotz (1917–18), though he did not originate it. This theory has not been widely accepted, but it has found modern adherents, such as Kirkwood (1969), though he never uses the term *Opfertod*. Dawe (1963, pp. 31–42) marshals what are probably the strongest arguments for the theory, though they are not finally convincing. Lesky (1961, pp. 5–6) argues strongly against the theory. The Opfertod theory seems to me right in stressing that the city is freed from danger by the death of the brothers; I should say that it errs in confusing this result with Eteocles' intentions.

Solmsen (1937) emphasized the role of the curse in the play, though his view of Eteocles' character was influenced by the Opfertod theory. Other scholars, in spite of variations of opinion on details, have come to a general agreement that Eteocles' "decision" to stand against Polynices is the product at once of his own resolve and of his situation. The basic position was formulated by Regenbogen (1933). More recently, Wolff (1958) tried to demonstrate that Eteocles makes his gate assignments before the start of the shield scene and so has only limited freedom of action; and Patzer (1958) built on Wolff's and Solmsen's conclusions to distinguish three stages in Eteocles' understanding of the curse in the progress of the play. Lesky (1961, 1966) put the matter into a new perspective by arguing that Eteocles, like Agamemnon and Orestes, is placed in a situation where he must perform an abhorrent act, but that in accepting this responsibility he comes to desire the deed passionately and to make it his own. In general accord with all of these is the study of von Fritz (1962) who, however, adds many interesting points of his own. Though all these views take account of the curse, they still stress Eteocles' character—excessively, I would argue.

The general problem of the play's coherence is addressed by Otis (1960). He too concentrates on the figure of Eteocles.

Far less admiring appraisals of Eteocles than any of the above are given by Golden (1964) and Podlecki (1964). Golden, indeed, denies the importance of the curse and sees the brothers' quarrel as a squabble over property, the play as a condemnation of the use of force to settle disputes. Why Aeschylus would choose to throw dust in his spectators' eyes by stressing a curse is left unexplained.

2. Arist. *Poet.*, especially 1450^a20-25. For a discussion of this and related passages of the *Poetics*, see Jones (1962), chapter 1 (pp. 11-62). Similarly, A. M. Dale, in her edition of Euripides' *Alcestis* (Oxford, 1954), condemns "our inveterate modern habit of regarding a drama almost exclusively in terms of its character," and speaks instead of "the trend of the action and the rhetoric of the situation" (introduction, pp. xxiv-xxv). Cf. also Easterling (1973). Dawe's revival of "Tychoismus" reaches the same general conclusion from a somewhat different viewpoint.

It is, then, difficult to accept Kitto's statement that "the *Septem* is our earliest tragedy of character, Eteocles the first Man of the European stage" (1950, p. 54)—an opinion that has been echoed often in one way or another (e.g., by von Fritz, 1962, p. 193).

3. See above, p. 95, with note 36 to chapter 4.

4. One of the unfortunate results of excessive concentration on Eteocles is a search for nobility in his character and a simultaneous tendency to view Polynices as the villain of the play. For arguments against this, see pp. 20-21, above.

5. I have in mind Patzer's theory of stages in Eteocles' understanding of the curse (see note 1 above), which may be disputed not only on specific points but more generally because of its emphasis on the person of Eteocles. The crucial point is not what *Eteocles* may or may not know, but how much of the true situation the *spectators* are allowed to see. Even though they must have known about the curse from the other two plays of the trilogy, they are not made aware that it has contrived the brothers' duel, and how it has done so, until the end of the shield scene.

6. Soph. *O.C.* 521-23, 960-1002.

7. "Oedipus must defend himself, and as an Athenian he speaks as if he were pleading before that solemn court Creon invoked, the Areopagus, the ancestral Athenian place of judgment for cases of murder . . . [his defense] is a plea which the Areopagus could admit. He killed his father and married his mother in ignorance, not voluntarily. . . . The speech is intended to justify him before the high court of the city which has adopted him; and it succeeds" (Knox, 1966, pp. 157-58). Cf. also *O.C.* 547-48.

8. Cf. Lesky (1961), p. 15: "Was von aussen über ihn verhängt ist, das wird zu seiner persönlichen Schuld, weil er das Notwendige in seinen eigenen Willen hineinnimmt, weil er das, was er tun muss, schliesslich auch zu tun begehrt." Thus Eteocles becomes "ein Frevler." On Eteocles' guilt, see also Patzer (1958), p. 114.

9. It should be stressed that the argument made here does not imply an attitude that Aeschylus is uninteresting as a thinker (as some have maintained). The point is rather that he did not think in the manner or in the terms to which we are accustomed today.

Bibliography

An asterisk [*] marks words which deal particularly with the *Seven Against Thebes*. Journal abbreviations are those of *L'Année Philologique*.

Arnott, P. *Greek Scenic Conventions in the Fifth Century B.C.* (Oxford, 1962).

*Bacon, H. "The Shield of Eteocles." *Arion* 3 (no. 3, 1964):27-38.

Baldry, H. C. "The Dramatization of the Theban Legend." *G&R* 25 (1956):24-37.

Beauchet, L. *Histoire du droit privé de la republique Athénienne*. Vol. 3 (Paris, 1897).

*Benardete, S. "Two Notes on Aeschylus' *Septem*." Part 1: *WS* n.f. 1 (1967): 22-30; Part 2, *WS* n.f. 2 (1968):5-17.

Bergk, T. *Griechische Literaturgeschichte*. Vol. 3 (Berlin, 1884).

Blaiklock, E. M. "The Nautical Imagery of Euripides' *Medea*." *CPh* 50 (1955): 233-37.

Bonner, R. J. "The Institution of Athenian Arbitrators." *CP* 11 (1916):191-95.

*Borecky, B. "Bemerkungen am Rande des Bruderstreites in den *Sieben gegen Theben*." In *Antiquitas Graeco-Romana ac Tempora Nostra* (Prague, 1968), pp. 263-67.

*Brown, A.L. "The End of the *Seven Against Thebes*." *CQ* 70 (n.s. 26, 1976): 206-16.

*Burnett, A. "Curse and Dream in Aeschylus' *Septem*." *GRBS* 14 (1973):343-68.

*Caldwell, R. "The Misogyny of Eteocles." *Arethusa* 6 (1973):197-231.

*Cameron, H. D. "The Debt to Earth in the *Seven Against Thebes*." *TAPA* 95 (1964):1-8.

*———. " 'Epigoni' and the Law of Inheritance in Aeschylus' *Septem*." *GRBS* 9 (1968):247-57.

*———. "The Power of Words in the *Seven Against Thebes*." *TAPA* 101 (1970): 95-118.

*———. *Studies on the Seven Against Thebes of Aeschylus* (The Hague, 1971).

*Campbell, A. Y. "Aeschylus, *Septem* 12-13." *CR* 45 (1931):5-6.

*———. "More about Aeschylus, *Septem* 10-20." *CR* 45 (1931):115-17.

Chase, G. H. "The Shield Devices of the Greeks." *HSCP* 13 (1902):61-127.

Croiset, M. *Eschyle*. 3rd ed. (Paris, 1965).

Dale, A. M. "Seen and Unseen on the Greek Stage: A Study in Scenic Conventions." *WS* 69 (1956):96-106. Reprinted in her *Collected Papers* (Cambridge, 1969), pp. 119-29.

———. *The Lyric Metres of Greek Drama*. 2nd ed. (Cambridge, 1968).

Dawe, R. D. "Inconsistency of Plot and Character in Aeschylus." *PCPhS* 189 (1963):21-62.

————. *The Collation and Investigation of the Manuscripts of Aeschylus* (Cambridge, 1964).

*————. "The End of the *Seven Against Thebes.*" *CQ* 61 (n.s. 17, 1967):16-28.

*Dawson, C. M. *The Seven Against Thebes by Aeschylus.* Prentice-Hall Greek Drama Series (Englewood Cliffs, N.J., 1970).

*Delcourt, M. "Le rôle du choeur dans les *Sept devant Thèbes.*" *AC* 1 (1932): 25-33.

Dumortier, J. *Les images dans la poésie d'Eschyle* (Paris, 1935).

Easterling, P.E. "Presentation of Character in Aeschylus." *G&R* 20 (1973):3-19.

*Engelmann, H. "Der Schiedsrichter aus der Fremde." *RhM* 110 (1967):97-102.

*Erbse, H. "Interpretationsprobleme in den *Septem* des Aischylos." *Hermes* 92 (1964):1-22.

Farnell, L. R. *Cults of the Greek States.* Vol. 5 (Oxford, 1909).

Fine, J. V. A. *Horoi* (*Hesperia* Supp. 9, 1951).

Finley, M. I. "Alienability of Land in Ancient Greece." In *The Use and Abuse of History* (New York, 1975), pp. 153-60.

Flacelière, R. *Greek Oracles.* Translated by Douglas Garman (New York, 1965).

*Fowler, B. H. "The Imagery of the *Seven Against Thebes.*" *SO* 45 (1970):24-37.

Fraenkel, E. *Aeschylus' "Agamemnon."* 3 vols. (Oxford, 1950).

*————. "Zu Aeschylus *Septem* 4-8." *MH* 18 (1961):37 (*Kleine Beitr.* 1:263).

————. "Aeschylea." *MH* 18 (1961):131-35 (*Kleine Beitr.* 1:265-71).

*————. "Zum Schluss der *Sieben gegen Theben.*" *MH* 21 (1964):58-64.

*————. "Die sieben Redepaare im Thebanerdrama des Aeschylus." *Kleine Beiträge zur klassischen Philologie* 1 (Rome, 1964): 273-328 (*Sitzungsber. der Bayern. Akad.* [1957] Heft 3).

————. "Der Einzug des Chors im *Prometheus.*" *Kleine Beitr.* 1 (1964):389-406 (*Annali della Scuola Norm. Sup. di Pisa,* Series 2, 23 [1954] :269-84).

*Fritz, K. von. "Die Gestalt des Eteokles in Aeschylus' *Sieben gegen Theben.*" In *Antike und moderne Tragödie* (Berlin, 1962), pp. 193-226.

Goheen, R. F. *The Imagery of Sophocles' Antigone* (Princeton, 1951).

*Golden, L. "The Character of Eteocles and the Meaning of the *Septem.*" *CP* 59 (1964):79-89.

————. *In Praise of Prometheus* (Chapel Hill, 1966).

Gould, T. *Oedipus the King by Sophocles.* Prentice-Hall Greek Drama Series (Englewood Cliffs, N.J., 1970).

*Groeneboom, P. *Aeschylus' Zeven tegen Thebe* (Groningen, 1938).

Guiraud, P. *La propriété foncière en Grèce* (Paris, 1893).

Haldane, J. A. "Musical Themes and Imagery in Aeschylus." *JHS* 85 (1965): 33-41.

Hammond, N. G. L. "The Conditions of Dramatic Production to the Death of Aeschylus." *GRBS* 13 (1972):387-450.

*Hecht, A., and Bacon, H. *Seven Against Thebes* (Oxford, 1973).

Hiltbrunner, O. *Wiederholungs- und Motivtechnik bei Aischylos* (Berne, 1950).

Howe, T. P. "Taboo in the Oedipus Theme." *TAPA* 93 (1962):124–43.

Huxley, G. L. *Greek Epic Poetry* (Cambridge, Mass., 1969).

Italie, G. *Index Aeschyleus.* 2nd ed. (Leiden, 1964).

Jones, John. *On Aristotle and Greek Tragedy* (London, 1962).

*Kirkwood, G. M. "Eteocles *Oiakostrophos.*" *Phoenix* 23 (1969):9–25.

Kitto, H. D. F. *Greek Tragedy.* 2nd ed. (London, 1950).

*Klotz, O. "Zu Aischylos thebanischer Tetralogie." *RhM* 72 (1917–18):616–25.

Knox, B. M. W. *Oedipus at Thebes* (New Haven, 1957).

——. *The Heroic Temper: Studies in Sophoclean Tragedy* (Berkeley, 1966).

*Kohl, R. "Zum Schluss von Aischylos *Sieben gegen Theben.*" *Philologus* 76 (1920):208–13.

Lasserre, F. "Mimésis et mimique." *Dioniso* 41 (1967):245–63.

Lebeck, A. *The Oresteia: A Study in Language and Structure* (Cambridge, Mass., 1971).

*Lesky, A. "Aischylos, *Septem* 576 ff." In *Studi in Onore di G. Funaioli* (Rome, 1955), pp. 163–69.

*——. "Eteokles in den *Sieben gegen Theben.*" *WS* 74 (1961):5–17.

——, "Decision and Responsibility in the Tragedy of Aeschylus." *JHS* 86 (1966):78–85.

——. *Die tragische Dichtung der Hellenen.* 3rd ed. (Göttingen, 1972).

Levy, H. L. "Property Distribution by Lot in Present Day Greece." *TAPA* 87 (1956):42–46.

Lewis, N. "Solon's Agrarian Legislation." *AJP* 62 (1941):144–56.

*Lloyd-Jones, H. "The End of the *Seven Against Thebes.*" *CQ* 53, (n.s. 9, 1959): 80–115.

——. *The Justice of Zeus* (Berkeley, 1971).

Lobel, E. *Oxyrhynchus Papyri.* Vol. XX (London, 1952).

Long, H. S. "Notes on Aeschylus' *Prometheus Bound.*" *Proc. Amer. Phil. Soc.* 102 (1958):229–80.

*Manton, G. R. "The Second Stasimon of the *Seven Against Thebes.*" *BICS* 8 (1961):77–84.

Méautis, G. *Eschyle et la trilogie.* 7th ed. (Paris, 1936).

*Mesk, J. "Die Parodos der *Sieben gegen Theben.*" *Philologus* 89 (1934):454–59.

Mette, H. J. *Die Fragmente der Tragödien des Aischylos* (Berlin, 1959).

——. *Der verlorene Aischylos* (Berlin, 1963).

*Moreau, A. "Fonction du personnage d'Amphiaraos dans les 'Sept contre Thèbes'." *BAGB* (1976) no. 2:158–81.

*Mühll, P. von der. "Der Zweikampf der Oidipussöhne im dritten Epeisodion der *Septem.*" *MH* 21 (1964):225–27.

Murray, G. *Aeschylus, the Creator of Tragedy* (Oxford, 1940).

——. *Aeschyli Septem Quae Supersunt Tragoediae.* 2nd ed. (Oxford, 1955).

Murray, R. D. *The Motif of Io in Aeschylus' Suppliants* (Princeton, 1958).

Nes, D. van. *Die maritime Bildersprache bei Aischlos* (Groningen, 1963).

*Nicolaus, P. *Die Frage nach der Echtheit der Schlussszene von Aischylos' Sieben gegen Theben* (diss. Tübingen, 1967).

*Otis, B. "The Unity of the *Seven Against Thebes.*" *GRBS* 3 (1960):153–74.

Owen, E. T. *The Harmony of Aeschylus* (Toronto, 1952).

Page, D. *Aeschyli Septem Quae Supersunt Tragoediae* (Oxford, 1972).

Paley, F. A. *The Tragedies of Aeschylus*. 3rd ed. (London, 1870).

Parke, H. W. *Greek Oracles* (London, 1967).

——. *The Oracles of Zeus* (Oxford, 1967).

Parke, H. W., and Wormell, D. E. W. *The Delphic Oracle*. 2 vols. (Oxford, 1956).

*Patzer, H. "Die dramatische Handlung der *Sieben gegen Theben.*" *HSCP* 63 (1958):97–119.

*Petre, Z. "Thèmes dominants et attitudes politiques dans les *Sept contre Thèbes* d'Eschyle." *Stud. Clas.* 13 (1971):15–28.

Pickard-Cambridge, A. W. *The Theatre of Dionysus in Athens* (Oxford, 1946).

——. *The Dramatic Festivals of Athens*. 2nd ed. (Oxford, 1968).

*Platt, A. "The Last Scene of the *Seven Against Thebes.*" *CR* 26 (1912):141–44.

*Podlecki, A. J. "The Character of Eteocles in Aeschylus' *Septem.*" *TAPA* 95 (1964):283–99.

——. "Reconstructing an Aeschylean Trilogy." *BICS* 22 (1975):1–19.

*Pötscher, W. "Zum Schluss der *Sieben gegen Theben.*" *Eranos* 56 (1958):140–54.

*Regenbogen, O. "Bemerkungen zu den *Sieben* des Aischylos." *Hermes* 68 (1933):51–69.

Reinhardt, K. *Aischylos als Regisseur und Theologe* (Berne, 1949).

Rivier, A. "Eschyle et le tragique." *EL* 6 (1963):73–112.

——. "Remarques sur le nécessaire et la nécessité chez Eschyle." *REG* 81 (1968):15–39.

Robbins, T. E. "The Lot Oracle at Delphi." *CP* 11 (1916):278–92.

Robert, C. *Oidipus* (Berlin, 1915).

——. "Die Parodos der aischyleischen *Septem.*" *Hermes* 57 (1922):161–70.

Romilly, J. de. *La crainte et l'angoisse dans le théâtre d'Eschyle* (Paris, 1958).

——. *Time in Greek Tragedy* (Ithaca, 1968).

*Rose, H. J. "Drama Areôs Meston." *Mnemosyne* 6 (1938):321–28.

——. *A Handbook of Greek Mythology* (New York, 1959).

*Rosenmeyer, T. "*Seven Against Thebes*: A Tragedy of War." *Arion* 1 (1962): 48–78.

*Schadewaldt, W. "Die Wappnung des Eteokles." In *Eranion, Festschrift für H. Hommel* (Tübingen, 1961), pp. 105–16.

*Sheppard, J. T. "The Plot of the *Septem Contra Thebas.*" *CQ* 7 (1913):73–82.

Smyth, H. W. *Aeschylean Tragedy* (Berkeley, 1924).

*Solmsen, F. "The Erinys in Aischylos' *Septem.*" *TAPA* 68 (1937):197–211.

Stanford, W. B. *Aeschylus in his Style* (Dublin, 1942).

Stoessl, F. *Die Trilogie des Aischylos* (Vienna, 1937).

*Tucker, T. G. *The Seven Against Thebes of Aeschylus* (Cambridge, 1908).

*Verrall, A. W. *"The Seven Against Thebes" of Aeschylus* (London, 1887).

Webster, T. B. L. *The Tragedies of Euripides* (London, 1967).

*Wecklein, N. *Aischylos Sieben gegen Theben* (Leipzig, 1902).

*Wilamowitz-Moellendorff, U. von. "Drei Schlussscenen griechischer Dramen." Part 1. *Sitzungsber. der berliner Akademie* (1903), pp. 436-50.

———. *Aeschyli Tragoediae* (Berlin, 1914).

———. *Aischylos Interpretationen* (Berlin, 1914).

*Wilkens, K. "Dikê Homaimôn? Zu Aischylos *Sieben* 415." *Hermes* 97 (1969): 117-21.

*Willink, C. W. "A Problem in Aeschylus' *Septem.*" *CQ* 60 (n.s. 18, 1968):4-10.

*Winnington-Ingram, R. P. "Aeschylus *Septem* 187-90; 750-757." *BICS* 13 (1966):88-93.

———. "Zeus in the *Persae.*" *JHS* 93 (1973):210-19.

*———. "*Septem Contra Thebas.*" *YCIS* 25 (1977):1-45.

*Wolff, E. "Die Entscheidung des Eteokles in den *Sieben gegen Theben.*" *HSCP* 63 (1958):89-95.

Woodhouse, W. J. *Solon the Liberator* (Oxford, 1938).

*Wundt, M. "Die Schlussscene der *Sieben gegen Theben.*" *Philologus* 65 (1906): 357-81.

Index of Aeschylean Passages

189